Jan Jordan (Robinson) was born in Devonport, Auckland, during the 1950s. Since then she has lived, worked and studied in a variety of places, including six months living in the heart of Amsterdam's red-light district. Currently she teaches criminology at Victoria University, Wellington, and is a trustee of the New Zealand Prostitutes' Collective.

WORKING GIRLS

Women in the
New Zealand Sex Industry
talk to
JAN JORDAN

PENGUIN BOOKS

PENGUIN BOOKS

Penguin Books (NZ) Ltd, 182-190 Wairau Road, Auckland 10, New Zealand
Penguin Books Ltd, 27 Wrights Lane, London W8 5TZ, England
Penguin USA, 375 Hudson Street, New York, NY 10014, United States
Penguin Books Australia Ltd, 487 Maroondah Highway, Ringwood, Australia 3134
Penguin Books Canada Ltd, 10 Alcorn Avenue, Toronto, Ontario, Canada M4V 3B2

Penguin Books Ltd, Registered Offices: Harmondsworth, Middlesex, England

First published 1991
1 3 5 7 9 10 8 6 4 2

Copyright © Jan Jordan, 1991
All rights reserved
The moral right of the author has been asserted.

Designed by Richard King
Typeset by Typocrafters Ltd, Auckland
Printed in Australia

Except in the United States of America, this book is sold subject to the condition that it shall not, by way of trade or otherwise, be lent, re-sold, hired out or otherwise circulated without the publisher's prior consent in any form of binding or cover other than that in which it is published and without a similar condition including this condition being imposed on the subsequent purchaser.

Contents

Acknowledgements	7	Bridget	136
Introduction	9	Desna	147
Sarah	15	Liz	165
Harley	36	Jasmine	177
Hinemoa	47	Kate	189
Lee	61	Julia	203
Victoria	73	Tracy Lee	214
Gloria	91	Caroline	229
Hilary	100	Conclusion	256
Genevieve	117	Appendix	271
Alexandra	126	Further Reading	275

ACKNOWLEDGEMENTS

Many people have played a significant role in bringing this book into being. I would especially like to thank the following:

Geoff Walker (Penguin Books) for having the vision to commission it and the integrity not to compromise its stance.

Linda Cassells, for approaching the task of editing the transcripts with such warmth and sensitivity.

Catherine, Kathy, Juliet, Elke and others from the New Zealand Prostitutes' Collective, for always being so willing to assist and comment.

Astrid, Link and Mary from Wellington Information and Drug Education (WIDE), for their help and encouragement.

Jenny Neale, for being such a wonderfully committed and enthusiastic mentor.

Johanna Moeller, Brenda Watson, and Barbara Cleverly, who so efficiently transcribed and typed a varitable mountain of tapes.

Sue Reidy, for producing such a strong, colourful cover.

Fleur Grenfell, for her assistance and support.

Julie Leibrich, Allison Morris, June Joyce, and Stevan Eldred-Grigg, for their willingness to comment on various drafts, and their friendship.

Numerous other friends, including Rosemary Novitz, Jane Tolerton, Charlotte Macdonald, Alison Laurie, Geoff Fougere, Rose O'Neill, Glenda Laurence, Peter Waugh, Rae Julian, Penny Fenwick, Phyllis Herda, Jocelyn O'Kane, Sam Lynne, Brendy Weir, Anna Woods, Fran Hyland, Allison Kirkman, Linda Gibson, and Jenni Bedford, all of whom have challenged, inspired and nurtured me at various stages during the production of this book.

Warren Young and other colleagues at the Institute of

WORKING GIRLS

Criminology, for their demonstrations of support for this venture.

The Internal Grants Committee of Victoria University, for funding to subsidise travel and transcription costs.

Kay Rosaline, from whom I have learned much about the power of truth-telling about women's experiences.

The greatest acknowledgement of all goes to the women whose stories appear in this book — its existence reflects their courage.

INTRODUCTION

I could never meet a man and sleep with him the same night — that's immoral. It's cheap and disgusting and humiliating. But I can meet a man and sleep with him for money — that's survival.

— Ex-sex worker

In this book seventeen women who have worked in New Zealand's sex industry tell their stories of 'survival'. Some are among the eight thousand or so estimated currently to work as prostitutes in this country, while others have 'worked' in the recent past. All have powerful stories to tell.

As sex workers they participate in an industry organised to provide sexual services in a variety of ways.

Ship girls operate around the wharf area of New Zealand's ports, forming liaisons with seamen that frequently last from one ship's visit to its next and sometimes evolve into long-lasting relationships. While sex may be exchanged directly for cash in some situations, often the arrangements are much more subtle than that. For the women concerned, being on the ships can become more a way of life than a job.

Street workers work on the streets in known 'red-light' areas (for the most part only in Auckland and Wellington in New Zealand). They generally wait to be approached by clients seeking sexual services and, once an exchange has been negotiated, take them to a nearby room or, more typically, use the client's own car for the transaction.

Escort agencies rely on clients phoning to request that someone be sent to their hotel/motel room or home. The agency then contacts one of its workers, who makes any sexual arrangement upon arrival. In these situations the client pays both an agency fee plus a fee to the worker, depending on whatever services are requested. Occasionally it may be only companionship that is being sought — in most cases it is sex.

Probably the majority of sex workers operate through massage parlours. In most cases the client pays the parlour a fee for a massage, then negotiates anything 'extra' he might wish with the masseuse. The masseuses are totally dependent on such 'extra' sexual requests for their income, since they are usually not paid any wage by the parlour. Recent developments suggest, in fact, that parlours are even beginning to charge their workers for the use of the premises. A $20 fee per worker per shift can easily bring in an extra $5,000 or even $10,000 a year to management, but from the worker's perspective this means she can end up paying the parlour money even on those nights when no clients request extras.

It is not illegal to be a prostitute in New Zealand. However, our current laws prohibit soliciting, brothel-keeping, pimping, and living off the earnings of money obtained through prostitution. They also provide for the close regulation and monitoring of massage parlour workers. In effect, it is virtually impossible to work as a prostitute *and* stay within the law.

The soliciting laws in particular reflect a double standard of morality — it is against the law for sex workers to solicit clients but not for clients to solicit sex workers. This reflects the bias of our early prostitution laws, which sought simultaneously to regulate women's lives while protecting men's interests. Today the majority of sex workers are still overwhelmingly female, and this book is deliberately restricted in coverage to 'working girls', since somewhat different sets of issues are involved for the small minority of gay, transvestite and transsexual sex workers.

The book's focus is also restricted primarily to those women who have grown up within the New Zealand context and then decided to enter sex work, rather than those brought here from countries such as Thailand or the Philippines expressly for the purposes of prostitution. It seemd neither feasible nor appropriate for me to interview these women and could possibly even

INTRODUCTION

have placed them in a dangerous situation. While they are still a minority within the New Zealand sex industry, their lack of economic independence and often insecure immigration status renders them highly vulnerable to exploitation and the abuse of power — their stories also need to be told.

My interest in the area of sex work has evolved over the last ten years. It dates back to the time I spent researching women and crime in nineteenth-century Canterbury for my sociology thesis, where repeatedly the women coming most often to official notice were those labelled as prostitutes. Later I was asked to contribute to *Public and Private Worlds* (ed. Shelagh Cox, Allen and Unwin, 1987), and I can still remember the day Shelagh suggested I continue my work on prostitution, but in the contemporary setting. I felt daunted! It was with a considerable degree of apprehension that I made my first approach to a massage parlour, unsure both of what I would find and how they would find me. As I talked to the women, I became more and more convinced that their stories needed to be told. Since then my involvement has grown beyond that required to produce this book, so that I am now an active participant in the New Zealand Prostitutes' Collective (NZPC) through my role as one of their trustees.

My aim in bringing this collection of accounts together is to contribute to the process of making women's lives visible. As sex workers these women live in a society that either refuses to acknowledge their existence, or seeks to condemn and ostracise them. We grow up with a set of stereotypes about prostitutes, convinced that we could recognise one at a glance by her fishnets, stilettos and sexy garb. One only has to look at the images of prostitutes in the media to have this caricature reinforced. We also think we 'know' why women sell their bodies — it's either because they love sex, crave drugs, or have some nasty pimp hovering in the shadows.

The lives of the women in this book challenge such popular images. They provide a window into a world that, while initially appearing very different from our own, on reflection often proves very similar — their struggle to survive financially, to build a better life for themselves and their children, and in some cases to overcome the effects of abuse and violence by exerting control over their bodies.

Time and time again during these interviews I was struck by how familiar much of what the women were saying sounded to me, yet I was initially surprised that this should be the case, given my non-involvement in the sex-work industry. As they related accounts of child abuse and forced sex, discussed their various coping mechanisms, and indicated the structural powerlessness they often felt with regard to achieving economic and personal independence, I increasingly realised the similarities in our struggles. Even though I had never worked in a parlour or on the streets, the bargains these women made around their sexuality often reminded me of the more subtle arrangements I had made with men at different times in my life. Their stories are their own, but in some ways they could also be mine and those of many other women.

In deciding who to interview for this book, I tried to ensure that women were included who had worked in a variety of different geographical areas in New Zealand and in different sectors of the industry, both past and present. I also wanted to ensure that both Maori and Pakeha women were represented, and that women who identified themselves sexually as either lesbian, bisexual or heterosexual were included.

Despite this, I would not wish to claim that the women whose accounts appear here are necessarily 'representative' of all New Zealand sex workers. With this kind of essentially illegal industry, involving mostly covert and highly mobile workers, it would be impossible to establish any scientifically drawn population base from which to select a sample. More importantly, the search for 'representativeness' itself constitutes a false scientific objective. It ignores the fact that each of these accounts is valuable in its own right, and enhances our knowledge and understanding of women's involvement in sex work.

INTRODUCTION

I met the women in a variety of ways. Sometimes one woman would give me the name of a friend, so I would be passed on that way. A couple of women I had met while doing the earlier research for *Public and Private Worlds*, and they referred me to others they knew. Some I had met whilst engaged in research on family violence at Arohata Women's Prison. Others contacted me in response to an invitation made through *Siren*, NZPC's magazine. The collective itself was very helpful in terms of assisting me to locate other women, and in allowing me to use their premises to meet with the women. Some also approached me of their own accord after hearing me lecture or speak, and one or two I met through personal contacts. A few women whom I approached declined for various reasons to take part. Most, however, were very willing to talk and several indicated that they had always wanted to write their experiences down but had never found the time to do it.

The interviews were conducted in a variety of venues. Some women chose their own home, while others opted for either my office or home. Several were conducted in a prison chapel, some at NZPC's rooms, and one involved my hiring a motel unit, on a casual occupancy basis, like a client, in order to get some guaranteed privacy.

Each of the women knew that these interviews were for a book on sex work in New Zealand, and they agreed to take part on that basis. The interviews themselves were recorded on tape, transcribed, then edited and restructured so as to read more easily.

Great effort was then made to relocate each of the women in order that they could see the final draft of their particular interview and make any changes they thought necessary. In some cases this involved their deleting certain details; in others it meant adding in experiences they felt to have been significant but which they had omitted earlier. One woman, for example, realised that she'd forgotten to tell me she'd been married! In most cases the alterations involved changing details of names and places so as to preserve confidentiality — the names included here are therefore mostly pseudonyms, and some place names have also been altered. Wherever possible the women themselves, either at the time of interview or subsequently, chose the name they wished to be known by in the book.

Five women, unfortunately, could not be re-located — their interviews have therefore had any identifying details changed and are included here on the basis that they knew from the outset that they were being interviewed for publication. Often they did in fact indicate in the course of the interview the aspects of their lives they wanted disguised or omitted.

One aspect I appreciated was hearing how the women felt when they saw their interviews written up. Several of them got, as one woman put it, 'a real buzz' from seeing their life in print. It was like an acknowledgement that all they had experienced was real, and often they said they were pleased and impressed at how eloquent they sounded and at some of the comments they had made. Even one woman who felt a little aghast initially at seeing all the traumas of her life written down, later said she liked rereading it so she could remind herself of where she had come from and affirm how much she had moved herself on since her youth.

For many of the women, then, it seems that the very act of being interviewed was quite a positive and validating experience. Several women found it helped them to own and reclaim past experiences they had tried to blank out, and some decided to make contact with other sex workers and later became involved with NZPC.

Some sex workers who participated in the production of this book said they would have preferred someone from within the industry to have produced it. In effect, however, they did. Without their support and co-operation the book would never have been written. I was simply the vehicle they used — it is *their* stories which appear on these pages. Consequently, it seems appropriate that any surplus royalties from the sale of this book will go to the New Zealand Prostitutes' Collective.

SARAH

Sarah is in her late twenties and has worked in the sex industry for the last nine years. She has worked mostly in massage parlours, as both a masseuse and a receptionist, and was interviewed shortly before NZPC was formed.

I grew up on a farm near Ashburton, part of a good Catholic farming family. Dad was farm manager, and there were eight of us kids altogether. I was one of the middle ones. We went to a local country school initially, and then to convent schools for our secondary education. I left after the fifth form and did a secretarial course.

My first sexual experience was forced on me when I was fifteen. We were staying at a holiday camp and I met this guy in the park. He was twenty-one. He came and asked my parents if he could take me to a movie. He told them he was nineteen. I'd never been out with a boy before and I didn't know what sex was. Instead of taking me to the movie, he drove me miles away and did his nasty deed. I didn't really know what was going on. That was my first sexual experience. I didn't tell my parents — they wouldn't have understood. They would have blamed me. It was best not to tell anybody.

When I was sixteen or so I had a boyfriend. My parents approved of him because he came from a good family. I went to a party at his place, and my parents thought his parents were there, but they weren't. Later I was talking to my girlfriend on the phone and told her about the party and the alcohol and how everyone had gone into the bedrooms and done their bit, and my mother walked in and said, 'That was a very interesting conversation.' She never mentioned the sex — she only ever told Dad about there being alcohol at the party and his parents not being present. I got grounded for the next two years. So when I was in the fourth and fifth form I never went anywhere but school and church — it was pretty tough.

Then, when I was nearly eighteen, I moved to the city and went a bit mad. I went night-clubbing all the time, and the freedom — my God! I had a really good time. I calmed down after a while, but the first few years were pretty hectic.

When I was eighteen I was raped by a friend of my flatmate's. I stupidly trusted him and went to his house to call a taxi after we'd had a friendly drink together at a hotel near his house. The main thing I remember about the actual rape was trying desperately to keep my legs together. I failed. Naively I took him to court. That was the worst part — the humiliation. My only memory of the trial was having him sitting almost right in front of me when I was on the stand. He was a black African and all I could see were his white eyes staring up at me and a big, white smile laughing as if to say, 'You'll never get me, bitch.' Naturally he got off, as so many rapists do.

The trial was almost worse and more degrading than the actual rape. He had been in court for rape and sexual assault on several occasions and had got off each one, although this fact was not brought up in court like my previous sex life had been. I remember nothing more of the trial — the beginning of the 'switch off' mechanism?

During those early years in the city I was employed in various secretarial jobs. I was flatting with this girl who was also a secretary, but then she left her job and had all these days off. I hated the fact that she was having a good time while I was working, so I quit my job too. We thought we would do waitressing, but after one night we just looked up the paper, saw 'Masseuses wanted', went down and had a couple of interviews, and started next night at Cleopatra's.

The first night we were very scared but when we got home I remember we sat on my bed counting our money and we couldn't believe it. It was so easy. When you go from working as a secretary getting $180 a week in the hand to suddenly coming home and there's $600 on the bed for one night's work and it's all yours, it's very easy. That was the average in those days, but the money now is nowhere like it used to be. Most of the girls are pretty happy if they go home with $250.

I worked at Cleopatra's for about three years, then left because I fell out with the woman running it. I'd been assaulted by a client one night and was in the kitchen crying my eyes out, when she came storming out and said, 'What the hell have you done to him? He's complaining like mad about you out there,' and she gave him a refund. It wasn't the first bad experience I'd had with her, so after that I thought, 'Fuck you,' and I left, and I didn't go back to Cleopatra's until I heard that she had gone for good.

I went to the Las Vegas then. It was a small, dark, divey little place, but the girls I was working with were a lot of fun. We had a great time, although we didn't do a lot of work. All my regulars followed me there, so I was pretty busy. You could do whatever you liked, bowl up whenever you liked. I enjoyed it, but I was dying to get back to Cleopatra's again. The girls at Cleopatra's were just nice, normal girls, whereas at the Las Vegas they were a bit odd.

The Las Vegas was a rap parlour then, which meant there was no massage. You took a guy to the room, you sat there, you had a chat — rapping was just chatting. Usually within five minutes they got bored and asked about sex, so in that sense it was a lot easier because you didn't have to go through the rigmarole of giving a massage. Massaging can be very exhausting. I still massaged most of the clients who'd followed me from Cleopatra's, though, because they were used to being massaged and I found that was the best way to get them turned on.

I've worked at other places in Wellington. I had one night at the Harem, which was dreadful. You were expected to dress up in underwear and all that sort of thing, which I find extremely tacky. I also worked up at Edward's, but I didn't like that either. That place was really dirty — he won't pay for a cleaner or anything. Mainly I didn't like it because most of the people don't go there specifically for a girl. Generally they sit around and drink Edward's booze and watch blue movies. I found that really embarrassing and very hard to be around. You feel cheaper up there when you're sitting in the lounge with all these men glaring at you — you feel more like a whore than you do at Cleopatra's. And these men weren't trained at all, given that you train your clients. They expected everything they saw in the blue movie, and there's no way I was going to do all of that, but I couldn't cope with having to explain why all the time, so it didn't work out very well.

There wasn't much difference in the clientele either. Half the clients went to Cleopatra's as well. You get the odd politician — nothing special. And they won't pay more than anyone else does. The rich and powerful aren't good clients. They say, 'Don't you know who I am?' and expect you to do it for nothing. You're doing the job for money, not the prestige of who you fuck.

After working for about three or four years at Cleopatra's, I decided I needed a new adventure and set off to Auckland. I worked at Flora's for the six months I was there. It was very busy, the hours were long and I made a lot of money, but I was desperately lonely. The girls at Flora's were great, but not into socialising outside of work. A friend of mine from Cleopatra's came to visit me and introduced me to a friend of hers. He seemed a really wonderful guy, a real comedian. I don't really know why to this day, but four months later we got married. The morning after the wedding, I realised I'd made a big mistake when he verbally assaulted me for the first time, and had me in tears. It was all because I'd passed out when we went to bed and hadn't consummated the marriage — as if we were virgins anyway! I had drunk too much champagne, when I don't normally drink.

The marriage lasted only five months and they were the worst five months of my life. He constantly abused me verbally — never physically, as he knew I'd never put up with that. He'd have me in tears at some stage of almost every day calling me a whore and a slut. He seemed to think that the marriage certificate was like an ownership paper and that he could treat me as badly as he liked.

During the whole time we were married he never worked a day. He quit his job as a silver-service waiter straight after we were married and would not even consider getting himself a job, claiming he wasn't able to cope — as if *I* wanted to be on my back. If I ever didn't feel like sex he'd get super mad and scream things like, 'Everyone gets to fuck you — except me, you bitch.' He never wanted me to stop working though — he wanted the money.

I fell out of love *very* quickly. I only put up with it all as long as I did because of pride. It was a choice between him and me, so I told him to leave and that I wanted a divorce. Luckily for me his best friend shouted him a one-way ticket to London —he was out of my life for good. Two years later we were divorced. It seems funny now to say I was married for my money!

I currently work as a receptionist at Cleopatra's, which is the best parlour in Wellington. It's the best in terms of the women who work there and in terms of the place. It's the cleanest and the nicest, and it's the best run in terms of the clientele — we don't let the sleazier people in. The actual building is owned by a guy, but he keeps right out of it. He lives in Auckland and the place is run by a woman. And I think the fact that it is run by a woman makes the biggest difference of all because it means there are no men telling the women what to do. In a lot of parlours the guys that run the place think they can get it all because they're the boss, and the younger girls think they have to give them sex.

As a receptionist I'm paid a fixed wage, so much per shift, but no commission, thank God. It's different when you're working. Working girls are basically self-employed. When a client comes into a parlour, he pays at the desk for a massage — about $30 for a half-hour, more for longer. The receptionist books him in with the girl whose turn it is, unless he specifically requests someone, and he takes a shower and comes into the lounge. The girl then takes him through and gives him a massage. Anything else that goes on in the room is private between the client and the girl, and he pays her for any extras. The management have nothing to do with that — they're not even supposed to know anything about it.

The policy is that the girls do not offer sex, and you have to be very careful about that. There's no way you can risk offering illegal things in case he's a cop. You can't tell who's a cop and who isn't — they can be fat little men or skinny young men. So the idea is that you hint at sex. Once *they* have said the initial words, then you can go into the prices. Sometimes you go round and round, because some of them just don't want to say the word and you can spend ten minutes going, 'What do you want?' while they say, 'How about a quick one?' and you say, 'A quick what?' and so forth. They've paid for their time in advance, so if they spend half of it trying to say the word 'sex' then they don't get any more. Usually there's a bit of leeway, so that clients may come out a little bit late from short massages. No one worries unless it's really busy. Then, if he wants more time, the girl comes out and tells the receptionist so he has to pay for the extra. Most of the clients pay by cash, or they can charge it, using a different name for the parlour to conceal its identity.

We just give ordinary relaxing massages. Legally we're not allowed to give therapeutic massage. Under the Massage Parlour Agreement it says that basically we're not allowed to try and fix people's backs. But most of the girls can massage really well because they've learned it on the job or from each other.

The kind of massage given usually depends on the client. I used to love giving a really good therapeutic massage, but the key to making money is to make it sensual, to turn the guy on. There's an amazing number of guys who come in and just want a massage. For instance, it's possible that some nights you might get five massages and four of them will be straight. Other nights you can do ten and none of them will be straight.

Most straight massages mean the clients haven't got the money. When they pay at the front desk, they think they're

SARAH

going to get sex as well; especially if they're from Australia, because that's the way it works over there. Or they think they're going to get sex a lot cheaper than they do. If a client doesn't want extras, you don't get paid. If you work a night and do five massages and they're all straight, you have to borrow the taxi fare home.

The basic prices are $40 for a hand relief where you sit beside them and do it but they can't touch you, $50 where they can touch you on the top half, and $60 for the nearest thing to sex without having it, when you lie down next to the guy and body massage while doing the hand relief. Straight sex is $70–80, depending on the client, oral with sex $100, oral with hand relief $80, and body massage also $80. It's up to the girl what she does and how much she charges for these little bits and pieces. When I started working nearly seven years ago, it was $60 for sex then, so it's only gone up $10 in seven years, which is really ridiculous.

At the moment day shifts are a lot quieter than nights. Other times it can be the other way around. During the day most clients come alone. You very rarely see drunk clients in the day, thank goodness. That's why the girls like working days, because everybody's sober, and when they're sober, they're quick. At night they tend to come in groups or pairs — moral support. They'll have been out to the pub. If they're a bit merry, it's okay, but if they're drunk we don't let them in. Some receptionists might, but I don't. I still remember what it was like working — there's no way I'm going to let people in I wouldn't be prepared to massage.

The girls at Cleopatra's do all the laundry — the towels and everything. We've got an industrial washer and drier. We don't do the cleaning though. We employ a cleaner, and we're the only massage parlour I've ever known that does so.

There's no particular sort of guy who comes to a massage parlour. We get the total range in here, from the blue-collar worker to big executives like bank managers and politicians. In terms of age, the clients vary greatly from about nineteen or twenty up to seventy or eighty. Mostly they're middle-aged, and also a lot of guys in their thirties. In the day-time you get mostly middle-aged people, all the businessmen, while at night you still get a lot of them coming in, plus a lot of younger guys.

Mostly they're married, but there'd be no way their wife would know what they were doing. Most of them come in probably because they're so bad at sex the wife won't do it with them any more, which is entirely understandable. Most of them complain, 'My wife's frigid.' Well, we all know *why*. After a few years of being fumbled over and fucked for a few seconds and then rolled off, I mean, who's going to want to keep doing it? The girls will only put up with that for money. It's very hard to respect a man who has to pay for sex. I would like to think that there are some men out there who have enough dignity not to see their penises as the be-all and end-all and who don't have to go and pay for sex.

A lot of the clients are regulars, and they request a particular girl they know and like. Some will constantly try out the new girls or have a different girl every time because they like variety. A request usually means money — he's not likely to be straight if he's asked for you. The only time a girl will refuse to do a client is if he's been particularly bad to her, if he's ripped her off, or, as sometimes happens, he's become so attached to a girl that he's driving her nuts. In the end she has to turn around to him and say, 'Look, you can't see me any more,' in which case you've got a sobbing male on your hands. But there's nothing much you can do about it except say, 'Go away, I'm just a whore — you're just a client. This means nothing to me.'

Relationships don't really ever develop between clients and girls. Some girls will see clients outside of work, but just as friends. A lot of girls have things going on outside of work business-wise, and a lot of clients turn out to be very handy with that.

I've got one client I still have lunch with regularly. I actually had lunch with him today and he offered me a job — interior designing. Now that I'm not working any more I get on better with him, because he's no threat to me. He's still madly in love with me. He's married, or course, I'm using him for everything I can at the moment.

The clients come to us basically for sex. Some come for company; some are just lonely; some want to have a cry on your shoulder and tell you all about their problems; but generally they just come for a quick fuck. And if they've got the money, that's what they get. They get what they want — we get what we want.

What you try to do is to click on to what a client wants and play out that role. Some of them want nursing; some want to be treated badly; some want to be cuddled and loved. In the first five minutes you can figure out exactly what role they want and switch into it, and you can even vary your accent according to what they want — French, German or whatever. It's really fun putting on an accent, but embarrassing when they come back and you've forgotten what accent you used!

You've got to be a total actress in this business — it's all acting. If you were just yourself, you'd never make any money. Because who wants to be there? Who wants to be nice to this creep? It's all a matter of pretending. You pretend you like them; you pretend you like it; you pretend whatever they want you to pretend. And if you can act, then you make money. If you can't, you don't do too well.

And the guys don't realise it, generally. Some might, but most don't even want to think about it. More often than not, clients will say, 'Oh, you must really like this job; you must really like sex', and you go 'Mmmm', thinking to yourself, 'My God, if only they knew.' There's so many things you want to say to these guys, but you can't — things like 'You disgust me! You're a prat! You're a pig!' If you could actually tell them what you thought, they'd probably have this huge complex for the rest of their lives.

If they ask, 'Am I any good?' you tell them they're fine. You never get too enthusiastic about it unless they're paying big money. Sometimes they can't come unless they think you've come, so then you're required to do quite a bit of acting. But you only fake an orgasm as an absolute last resort, because it's very embarrassing.

When a new girls starts, we usually have to chat to her and tell her to be very careful about what she says. One thing you don't do is talk about yourself. If you do, then you make sure you lie, because you don't want the clients knowing too much about you. It's okay for them to pour their heart out to you, but we're in a delicate position. That's one reason why the girls have working names. For a lot of them the situation outside of work can be quite dicey, with partners or family members not knowing that they work.

Each girl has her own rules in terms of what she lets clients do. Like no girls will let clients kiss them; it's too personal. The whole neck up is a taboo area. To have any client even touch your face is incredibly claustrophobic. From your neck up is *your* space. You can switch off to the rest of your body, but you can't switch off to your face.

Girls don't let clients go down on them orally because it's unhygienic. That's another reason why they don't kiss clients — hygiene. The same with oral. Girls don't let clients put their fingers inside them because that's unhygienic, plus it's not exactly pleasant.

Some girls will put up with more than others. It's a matter of experience. The longer you're in the game and the wiser you get, the less you can put up with. When I first started working, clients used to get away with all kinds of things. If you're a new girl, it's hard to know what you're supposed to do. But the longer you're in the game, the tougher you get, and the more you learn that you can in fact just slap their hand away.

Cleopatra's doesn't handle requests for bondage and stuff —we leave that to other parlours. This place is too small for a start — the rooms are so close to each other that if you were whipping a guy the whole place would hear it. We do have lots of people ringing up for things like that and I just say, 'No, I'm sorry, we don't do that'. Generally the girls who work at Cleopatra's are so straight that they just couldn't do it anyway — they'd crack up laughing!

SARAH

We don't show pornography at Cleopatra's either — in fact, we consider that extremely tacky. We're basically anti-pornography. It's amazing the number of people who ring up asking if we show videos, though. A guy shouldn't have to watch disgusting blue movies to get turned on. We're not really interested in that sort of client, because we consider pornography pretty tasteless.

The busiest time of year in this business is pre-Christmas. People have more money then — they've been given their holiday pay. After Christmas it's very quiet for the first month because nobody has any money left. When there are special events on in Wellington it can be pretty busy. A lot of out-of-town people will come in for their special trip to a massage parlour. Groups of men will go and have a night on the town and everything is included — going to the pubs, the nightclubs and the massage parlours. That's especially true after big sports events, and particularly after the car races.

It can also be busy when the fishing boats come in. The Japanese usually come en masse and they are really good clients. In Japan some of these men would be considered the lowest of the low, but they are the politest, sweetest, easiest clients you could ever imagine. They're quick — they're just in, they want sex, and they're out again. They have the most expensive massage — they don't realise they're paying for time; they think they're paying for the best. That's fine for the desk, since they're only there ten minutes and the desk gets the seventy-minute price! They're extremely clean, and some of them even bring their own condoms because ours don't fit — the Japanese are tiny. They want basic sex, and they're very grateful. The only problem is that working-class Japanese men sometimes have pearls implanted under the foreskin of their penis. This is similar to the use of tattoos in Western society and signifies the same 'I'm a man — I can take pain' thing. I've been hurt like hell by over-vigorous Japanese contortionists with pearls.

The Koreans are a different story. We don't usually let them in. They're cheap, they're dirty, they won't use a condom, they stink, they're just horrible. We also get some clients from the cruise ships. Not the passengers, but the crews. Mostly the cruise ships that arrive here are full of really old passengers anyway. Generally the crew are quite good as clients.

We try to play an educative role with a lot of clients. Education is a very big part of the job. The thing I most used to try to educate them about was safe sex, because I consider that extremely important today. All the girls in the parlour have regular check-ups, and a while ago we made it a policy for all the girls to bring in a doctor's certificate. It's the new girls we have to worry about. Basically it's a matter of getting it into their heads that if they don't have safe sex, it's not only bad for everybody else, it's bad for them too.

Most girls have check-ups once a month for STDs, and if one comes back positive, and then it's usually from her private life, then she won't work until it's cleared up. There's no sick pay or anything like that — it's a matter of trying to save some money in case it ever happens. As long as you adhere to safe sex principles and use condoms, there's no reason for anything ever to happen. Not all parlours are necessarily like that, though — all it takes is some dirty little man who won't use a condom, and a desperate, uneducated girl, and you've got problems.

Occasionally girls may use douches to clean themselves out, but that's not usually necessary with condoms, unless they break. In terms of contraception, all the girls are on something — the pill, injection, IUD, or whatever. There's no way you can rely on condoms as a contraceptive measure — they're purely for the venereal disease thing.

AIDS has had a lot of impact. It has made a lot of people scared and a lot of people aware. You don't get guys arguing about condoms any more like you used to. In fact a lot of *them* now say to us, 'You do use a condom, don't you?' They're paranoid about it too.

There's all sorts of other things we try to educate clients about. A lot of men come in here and tell you about the problems with their wives and you try to point out a few things to them like how to treat women, since most men have no idea. It's quite good to be able to tell them a few facts about what women feel and why their wife was probably acting like that, and to teach them sexually that there is such a thing as a clitoris, which most men don't know.

Most men think sex is just fucking. It involves putting their penis inside a vagina and pumping it around and that's it. That's supposed to make the woman come, because, of course, they think women have vaginal orgasms all the time. Mostly it's the middle-aged guys who are the most receptive to 'anatomy' lessons. Some of the younger guys know about it from having read *Cleo* and things.

Sometimes we get young guys coming in for their first sexual experience. But we also get guys coming in and telling us they're virgins, because they hope the girl will give them a better time. Occasionally a really young boy does come in who is a virgin and is absolutely terrified of the whole thing. He'll lie there like a stiff board, eyes as big as saucers. You handle them with kid gloves and try to calm them down — otherwise they're likely to freak out and you won't get any money.

Some guys will come in just to talk, which can be really frustrating. Occasionally they will actually give you money for just talking. They will realise that they've wasted your time and give you either a generous amount of money or a token payment. You don't mind helping people as long as you get some reward for it — we're not charity workers.

Generally the parlours are safe to work in, because there are other people around. If a guy gets rough, the girl can just get up and walk out of the room. In one particular incident I had, an Islander tried to strangle me. It was when we were in our old premises, which were really big, and the room we were in was miles away from everybody, so I screamed but nobody heard me.

I think it was because of a self-defence course I'd done that I managed to talk my way out of it. I remember lying there, with his fingers in my neck, thinking, 'Keep calm, keep calm, focus on what *you* can do to them, not what they can do to you.' I thought maybe I could poke his eyes out, but then he would just get really mad and hit me, so I decided to try and talk my way out of it. I relaxed and went totally limp and said, 'Okay! Okay! If you want a fuck, fine. Don't worry — just let me go and get a condom.' And he goes, 'Oh — okay!' so I got up and left the room. Needless to say, I didn't go back.

The place we work in now is a lot different. You can be in the lounge and you'll hear someone laughing in one of the rooms. It's small, and that's good because you know it's safer that way. If you do need to scream, people will hear you. There was one place I worked that had a button by the bed you could push if anything went wrong.

Outcalls can be much more dangerous. Sometimes we do send girls out, but only to the major hotels, and even then they're not always safe. When I'm on reception I don't send anybody on outcalls. No way. You could go to a room and there could be six guys there, or a guy with a gun, or a psychopath with a knife — you've no way of knowing.

I was raped on an outcall many years ago. It was by an associate of the lady who used to run this parlour then. She sent me out to the private home of a pig of a man in Upper Hutt who, when I got there, said he wanted anal sex. I said no, but he took it anyway, which wasn't very pleasant — being sodomised is not nice.

I went back to the parlour that night expecting some kind of support or sympathy from this woman. But she was a really horrible bitch. She didn't care. She told me not to be ridiculous and said, 'You've just got to put up with that.' This woman was a Hitler. She ran the place so smoothly, it was incredible. But she ran it from the clients' point of view, not the girls'. Lots of parlours are like that, but good managers know that if they want to be busy and have good staff, it pays them to run the place from the girls' point of view. If the girls are happy, they will make the clients happy.

If we have trouble with a client in a parlour, I know we could rely on the police to help. They're generally pretty good.

SARAH

I had a situation the other night when I was on reception where this guy was threatening to call the police and I said, 'Okay — call them.' I would have just said to them, 'Will you escort this gentleman out?' In the end I didn't need to, but I wasn't worried about it.

What the police are most worried about in parlours is drugs, and there are girls with drug problems in some parlours. Mostly the police are really good as long as you keep a straight place and all the girls are okay. Sometimes we get police coming to the parlour off-duty as clients, but they don't give us a hard time — they know they could end up in a lot of shit.

I do think the laws on prostitution need to be changed. I'd like to see it decriminalised, not legalised. If it was legalised, we'd end up with the same sort of situation as they've got in Melbourne. The guys pay for everything at the desk, and then the girls have to do them whether they want to or not. And the prices would go right down because competition would be rife — legalised pimping.

If it was decriminalised, we could run the same as we are now but without having to live in constant fear of getting busted. At the moment you've got to be so careful with every client, and so suspicious. And the clients feel paranoid too. Decriminalisation would be the best option for everybody.

There's only once, since I worked in parlours, that I've been back to a straight job. It was dreadful. I did it for my boyfriend — I didn't do it for me. I went and worked three months in an office and nearly went crazy. I think I could handle it better now, if I was paid enough money and it was interesting enough. But this work is a bit like heroin — it's totally addictive, and it's very, very hard to get out of. It's not only the money, it's the freedom. You can work when you want; you can take holidays when you want; you're not tied to an office five days a week all those weeks of the year with two weeks off at the end.

I know a lot of girls who really want to get out. They go back to working in an office and absolutely hate it. Women aren't treated too well by men in offices anyway. It's a very subservient role and it's not easy to go back to saying, 'Yes sir, no sir,' when you're used to being in charge. Our workplace is our space, and it's important to have that control.

A lot of working girls have been sexually abused — not all, but a lot. If you have been abused from an early age, sex doesn't mean a hell of a lot to you anyway. If your first sexual experiences are wonderful, warm things, then you'll have a good view of sex, but if you've been abused or raped young, it doesn't mean a hell of a lot. You can switch off easily in the job because you've had to in the past.

That switch-off mechanism is essential to being able to stay in the job. When my switch-off mechanism stopped working, I just couldn't handle it any more. Every time I was with a client I felt like I was being raped. I just wanted to push him off and scream — it was awful. When I woke up one morning crying and I'd had a nightmare about it, I knew it was time to get out.

I tend not to have personal relationships with men while I'm working. I've been celibate ever since the boyfriend I gave up work for left. It's very hard to handle relationships while you're working, because no good man can put up with you working. Or even if he can put up with it, it doesn't do the relationship any good. There will be a lot of pain involved in it for him as well as yourself. Some women become lesbians because of the job, but there don't seem to be as many in the parlours now as there used to be.

When people ask what I do, I give different answers depending on the person. My brothers and sisters know, but my parents don't — they still think I'm a secretary. Some people I make up a story for, but generally I tell them, and I've found good friends can cope with it — it means you find out who your friends are.

I don't tell landlords what I do — I say I'm a secretary or an interior designer or something like that. Bank managers are a problem. If the girls earned that kind of money in a legitimate job, they'd be a lot better off. They could go and get a loan on the basis of what they earn each week. That's why girls don't often buy houses, because it's very hard to keep putting your money away until you've got $60,000, yet you can't get a loan on illicit earnings.

When I was working, if anybody asked me what I did, I called myself a 'working girl'. If I really wanted to shock someone, I'd say, 'I fuck rich capitalists for money.' I didn't say that very often, but it was fun!

There is some exploitation in the job, but that all comes from there being set prices. We're exploited as much as shopkeepers are. It's all a matter of supply and demand, and outright exploitation only occurs to the extent that we can only charge so much because that's all they'll pay.

I didn't feel like the men were buying me, as such. I felt like they bought the use of my skills. They didn't buy me because 'me' is my head. That's what is inside me and nobody can ever buy that.

I see very little difference between housewives and prostitutes. A lot of housewives are doing the same sort of job that we are, and they're exploited in the same kinds of ways. They're saying to their husbands, 'I'll give you sexual favours and give you children if you support me and feed me and bring me home money.' They're doing it for their livelihood as much as we are, and the only difference is that they've made a commitment to *one* person, presumably for love. But that fades away often. Then they lie there like we do and think about their shopping lists.

I see myself as a feminist, a very strong feminist. I probably became one when I was fifteen years old, although in some ways I think I've always been one. But I think that's how old I was when I read *The Women's Room*, and it made a big impression on me. From then on I could see how women are treated — the way we get lower wages, poorer jobs, less opportunity, the whole thing.

I think a lot of feminists don't understand prostitutes, but prostitutes understand feminists a fair bit. We can understand about the way they feel about what we do. But most feminists don't understand what it's about, or that there's very few women who can do it.

I do see contradictions in terms of my being a feminist and working in prostitution. As a feminist I don't like pornography; I don't like men whistling; I hate the whole way that women are treated as sex objects — which prostitution is. But at the same time, while you're doing the job you look at it in a different light. You see yourself as exploiting *them* more than they're exploiting you. You have to see it that way, or you couldn't do it otherwise.

A man's biggest weakness is that his brain is ruled by his penis. It's a status thing — the more women they can get, the better; the longer they can hang on, the better; the bigger their penis, the better — it's all absolutely ridiculous.

Men just need the sexual act a lot of the time. Women need the love that sex brings and the affection and the warmth. Women may want sex for sex's sake too, sometimes, but it's not so strong that they'd go and pay for it. You don't see any massage parlours around for women.

For me, working had nothing to do with the sex. I worked for the money, the freedom, and to be with the other girls. There's a very strong bond between the girls, a strong women's bond, which is really good, because you need that. It doesn't get spoiled by competition for clients, because there isn't really any. Occasionally there may be a little bit of bitchiness, but that's usually called to a halt pretty soon.

The actual working part was never enjoyable, not sexually. At one stage I did enjoy the power I felt I had, but I realise now that the only power a woman has over a man is the ability to say no.

I think the power thing was one of the ways I coped with it. You knew that if they had money in their wallet, you could get them to spend it, no matter what. Even if it was for their rent, it was great fun getting it off them, because you could think, 'You pathetic little man, you're so weak I can get your money.' You had power over their wallets, penises, brains, because one big cord connects them.

SARAH

I've been employed as receptionist here for about four months now, and I love it. The best thing is I don't have to go through with any of those men. I'm still in the scene, I'm still with the girls, I've got all the good parts, but I don't have to fuck anybody any more. The money's not nearly as good, but that doesn't matter. My body's all mine and it's great.

I think there's a real need for some kind of organisation to represent the interests of working girls, some kind of union or body that will stand up for the girls' rights. The girls should be paid by the parlour. But the way things are these days, the parlours couldn't afford it. But the girls should be paid for the straight massages they do at least. I'd love to organise a union for the girls, for all working girls, but at the moment it would be too hard.

The girls should also be able to have a say in who can work on reception and who can't. Otherwise you feel like there's no one to back you up if there's a dispute with a client. The receptionist determines who is let in, who you have to do and what you have to put up with.

The New Zealand government is far too backward to give prostitutes any funding here. The government isn't really doing a hell of a lot to help out with the AIDS thing at all. For a start they should be giving condoms away, not selling them for $15 a packet. A lot of people just can't afford condoms, or they're too embarrassed to go and buy them. They could give away free condoms and save a hell of a lot of money in hospitalisation in the future. Prevention is better than cure, but the government doesn't seem to understand that. They should be educating school children. They talk about 'safe sex' all the time on TV and yet they never tell anyone what safe sex really is. They need to spell it out — that, for example, no exchanging of body fluids means condoms at all times for everything.

What I want to do now is be an interior designer. If I wanted to do the course I'd have to go to Auckland for four years, and I couldn't handle that — I hate Auckland. But I have the chance of getting into business now, so if I can prove myself hopefully I'll work my way up. This ex-client is willing to help me out.

I want a career for myself, before I think about marriage, children and all the rest of it. I'm certainly not going to sit around waiting for some man to come and support me. Can't suffer from the Cinderella complex forever! Women today have got to get out there and earn their own money.

Besides, I don't want a man at the moment anyway. It would be nice to have someone to go out with and all the rest of it, but I'm certainly not into sex and I'm not into answering to someone else and I certainly don't want to go through the pain of a relationship again. I'm really happy on my own, just me and my animals.

I'm definitely through with prostitution. I'd like to get out of it altogether soon. I'm doing reception work because it's getting me some money and it's something I can do, but soon, hopefully, I'd like to leave it all behind.

I've given up going for job interviews though, because it's just so much hassle. Trying to explain the last seven years away is just too hard, even with telling lies and that. The last resumé I got together I even got references for — I wrote them myself and got people to sign them. I was over-qualified for everything then! So that didn't work out.

The only thing I want to get into now is interior design. That's where my passion lies. It's the only thing I can see that I could actually do and enjoy and be good at, so I'm determined to slog my way up there some way or other. I'll have to start at the bottom again, but that's life.

Since this interview was conducted over two years ago, Sarah decided to return to sex work in order to pay off some debts she had accumulated. She also became involved in setting up NZPC. During this time she started a new relationship, and has recently quit working to return to reception duties again. This decision arose from her feeling that she really wanted this relationship to work, and that she'd definitely had enough of working after nine years in the indus-

Sarah

try. Sarah says she is still terrified that if her circumstances change she'll end up back working again. Part of the difficulty involved in leaving sex work is that 'it's hard to get a job in the straight world without running into clients everywhere'.

HARLEY

Harley is in her early twenties and began working in an Auckland massage parlour when she was fourteen. Since then she has also worked as an escort and on the streets. She was interviewed in Arohata Women's Prison shortly before her release.

I was born in Auckland but taken up north before I knew it, and grew up in Northland. When I was about ten or eleven my mum got a boyfriend and divorced the guy I thought was my father, and we went to live on a farm with him. I felt pretty torn between my parents. I lived with my aunties a lot, and one of them had some gang guys living next door who I got to know. Once when I ran away from the farm, I went there, but they came and got me and stuck me in a hostel in Auckland.

One day I was called in to this guy's office and he said, 'You're about to meet your real father.' I said, 'I beg your pardon — I know my real father.' It was really funny. First of all this guy with a suit on walked in. He completely ignored me and just started talking to this other guy, and I thought, 'Wow, that's my dad, is it?' Then he walked out again and it wasn't even him! My dad did walk in after that and he was nice, real tall and dark and lovely. He stuck around for two weeks and then I never saw him again.

So about the time I met my father, I'd decided I was going to live with a gang guy I'd met who'd just got out after doing seven years inside for murder. He was only seventeen at the time it happened, and I still don't know if he did it or not. Anyway, I told my dad I was going to live with this guy and that was the last I heard of my father.

I was fourteen by this stage, and I'd left school. I ended up living with that guy until I was eighteen and a half. He didn't like me working though, but I got sick of being broke.

It was the guy I'd been with before that who got me started working. I think he told me it was a modelling job. I went along and found out what it really was in a hurry. It was a parlour called Pleasures. All of a sudden I had all this money, so I kept on working. Although I was only fourteen, I had lied and told them I was seventeen. I used a lot of the money to buy him things. He was a pimp, really. I went with him and worked there for six months before I took up with that guy who'd been inside.

Pleasures was just an ordinary massage parlour. Quite small, with about four girls working a night, six on busy nights. It was managed by a woman usually. When a client came in, we'd show him a room, tell him to have a shower, and then give him a massage. You'd wait for him to ask for extras, just in case he was a cop. I'd only do hand relief or sex, although I'd sometimes get kinky ones who wanted golden showers. That involves pissing on them, and sometimes they'd just lie there with their mouths open and jerk themselves off. They'd pay heaps though — $300 a time.

Sometimes we'd get those clients to lie down and tell them we needed to go and have a drink first before we could piss on them. Then we'd watch TV for half an hour, come back and tell them, 'Listen, I can't right now. Come back tomorrow.' But you don't give their money back. You always get their money first, and keep it. They're hardly likely to go off to a cop and say, 'Hey listen, I just paid this woman $300 to give me a golden shower and she didn't!'

Most of my clients were in their thirties and forties. I did have some young ones though, about sixteen or seventeen. I also had some virgins who came in because their mates had set it up, or once a guy came in because his father had arranged it. The oldest client I had was real old, seventy or something. You get worried when they're that age that they're going to croak, so you don't want to turn them on too much.

When I started work there I found out that the bosses often

wanted the girls to give them a massage — it was just a polite way of saying they wanted to have a perve. Often they'd try to put it on you to give them sex for free. And if the guy owns the place and you want the job, it seems like there's not much choice but to give it. I've always refused — I figure they can get stuffed.

You get some weird clients. I used to have one guy who'd come in, pay me $200, and open his briefcase, and inside he had handcuffs and different kinds of whips and these lacy knickers which he'd put on. And I had to handcuff him to the table and whip him, as hard as I could without drawing blood. He'd just come from the whipping. Most of the guys who wanted this sort of thing were businessmen, company heads, pretty well-off guys.

We used to get mainly Pakeha guys coming in. Except for the Japanese — we used to get heaps of them, off the fishing boats. I'll never forget them, because they have pearls in their dicks. When I first started working I wouldn't go near them or touch them because I thought they were warts, until one of the girls told me. The number of pearls they've got shows how wealthy they are.

Some of my clients became regulars, probably thirty or forty per cent. With some it seemed that the worse you treated them, the more they loved it, and they'd come back again and again. I don't understand men!

I used to work a mix of day and night shifts, depending on whether I had a habit or not, or whether I wanted to go out raging. It was always a much busier at night-time.

If guys were drunk and I felt stuffed, I'd just say to them, 'Listen, honey, you won't get it up tonight. Come back another night and I'll only charge you half price.' They'd never come back, or if they did I'd just look at them and say, 'No, not me.' It was just too hard trying to do them when they were drunk, so I didn't bother — just took their money.

Some clients want someone to listen to their problems —they're good, because they just sit and talk. They pay for sex, but really just want to get their problems off their chests. I never got close to any of my clients, though. I wouldn't — it just feels too dangerous.

I've also had a few sugar daddies. A sugar daddy buys you things and puts you up in a flat and looks after you. What he's supposed to get out of it is sex occasionally, but they didn't often from me — maybe I'm just cruel!

Usually I'd be in a relationship with one for a couple of months at a time. The last guy I had was really rich. He had a family and he owned all these offices and he put me up the top of one of his buildings. It was all decked out like a neat little penthouse, and he'd give me $50 a day spending money as well. He called around to see me all the time, but it was just for the company.

I wasn't supposed to be working while I was with him, but I was going up K Road still and he was angry when he found out. He was angrier when I had a party there one night, though, and his car got stolen by one of my mates. He asked me to move out. He was real cunning, though. He got this girl to move in who was going out with a policeman and I found another place quick — you don't want policemen hanging round the place when you've got a drug habit.

Working for escort agencies is good because you make heaps of money from all the overseas clients with their foreign currencies. All you need to set up an agency is a house and a telephone and advertisements in the paper. If a guy rings up to say he'd like a lady at six o'clock, you say, 'Just a minute, sir, can I have your phone number and address please?' Once he's given it to you, and his room number or whatever, you tell him you'll arrange the details and call him back. Then you check out the address in the phone book to make sure it's a private house and ring back to make sure it's the right phone number and the right person.

A lot of guys who rang up were lazy, I reckon. They'd be the sort who live by themselves and they'd get home after work and ring up for someone to come over. Or they might be from out of town or overseas and they'd have a nice meal and start relaxing and think, 'Oh, I wouldn't mind a woman,' so they'd ring up.

Sometimes you'd get couples ringing up. Often he might just want to watch while you had sex with his wife, or he might join in. And sometimes you might get one guy ringing up for two girls.

I've also worked on the streets, when I was nineteen or twenty. I couldn't be bothered going and getting a job in a parlour then, having to work all those hours. On the streets I could do my own advertising, wear what I wanted, be my own boss. I'd walk up and say, 'Want a girl, mister — cheap?' They might turn around then and ask where we could go, so I'd say, 'In your car,' and tell them where to drive to. I won't go to parks because they're too far away and too deserted. Lots of clients say they'd like to go to the Domain, but heaps of things have happened to girls there — they've been raped and all sorts. Normally I just go to a couple of streets away, up a driveway or behind a shop or something. Usually they want hand jobs or straight sex. Most ask for oral as well, but I won't do that. I don't tell them until I've got the money first, though.

Mostly I work with the queens on the street, even though I'm a fish (the queens call us girls 'fish'). They let me work with them, though, because I've sort of grown up with most of them, and they've often kept an eye out for me and looked after me. The queens provide the same as we do — sex — but using the other passage. They'll do oral a lot too. The queens undercut us. They won't admit it, but they do. I don't really feel like we're in competition, though, because I think everyone has got their own speciality.

It's more of a con game up there on the street. You hop in the car and you're so sweet to them. You run your hand up their leg and say, 'Would you like to have the best time of your life tonight?' and all that sort of crap. I have to be pretty out of it to say some of the things I say.

If I had the choice, I'm not sure which I'd rather work. Escorts are good, but they're really time-consuming; parlours are okay, except you have to work that certain time-span. I

HARLEY

think I'd choose the streets, if it wasn't for the risk, because you can work when and as often as you want, and you're your own boss.

I had one client out on the streets who looked like a sales rep, suit on and everything, nice, well groomed, flash car, baby seat in the back. I hopped in and he didn't drive where I told him. Instead he drove miles away and then he started beating me. He broke three of my ribs. He just beat the shit out of me, then threw me out of the car.

I went back to where I was living on K Road and, as I let myself in, this girl saw me who I used to go to school with. She's a cop. She was practically crying because I was a real mess, and I had to go to hospital, but I wouldn't tell her what had happened. I figure the cops are against us. I just told the queens and gave them a description of his car, because I knew he'd get nothing but hell after that.

The second night I went out after recovering, a young guy, about eighteen or nineteen, wanted to do business so I jumped in the car. He said to me, 'Roll a joint,' and gave me some dope, then drove to a carpark, took out a gun, stuck it against my head and said, 'Get your clothes off.' So I just wound down the window and screamed at the top of my lungs until he booted me out of the car. He tried to scare me, but I scared him.

No one came, but then no one ever does. Even when that other guy was beating me up, I screamed and screamed and there was a whole row of houses there, but nobody came. After he dumped me out of the car I walked up the hill and there was a guy out on his front lawn who said, 'Oh yeah. I saw you, but I thought it was your boyfriend. I thought it was just a domestic.'

Another time a guy ended up raping me. These are probably the worst things that have happened to me. That's not too bad in all the years I've been working.

When I'm working I have to feel that I'm in charge, because otherwise you'll get raped and things. You can't let them think they've got the power over you.

I won't go to the cops, though, no matter what happens. They're always after us. They search your bag looking for condoms and things so they can do you for soliciting. They always ask where you're going and everything. I normally work where there are takeaways or a coffee bar nearby, so I can always say, 'I'm just going to have a cup of coffee.' At one o'clock in the morning they don't believe it, but if they can't catch you, you're okay.

The ordinary cops pretty much leave us alone because we're too cunning for them. But the Vice will plant guys who will sit in their cars and call you over. You just wave to them and walk past and carry on working right in front of them. Sometimes you can tell which ones are cops because of the cars they use. Although they can be quite smart and use beat-up Minis to put us off. Normally, though, word gets around real fast. Often they're just a dead giveaway. Even the clients will tell us there's a cop parked down the road. They wait for you to lead, to say to them, 'Well, if you want sex it's such and such a price.' They can't ask you — otherwise it's entrapment.

Once they terrified this poor guy I was with by picking him up. I'd seen them coming down this no-exit street and I told him not to panic. I gave him my name and he told me his, and I told him to say that we were friends and he was giving me a lift. He freaked out and told me to jump out of the car, but said he'd stick to the story. The cops asked for his driver's licence and said they'd ring up his wife, then took me away for soliciting. In the end it got dismissed because there was no witness.

Sometimes it feels like a bit of a game with the cops, but it can be a vicious game. As far as I know, I've never had an off-duty cop as a client. I wouldn't do a cop on principle. You get clients who *say* they're cops, though. He'll pay you and get it over with, then turn around and say, 'We're going down town — you're under arrest.' So you laugh and say, 'Get fucked, mister. Like hell.'

Sometimes guys will take you somewhere and say, 'If you don't front up I'm going to take you down town and have you for soliciting and prostitution.' They won't have paid, and you're in their car, so you're sort of trapped. But you just tell them, 'Get stuffed. No way. If you're going to arrest me, take me there now.' Then you hop out and walk back.

The police come around the parlours too. We've got warning systems in the parlours, though. There's a naked bulb in each room and a button out by the front desk, so if the cops come in you just press that button and all the lights flash on in the rooms.

The cops come charging in usually, bursting through the doors. If you're halfway through with a client it's just too bad. You stop and make him lie down and pretend you're just massaging him. Mainly the cops look at the register when they come round, just to see who's working there and if they've got any criminal convictions or drug convictions. I won't be able to work in a parlour when I get out of jail because I'll have criminal convictions, so I'll have to work the streets.

Before I go out working I have to have something, even if it's just a few drinks. I can't walk in cold. If I do, it's torturous. When I'm working nights, I'll spend all day at the pub, if I'm not using at the time. Or else I might get up and have a blast to start the day, then do some housework. I used to love doing housework when I was out of it. Or I'd visit people, or go to the beach, get a tan. Often I'd go to the doctor's and score as many pills as I could. I'd spend heaps of time on doctor's appointments. I'd ring up new doctors and tell them, 'I've run out of this and I'm up here for a funeral and I don't know what to do.' I'd score heaps.

I'll probably go back on the streets and get a habit again. The only reason I want a habit when I get out is to lose some weight. I lost three stone in three weeks last time I got out, and that's the only way I did it. I hate being fat. If I get back on the same stuff, it will cost me nearly a grand each day.

On quiet nights I might only earn a couple of hundred, and that wouldn't be enough. You have to have another income as well. So before I came in here I was getting Temgesics from the doctor and selling them for $25 each. That's something I've been into since my accident. That was when I had PD on Saturdays. I woke up and went to the doctor's to get a medical certificate so I wouldn't have to go to PD. I'd already had my blast that morning, but it didn't get me out of it. The doctor gave me peth in the bum, and it didn't hit me straight away. I hitched a lift and was set down on the motorway. Got out of the truck and wham. The peth must have hit me when I stood up, because apparently I crossed the motorway like I owned it. Ended up with both legs broken and my pelvis.

My own habit is usually homebake. Or I get white when I can, or pink rocks or brown rocks. I know people who make homebake. About $100 worth does me for about six hours. I'd be reasonably comfortable for about ten hours; I would be nicely out of it for about four, come normal again a couple of hours later and be just okay for the next few hours. Then I'd start feeling downhill, getting cramps and things. I was about eighteen and a half when I started developing a habit. I was using speed when I started in the parlours, and later Valium, alcohol, then the Temgesics. Now it's mostly homebake.

I think I was eleven when I first had sex. It wasn't by choice. It was my mother's boyfriend's brother. I didn't know how to tell my mother, so I wrote her a letter and put it on their bed before I went to bed. The next morning they asked me about it. I said it was true and they called me a liar. It wasn't long before I came down and stayed in the hostel. I think that was the final straw. He only did it once, but he used to make passes all the time. I hated him. Just about everyone I know who's working has had some sort of experience like that.

I have an automatic switch when I'm working. It comes on so that I just can't remember a thing about the nights I work. Even an hour later, it's gone. That's where the drugs work, too, because they make you not remember. On a good night I might have seven clients. I couldn't switch on to my own man after that. It's hard having a relationship while you're working—they don't like it. I don't have a boyfriend on the outside—every time I come to jail they disappear.

HARLEY

Sometimes sex with women is easier. I lived with a lady for two years. She's dead now. We would normally work together, so we both knew how it felt.

Probably about half of all working girls are lesbian — or maybe it's really bisexual. I don't think working really affects them. Women are just more sensual — none of this wham bam stuff.

Sometimes I feel like the clients we go with only want us for sex. They want to be regulars, and some will ask us to go out for dinner without paying and everything, but I always say no. I don't think we get ripped off, though — if anything, we're ripping them off.

I always insist on clients using condoms when I'm working, always have and always will. There's not one client who could bribe me with any amount of money not to wear a condom, no way. I have a medical check too, about every six or eight weeks. Once I had gonorrhoea, but that was from a dear friend, and that's all I've had.

AIDS has affected the industry lately. There's not as many clients around now as there used to be. But at least some of them are bringing their own condoms now. And the queens and everyone on the streets are using condoms more than they used to.

I'd like to settle down eventually and have a family, but at the moment I'm still too young, too reckless. It wouldn't be fair if I had a family. I'm not one of these women who call themselves feminists. I enjoy having a boyfriend and looking after him.

When I get out I'll work occasionally to give me some extra money on top of my sickness benefit. I got on the sickness benefit after my other accident, a few years earlier. I broke my leg then too, in a bike accident, and had a metal pin put in it. That's a lot of the reason I use, because of the pain.

I have done straight jobs. When I had a boyfriend who didn't like me working, I had jobs waitressing and in cafeterias and in a video shop. I didn't last more than a couple of months in any of them. I would have stayed at the video shop longer, but the guy went bankrupt. I wouldn't even think of getting a straight job now.

If people ask me what I do, I sometimes tell them. If it was a really nice guy, I'd probably tell him I was a part-time model and sickness beneficiary. But if it was just somebody inquiring, I'd probably tell them I'm a hooker. And most people then ask me questions. They want to know about the clients and the money. I don't think my mother knows I'm working, but she has a fair idea.

Physically it's an easy life working on the streets. It's not easy mentally, though, because of having to put up the false front all the time. That's a real effort. I don't want to work — I'm just too used to the easy life now. Why should I get a straight job and work eight hours a day, five days a week, when I can earn more than that in just one night on the streets?

After she left prison Harley headed for Auckland. Unfortunately, it has been impossible to establish what she did or where she went from there.

HINEMOA

Hinemoa describes herself as a full-blood Maori of Ngarauru descent. She was a ship girl in Taranaki in the late 1950s and 1960s, before moving to Wellington, where she worked as a DJ in various strip and nightclubs.

I was born in Wellington and at six weeks travelled with my grandmother to St Joseph's Orphanage, Christchurch, run by the Sisters of the Good Shepherd. The orphanage was made up of a baby nursery, primary school and secondary, all run by nuns day and night, with the exception of the boilerhouse, which was manned by men. The cloistered order of Magdalen's prayed and toiled within its grounds as a separate religious community, with a Good Shepherd sister as their Mother Superior. There were acres and acres of land. They raised sheep, cattle, dairy herds, wheat fields, barley, oats, all manner of vegetables on a large scale. And lots of different fruit orchards — gooseberries, strawberries, raspberries, blackberries, black and red currants, nectarines, all manner of plums, peaches, apples, lemons, pears, crabapples, tomatoes, potatoes, beans, peas, pumpkins, cabbages. I have never seen a more successful self-sufficient place on such a large scale, and run totally by women.

Our day began and ended with a prayer. I would say everything was done by prayer. The power of prayer is something to behold.

I never heard a swear word in all my time at that convent, and that was a long time spent with a lot of people, predominantly female. So, you know, innocence is something I value.

I always felt like a queen or a little princess in those vast big buildings and open spaces. The memories of my childhood days are full of fun, excitement, learning, dressing up, parties, outings, lots of games and people. Life really was beautiful there.

Finally I left and came north to Te Horo, just out of Wellington, to a kind of finishing school which prepared you for the outside world. From there I went to Waitara in Taranaki, where for the first time in my life I met my flesh and blood mother. I was now on my own.

From Waitara I moved to New Plymouth, where I worked very hard and had my first date with the international circuit. He was a lovely, blue-eyed, blond Swede off one of the merchant ships. I can't remember his name, but we called all Scandinavians 'Der' anyway. Der was a word which stood in when you didn't know a person. It was like 'Hey, girl' or 'Hey, boy.'

I can still recall my first meeting with that Swede. He was drinking vodka straight from the bottle, and I was making tracks to the taxi stand to go home. I heard a lot of chatter and these four Swedes came up and began speaking in broken English to me. I just smiled. I must say being pursued by four lovely blue-eyed blonds was an absolute smorgasbord to me, and I have to be truly honest — those men were the very first males to make my heart skip a beat. It didn't matter who or what they were, what they were saying, or where they came from — they knew enough English to persuade me not to go home!

We all caught a cab down to their ship so they could change for the evening. I didn't go on board, I waited in the taxi. From the wharf we drove to the White Hart Hotel for drinks, then to a milkbar, on to Ping's Pie Cart to eat, and then to the Calypso Coffee Lounge to see Kahu Peneaha entertain. After that we went off to a party. There my entourage of four dwindled to one.

It got to 1 a.m. and I realised I must sleep to face another working day, so Der and I walked around for what seemed like hours. It was the long way home, but very romantic. We thanked one another for the pleasantries and parted, no kiss, just a hug, a smile, holding hands as though it was forever. And my heart fluttering as if in a time warp, measuring a colourful space of emptiness with just him and I. So that was that.

HINEMOA

You know, I can actually remember when just holding hands with a guy would make your feet lift. Such was the innocence of those days.

Mother Superior talked to us and told us about sex. I remember I sat through the sex talk three times, and by the third time I almost knew word for word what she was saying.

A lot of us took pledges in the convent that we would never touch alcohol until we were twenty-one. I made an internal vow to myself that I would remain a virgin until then. I just felt that I wanted to live my childhood as a child. I had seen others in the convent 'fall' — today it's called 'getting pregnant', but then it was called 'falling by the wayside'. And in those days if you became a solo parent you were shunned.

Boyfriends in those days were just that — boy friends. If you didn't want sex, or you didn't want them to kiss you, they didn't. But there was always the odd jerk, like there is today and always will be, who'd try his luck.

Now that vow I made about being a virgin I kept. That's one thing I did keep. Although I wasn't a virgin when I married. You hear about the wedding night, and let's be very real here — I can't see how on earth a virgin, or two virgins, can on their wedding night have the best night of their lives.

I used to believe I would never ever get married. I actually didn't want to get married. There were a lot of maidens around when I was a child who were elegant, good-looking, smart, clever, pillars of the community. Society looked up to them; they were important. I suppose in those days they would have still been virgins as well. They were something to behold. And that's what I wanted to be. But it never turned out that way.

I met my husband up in Taranaki, a local lad. It was three years, though, before we got married, not until I was twenty-three. He actually proposed to me three times. But I ran away from him initially — that's what brought me to Wellington. It was the furthest place I could think of to go.

I ran away, but my friends used to tell him where I was. I was going on the ships then; I was a ship girl. But as time went on he used to be there too. Later he told me the seamen used to have a collection for who would be the first to sleep with me. I never knew this, until one day he told me.

It took us about nine months or more for my virginity to be broken. He used to tell me that I was ruining him and I'd say, 'How the hell?' Still, I went to my doctor and talked about it, because I'd heard others say you could go to your doctor to get broken in. And I remember the doctor being so very nice and saying to me, 'But you don't really want that.' And I said, 'Of course I do. It's killing him.' He laughed, took me by the hand and sat me down and said, 'No, Hinemoa, you don't really need my services.'

After the wedding I still didn't want to give up seamen. I used to see them in the pubs, and I had that urge, even after marriage. I don't know what it was, but they were always a drawcard to me, especially the Scandinavians.

So I was a ship girl for years. The only thing that was different was that after marriage, I never slept with them. Or rather, I slept with them, but I never had coitus. I would never let a man touch my vagina with his hands even, because that to me was no different from a penis.

I did absolutely nothing with those men. I had a very beautiful body then, and I used to just go and lie nude in their cabins. I was a total exhibitionist. I had it to flaunt, and I flaunted it. They were quite happy for me just to do that. Although sometimes I used to freak them out. They'd come in and I'd be on their bunk, or I would just lie in my underwear, stuff like that. My friend used to say what I was doing was teasing. She used to sleep and have sex with my boyfriends. Sometimes she'd say she was still a virgin, though. But she and I both learned that there are times when you never told anybody that, even if you were. Like I knew not to tell people at work, businessmen especially, that I was a virgin. Because that's the first thing they go for. And I never liked businessmen at any rate.

When I met up with those four Swedes, they were the first men I ever looked at differently. And after going to that party with them, I met up with other 'tima' — ship girls. But I started off just courting, and it wasn't until I went on board the ship itself that I became one. And from then on I loved every minute of it.

In those days you didn't need to travel overseas. The international circuit came to you — Danes, Swedes, Germans, Finns, African natives off the ACT boats, Pommies from all the different parts of England, and nearly every nation's navy — the Chileans, the French, the Aussies, the Americans. The Japs were actually the last of any nation to visit our shores. And the Deep Freeze Air Force Americans — wowee!

They really were the good times. The ports were always full of ships. Now you're lucky to see even one in port.

Usually you knew beforehand when a ship was due. If there was a new boat in port you would ring them and ask to speak to somebody. Most of us were interested in the deck boys because we were the same age.

The officers were good value, but if you went with them you had to stay with them; it was a prestige situation. Whereas the cabin and deck boys, the engineer, the cook and all the rest of them were much more fun. With the officers you have to show respect and all the rest of it. When you're having a good time, respect isn't really one of the things that is foremost in your mind.

You went with who you fancied. And whether it was an officer or a cabin boy, you stayed with him throughout that boat's visit. It was just like the men saying a seaman has a girl in every port — what they never advertised were the girls who had a seaman on every ship!

There was a code of ethics involved, too. The older ones taught the younger ones. There were those who fell in love, too. How stupid, though, to fall in love with a seaman. I mean, it's preposterous really. But when you're a young girl . . .

I did end up falling in love with a couple of them in my time. But there was always that code of ethics you learn, and you know you're there for the good times. But you could still find yourself going for a tumble if you knew they had someone.

And some of them would sit down and talk to you about all their different girls and ports they'd just been in and the good times they'd had. So you weren't only having a good time with an international seaman; it was also learning the geography and history of the different countries.

I still used to go on the boats after marriage. I would look after them, and I became a 'safe house' for them. In those days you could get into trouble for harbouring seamen. It was against the law to run a safe house for seamen, for the guys who wanted to jump ship and stay in New Zealand. The police were always around in those days. They were the law, and they really did their work.

Usually you'd only go on the boat when the seamen were working, and then you'd stay overnight or whatever. It was like a floating hotel. There was always the chance of free travel, if you wanted to go from port to port. I only did that a couple of times. That's all I did. But all my friends did it constantly, and the lucky ones even went overseas.

If you were hidden and ringbolted out of the country, you had to hide until the ship left port. They'd hide you within the walls or under the beds or wherever. Ringbolting is just like hopping on a plane — the only difference is that you pay for the plane. We always used to say 'courtesy of Shaw Saville line' or whatever. There were girls who ringbolted just for the travel, and others who did it because of their boyfriends.

I was never all that involved in it, because I was working at the hospital, nursing. And sometimes I worked at night at Ping's Pie Cart. I had a lot of energy so I needed to do something with it. Later I worked as an au pair girl, nannying. But I would fit it all around the boats.

There were lots of times when we sat up on top of Paritutu Hill and drank the ships in. As soon as they docked, down we ran. If she was a new ship, we would look at her and analyse her. Then we'd go straight to the wharf and ring the ship and ask, 'Is that the purser? Oh, my name's so-and-so. There's a group of us girls all wanting to know if any of your crew would be interested.' And they would say yes, or put us on to somebody, or we'd ask for the bosun, or the engineer or whatever.

Sometimes we'd just stay at a coffee bar and meet them there first to see what they looked like. But you had no problems like that with the Scandinavians. Everyone liked them, the good old Scandies. You knew their looks — they were beauty personified.

At times it was really busy, because you could have all your seamen in port at once. But then if something like the *Esmeralda* came in, it would all change. I mean, the *Esmeralda* only comes along once in a blue moon. So every time she came in, off we'd go. They were little honeys, those Chileans, absolute little honeys. It wasn't only that, though. She was a beautiful ship, and so tidy.

A whole group of us girls would hang out together, going from ship to ship. And we'd share cabs down to the port. The distance between Waitara and New Plymouth was a fair way, and often there'd be half a dozen of us wanting to go down. And everyone used to say at the end, 'Where's Hinemoa?' and I'd give the cabbie a kiss on the cheek and that would be the fare. Many a time I've kissed a cabbie for the fare.

The men didn't give us money. I suppose you could ask for money if you wanted it. But they'd pay for everything, so when you were with them you didn't need money. A lot of my ship girlfriends never worked, that's how good times were way back then. Nobody really slept for money then. The first real situation for that would probably have been when the Japs came ashore, but for us it was all free. Maori girls have been known, though, throughout history to give it away, while the European yuppies were selling it in the pubs. But we were always out for the good times.

Ship boyfriends and ship relationships are different from local ones. When you go on board and you look at a ship, it's very small. But it's the fun and togetherness everybody has that makes it special. Everybody knows everybody else. You didn't dare take another girl's boyfriend. You got your beans if you did. If anyone did anything outside of the code of ethics, they could get a hiding. It would be the girls who would give it, never the men. The men never liked it, because after all we were meant to be ladies. I will admit, although it's a horrible thing to admit now, but I threw a girl down the gangplank once and she rolled all the way down.

Sometimes you'd shower with the guys, but you'd do that only when it was just you and your fellow. I even took some of them pig hunting, because that's something I liked to do. You did things with them that you'd do with a normal boyfriend — the only difference was they were guys off the ship.

And yes, seamen carry STDs and have a bad name. But if they came into port with it, they'd always tell you. My doctor was always marvellous. He was the one who first got the contraceptive pill going in New Zealand. But again, the ship girls were way ahead — they'd had it three, four, even five years before then.

In the late fifties, early sixties, we had to watch out for the police sometimes, because they were rounding up the ship girls and sending them off to Arohata. But I never had any trouble, except once in New Plymouth when ten of us ended up in court, but I'm not even sure now what that was all about.

In Port Taranaki there used to be a Maori cop who had a lovely little grey motorbike — we used to call it 'Beetlebomb'. He was clever, damn him. But I got away from him several times. We'd jump overboard and swim for our lives up to Ngamotu Beach. I'd get on my back in the water and move without making ripples, and I'd get away. The others would be overarming and kicking, and there would be Harry with his torch, shining it in the water.

The main batch of cops would be on the wharf waiting for us to come off, while sly old Harry would be out there on the other side. He knew some of the girls would jump over and try to swim away. You'd get soaked, of course, so you'd head for the nearest house and get changed, pronto, before he caught you. He was trying to get us for being unlawfully on board ship, especially after hours.

What we did after hours was to hide in the cabins. You were

supposed to be off at certain times, but if you were a ship girl you never got off. When the port was full, though, you were just running from ship to ship. You'd tell your boyfriend to go with someone else while you went off. You looked after one another's boyfriends.

I was probably unusual in not sleeping with the guys. Most of the girls probably did. There was always an initiation because there would be innocent girls, and our group always asked if new girls were virgins. We used to say, 'You don't have to if you don't want to,' and 'If you want any help, you know . . .' A lot of girls would just hover.

When I had first come to Wellington, which was about 1956, maybe 1958, the people I was meant to stay with had forgotten all about me and gone away on holiday for a week, so I spent the first night just walking around. Wellington seemed like such a beautiful big place. I didn't want to go to bed, I was so excited. There was only one night place open then — a little takeaway thing called the Hot Dog, run by a Greek guy called Angelo. He was fabulous, and everything was just beautiful.

A truckie told me the Valley Inn wanted workers, and one of the girls mentioned that the owner liked Maori girls. He was losing his head waitress at the time so I said I'd like to work for him, but start off somewhere else first. So I went into the kitchen for a while and loved it. But he pulled me out of there and I ended up waitressing.

I think what got me everywhere in those days was me being a Maori. Maoris were considered illiterate then, and very shy and all the rest of it. I was a Maori with a difference. A blue-blood Maori. I used to be a lot darker than I am now, I spoke very well, and I always used to walk erect with my head in the air. Bosses and people who mattered in jobs would look twice at me and tell me how different I was and ask why. I would never tell them I was brought up in a convent. I just used to say, 'My name is Hinemoa — what's yours?' I was really alone, I had nobody, and I couldn't talk about where I had come from or where I was born. It was better to remain aloof, dumb.

WORKING GIRLS

I played the dummy for a long, long time. But I hated to walk around with my head down, like a lot of others, because it showed little character. I didn't like my own race for that. They used to disadvantage themselves so much, and yet a lot of them were clever, just very shy. I was shy, but in a different way. I was proud of what I was, and I think others were attracted to that.

Like Zorba. I worked for him for a long time. I think I met up with him when I went into the Royal Oak with the seamen one time. We often used to go in there with our men. There would be a whole table of ship girls. And all the pros used to be down the other end.

In those days there were no street-walkers. You worked from the pubs then. It was only when the queens came in that beating the feet on the streets began. The first to do that were the Australian queens. They did it here at a time when the New Zealand queens were doing it over there.

That's how the whole perception of prostitution really began. It was overseas men coming in, who were used to sleeping with girls and paying for it. It happened to me with a Norwegian guy. We booked into the White Hart and went to go to sleep, when halfway through the bloody night his little hands were pawing, pawing. He wanted sex, and he was in a tantrum, so I jumped under the bed. It was very low to the floor and I was very slim, but he, being a big man, couldn't fit under. The beds were secured to the floor so they couldn't be moved, and I slid right under, right up against the wall. He was making a huge uproar, and when I came out the other girls were there and there was money all over the place, and Lee said to me, 'Why don't you take it, girl?' But I didn't want to. She asked if I knew who I'd got, because I think it was the captain. And I'd broken the code again, without knowing, because when you go with the captain you treat him right.

Life on board the ships is a lot different now. In those days a lot of the men just wanted to be out with the girls, and be seen in their company. Sure, if they scored, they scored; but a lot of them just liked going out with the girls and having fun.

I do think they crack it now, though, because someone told me just the other day that she'd been down on board and one of the guys had told her he didn't want a condom so she'd sent him off to the next bunk. But that hardly ever happened in my time. The cracking part really came in with the Japs.

You could only find out what they were like by going on board. Even the Royal Navy was good — not our navy, though. I mean, you wouldn't be seen dead with our navy. All the yuppies and squares would come out and go with the Kiwi navy, but you wouldn't have it on.

We were all so very naive and morally pure in those days. If you told a policeman to shut up, you'd be dragged in. Nowadays you can use four-letter words and still not get dragged in. You have to knock him down and just about murder him before you're taken in.

Being drunk and disorderly was the main charge then. The police used to have quotas, and I ended up being many a young policeman's first quota. They would be like little boys getting a new toy when you got down there — 'I've got my new arrest.' Never mind you or how they got it. Nine times out of ten you shouldn't really have been arrested.

I got involved in the strip scene in Wellington when it first started here. It was through Zorba. He ran a restaurant then, where the food was delicious, and I went and ate there often. My meal used to be a standard meal of roast lamb, vegetables, and half a dozen eggs. You'd go across there from the pub, at six o'clock closing, and then go off to a party.

Later I worked for Zorba in his restaurant, but he wanted me to work in the club. He'd taken it over from Wally Martin, who had opened the very first strip club in Wellington. It would have been about 1960, and it was in Manners Street. The Wesley Church owned the passage-way leading to the club, and there used to be a lot of ado about the moral side of it. It was the Club Exotic, and still exists today, although it's moved, but it's a far cry from what it used to be way back. It wasn't my idea to work in the club, but Zorba wanted me to serve at the door and stopped me from working in his restaurant to get me there. Mostly I got into doing DJ work there.

We used to work very hard. We would start at 6 or 7 p.m. and sometimes go through until 8 a.m. or even 10 a.m. Zorba used to come out and say, 'Hinemoa, stop the show. Look at them — they look tragic.' But if the house was full and the girls were in demand, then sure, the make-up might be coming to grief, but so would yours be if you worked those hours.

Nightclubs and strip clubs are often seen as seedy, but that's just a label we've been given by society. I think it was about 1970 that Pasi and Anita Daniels came over and opened the Purple Onion in Vivian Street, where Playgirls is now. That was the first transvestite 'Les Girls' situation and it became a real tourist attraction. When the Osaka Expo was on they were even taken over there by cruise ship to be in the New Zealand pavilion.

Later on, when I was working as DJ at the Perfumed Garden, we used to have telethon-type fundraisers there. We'd go for twenty-four or forty-eight hours non-stop, raising money. Later we did the same thing at Club Exotic. At times like that I wouldn't even eat so I wouldn't have to take time out to go to the toilet.

I loved the DJ work. I'd still love to get back to that again. I never wanted to go into radio, though, because you have to do what they tell you to do. Whereas in a nightclub, and especially in a strip club, it was very much your own work. You supplied your own records and that cost you a sweet little fortune. Sometimes I'd end up looking after the dancers, doing it all, virtually running the place — but I loved it.

Before the clubs got going, parties were the main thing, and going to the pub. Our meeting house in Wellington was the Royal Oak, with its Bistro Bar, which became world-famous. It was the meeting place for the international circuit and everybody went there. Zorba's eating house was just across the road, and down the street, on the corner, was the hairdresser.

So we'd finish work and go downtown, and every Friday we'd buy a new outfit. It's true — you could do that in those days. You bought yourself a whole new ensemble, from your head to your toes. You didn't just buy a frock, but shoes, accessories, handbag, the whole bloody lot. And you'd appear in that hotel dressed to kill.

And everything was there. All the men that you wanted, or didn't want, in the pub. So we'd get our new ensemble, get our hair done, go to the pub, then across to Zorba's. All the ones who wanted to party hearty would go there and line their bellies, then go and party all night and come back to him for breakfast. You'd see exactly the same faces there again next morning.

There were about ten of us girls who used to do the circuit. We stuck together, and more or less lived together. If one girl left the hotel, the whole lot of us left. We'd sit in the bar and every man who walked into that hotel would buy drinks for us, because the ship girls were the most popular.

The Greeks used to come in, wearing their hats and dark suits — we called them the Mafiosa. They were enormous giants of men, looking like the Godfather, and they would look over at us and smile and send us over a jug.

The locals, I must be honest — and do forgive me, but the locals were always a joke. A lot of them loved us, though. Now I think, 'God, Hinemoa, you must have been a real bitch in those days.' Because those guys would do anything for us, and we'd just use them. Here you were, whooping it up with these foreign men off the ships, but using the local guys for transport and things like that. But it was good for them as well, because they'd come along to the party too.

It's much tougher out on the streets now than it was then. The women now aren't earning as much as they did way back then. In those days a white woman only had to be white and she got money — she didn't even have to lie on her back for it.

I stayed in the scene after I got married because I couldn't leave it behind. I believed I had married for life, but unfortunately it wasn't to be. I really loved him, but I don't think we were married for any more than ten years, at the most. It wasn't either one's fault — it was both of us. For me I think it was, once again, the fact that I was too naive.

My big battle with him, ironic as it may sound, was that I actually caught him with a prostitute. And that to me was the lowest of the barrel, because he had to go and pay someone to get laid when I was there for nothing. That just blew my little brain away, and I wouldn't have him back again. And it was on the steps of the Elizabeth Street church. You can imagine what that did to me. I never ever forgave him.

We did go to counselling and I went to the priest and to the bishop. I went to marriage counsellors, but I couldn't find anything that could help me. Because no one explained to me about men. I was still very green; I had no knowledge of men. I knew about young men who wanted to have fun, but no one told me about the pros and cons of men, about two-timers and all of that.

That's why I think now, if I had my life to live all over again, I would live it free of men, without men, simply and solely because I've found that, apart from sex, there's not much to them.

Hinemoa now divides her time between part-time office work and evening work as a community worker running a coffee bar for sex workers. The AIDS scare prompted this place's establishment, which as well as providing a warm safe space for those who work the streets also encourages safe sex practices through the sale of cheap condoms.

LEE

Lee began working as a prostitute in Auckland when she was twenty-two. She moved to Australia in the 1960s, and spent some time working in a West Australian brothel before she was deported back to New Zealand.

I grew up in a suburb of Auckland during the 1950s. My father had his own business working from home, and he was a musician. He played the piano accordion, and my mother played the piano. We all played music at home together and sang around the piano. I had a younger sister, and I suppose I was very privileged and middle-class. Certainly my parents encouraged me in anything I showed an interest in.

I went to a boarding school with a very progressive lady headmistress. I'd been sent there because they had a marvellous Hungarian music teacher and I could also study art there. Although I was doing the usual academic course with French and Latin, I was expected to do something with art, and my ambition was to go and study art in Paris. After sitting UE and leaving school shortly before I turned seventeen, I went to enrol at Elam School of Fine Arts but found an artist I thought could teach me more.

Meanwhile I decided I wanted to go and study at the Sydney School of Art. I'd been waitressing part-time, and met this homosexual seaman who took quite a shine to me. When I said I wanted to go to Sydney, he and his friends helped me ringbolt over there on the *Monowai*. These men were lovely friends to me and protected me from the rest of the crew, who weren't gay.

When I arrived in Sydney I walked up to King's Cross and

found myself a little room, then walked down to the School of Art and enrolled there on my first day. I didn't realise a lot of the girls on the streets were prostitutes — I honestly had not even heard the word. So I was walking around King's Cross a lot, living in a little room and working nights in a nightclub. That's where I came undone, because the police raided the club for selling sly grog. But I didn't even know there was booze in the cups — I was so naive.

I ended up being beaten up and raped by the police, and in the end I was put in prison on vagrancy charges. I spent two months in Long Bay prison, and boy, was that an eye-opener. I said I was a Buddhist — I had been a Marxist but that was too depressing, and then I discovered some Buddhists and that really appealed to me for a while, but it was a bit passive, so I drifted out of that. Anyway, when I went into prison saying all these things, they thought I was a little bit insane and I was remanded for psychiatric observation.

When I got out of there, the police just never left me alone. That's just the way things were then; all the runaway girls went to King's Cross. I didn't know that, though. I liked it because it was full of little dives and coffee lounges with all sorts of bohemians, eccentrics and interesting people in them. I was very shy and naive, but I loved to watch people.

Once I knew prostitution was going on, I was intrigued, but I wasn't attracted to it at all. I had enough money to live on, eking out an existence in my little attic room. I got mixed up with an occult group, using a few herbs, doing a few incantations, weird paintings and all the rest of it. Eventually I scraped up my fare to catch a boat back to New Zealand, landing in Wellington, where I fell straight in with a bohemian crowd and was right in my element.

Then I went up to Auckland and met a man who was interested in all the sorts of things I had been in Sydney — yoga and everything. I got pregnant, so he did the right thing by me, and I got very confused about this. I had a child and we got married and set up house. But after a while, when the child was about four and I started asserting a little bit of independence and wanted to meet my old friends again, he objected. He didn't like my friends and started beating me up, so I ran back to Wellington. I thought to myself that marriage and being tied down wasn't for me, and I went back to Auckland to try to get my child back. After about a year of fighting through the courts, I ended up losing custody. There were no benefits then, and I tried to get live-in jobs where I could have the child, but I was completely at the mercy of these people, and I lost custody.

So I just went wild, drinking and leering up. I went to jazz clubs and I started thinking about how to earn some money. I decided it was only money that was stopping me, and that if I got enough I could get a decent lawyer to fight for my child. So I became the mistress of a wealthy businessman, and all of a sudden I was getting big money. I set myself up in a flat, bought a car, and time went on.

Eventually I decided I couldn't live in Auckland. It was impossible. There was no way I could see my child and it all seemed hopeless. I'd bought a house and everything by this stage, but I just walked out of the house, drove to the airport, got out of my car and hopped on a plane to Sydney. And I never looked back.

I lived in Sydney for a while and found all the big hotels where the wealthy farmers stayed. I'd go and sit in the lounge and it would only be a matter of time before I'd make a contact. Because I dressed well and spoke well, they had no idea I was on the game. I played very hard to get, and when anyone started to pick me up I'd talk about music and things like that.

Once I'd made the first contact, I never went back. Sometimes one of the hotel bellboys would get me an introduction, and I'd give him $10, but it was worth it, because that contact's yours then. And it meant I didn't have to hang around the hotel. I didn't have to go out much at all, except to shop or go to a concert. I never gave my music up, and I still paint even now.

Usually it was businessmen that I did business with, and they would tell their friends about me — at one stage I was doing business mainly with one firm. I had them come to my flat by appointment, but I kept it down to a certain number because I didn't want to get noticed.

After a while I realised I had stayed in Sydney too long. So I went to Melbourne and did the same thing there for ages. But then I heard about this mining town in the outback where prostitution was legalised and so were brothels. I really wanted to see more of Australia, so through a contact I made arrangements to go west. I had all sorts of contacts who helped me get a new driver's licence and new registration plates — in Australia you can do anything because everybody is so corrupt. I put my car on the train and set out across the desert. And that was the beginning of a different story altogether.

Over there you were expected to just go with the men that came — they lined up at the doors and you went with whoever. It didn't take me long before I decided I was going to try them out first, and it was only if they were okay and gave me no trouble that I'd agree to see them again.

I was much younger than the other girls, and the madam gave me more or less a free rein. So I picked the best, the best payers and the best behaved, and I was still busy all the time. Even though I had to hand over half the money to the madam, I was still making really good money and thought it was my chance to get a real nest egg.

The madams there were avaricious women. They were ex-prostitutes — too old to crack it any more and too smart to go under. You'd take the money from the man and put it into a locked box, and at the end of the day you counted up your money together and split it down the centre. Sometimes, though, the men would give me a tip and say, 'Don't give this to Nancy — this is for you.'

Out of her share the madam had to pay the police for protection. And she had to pay the politicians for being allowed to operate. The police virtually ran the prostitution industry and the gambling dens. There were certain rules that the girls had to keep — for example, they weren't allowed in public places like hotel bars or the swimming pool, but once a month they were allowed to go to the pictures on a Sunday night. In between-times you were locked in the brothel.

At night-time the gates were bolted from the inside and the men would all line up outside. I used to sit there and file my nails with Beethoven playing in the background, and I'd say, 'Yes, you can come in,' or 'No, you can't because you're a naughty boy.' There was a long verandah with the rooms going off it, and you could just unbolt your gate, let your man in, bolt it again, take him into the room and close the door. The whole place was wide open and everybody could see, but nobody minded. Sex was like eating — it was a necessity.

I found the only way to handle it at first was to brazen it out. I was very surprised and shocked and embarrassed, but I didn't care because I knew that nobody knew me there. I couldn't have done it anywhere closer to home. I thought it was like something out of a film, and so I behaved like a movie star.

I had to lock up my car while I worked there, and I was only allowed to use it if I took it out of town. On my days off I had to report to the police and show them a map of where I was going, and I went off to look at all the ghost towns and everything. It's also a bit dangerous driving on your own there anyway, because of the heat and the risk of getting lost.

Sometimes the police came as clients, but mainly the visiting police. The local police came too, but they were guests of the house so they didn't have to pay. The madam would fix us up for it later.

That whole place was a study in human nature. The men didn't care who you were or what you looked like — it was just relief, and that was that. The madam had an egg-timer with a bell on it — three minutes and she'd be knocking on the door. And that's as long as they had, unless they paid more. I learned certain ways of making a man climax early. Some of them, though, would throw things at the cage from outside afterwards if they were angry or couldn't climax. There were no real hassles, though, because we were under police protection and they knew it.

The average price was $5. Some would pay $20 for an hour.

Sometimes I could make $100 a night or twice that, since half would go to the madam. I had quite a bit of control because I was in demand. So if I'd had enough of them, that was it. I could just shut up and go.

Also, because I came from New Zealand I had no colour prejudice, although of course I had certain class prejudices. When the Thursday Islanders came by, they were charged $100 for half an hour and they would pay it because there was no other way they could get women, except maybe Aboriginal women. But those Australian girls, as low as they were on the social scale, wouldn't go with those men. And they were beautiful men, real gentlemen. They were gentle, respectful and just so grateful. When they came in I could earn about $500 in three or four hours.

Most of the men who came as clients were single men. This was 1966, and they were mostly Europeans, Greeks and Italians who had come over to work in the goldmines. It was good business, quick and clean. You didn't have to use condoms in those days, but I preferred to, and most of the men didn't mind. We had doctors' check-ups once a week. If anyone got VD the news swept through the street immediately. I can only remember hearing about one girl getting VD, but that meant all the houses were closed down. All the girls were checked out, and it was only when their blood tests and everything came back clear that they were allowed to operate again.

I had one regular client who used to talk as much as he wanted to have sex. Sometimes he'd just come, pay and talk for his three minutes, five minutes or whatever. Then one day he said that his wife knew he came here and she wanted to meet me. So on my day off I went over there for a meal with them. She was really neat. Her parents had come out to Australia years before with all their beautiful white starched linen to this dust bowl, never knowing what they were coming to. Anyway they ended up telling me a lot about the history of the goldfields and we'd go out driving together. But once I got to know his wife, I could never go as a customer with him again. He didn't mind — there was always someone else.

The attitude of the women in the town was strange. They were generally very supportive of us, because they thought we kept the men from straying anywhere else. They'd rather they came to us instead of messing around with other women. And there was no rape, no sex crime at all in that town in those days.

I stayed there eight months, then had to move on. I'd been having a love affair with a senior police officer, and he wanted me to set myself up in a house of my own. But the woman I was working for was very jealous, and when she found out what was going on she pulled a few strings in Perth and had me thrown out of town. One thing led to another and I was declared a prohibited immigrant and deported.

I thought I might as well go out with a bit of glory. They were going to fly me back to New Zealand, but I didn't really want to fly. I knew ships were going back and forth all the time, and I liked the idea of sailing the open seas with moonlight and shipboard romances and all that. So when they tried to take my fingerprints at the airport, I refused. I stood on my dignity and said I was not just a police prisoner, I was a federal prisoner. Two men then tried to take my fingerprints by force. They threw me on the ground with my arms up behind my back, then discovered I had very little clothing on underneath my big long coat. Virtually nothing in fact. They were shocked and scared that I was going to do something outrageous, which I was — I was going to take it all off on the tarmac. So the Qantas officials rushed in and said, 'We're not flying her. No way. We've declared her an air hazard!'

They took me back to Long Bay prison again and locked me up for another six weeks until the *Canberra* was ready to sail, a nice big luxury liner. They assigned a federal police officer to come back with me, a really lovely woman. We had a great trip!

I had some terrible experiences with the Australian police though, and in prison. I'm frightened to go back there even now, but who cares? Who wants to go there anyway — it's full of bloody Australians!

Back in New Zealand again I did a few dodgy things, like running a striptease club up in Auckland. Later I got a job in television designing costumes. I found it much easier to deal with the New Zealand police. They never raped me or took money off me. They never planted anything on me either, whereas the Australian police did that all the time.

It was only the higher-ups here who were against me. They were worried about some of the younger ones acting like human beings towards me, drinking with me in the hotels and chasing me in their cars and making fools of themselves over me.

In Melbourne it was quite a different story. I knew they were the enemy, and I had to get in underneath and get something on them before they got something on me. So I let them seduce me, and they're such arrogant pigs that they were pushovers. Then once I had that on them, I felt a little bit more secure. I got all sorts of information from them then. But I had to let them think *they* were seducing me — awful isn't it? But you've got to use whatever weapons you have, and that was all I had.

I never went back to prostitution, though. I didn't particularly want to and I didn't need to now I had a job I loved; and besides, the scene was changing and becoming too organised, and I didn't want to be beholden to other people. I think I had the best times of it all. It's harder now, and there's AIDS and everything to worry about. So when I say I don't want to be involved in it again, it's not because of the moral act. I've got no morals anyway; I'm amoral, so they said. That's what a probation report about me said years ago, because I said, 'I want to be a lesbian, and I don't see anything wrong in it.'

I don't think I did ever become one — I don't even know. To me a lesbian is someone who likes only women, whereas I could fall in love with anyone. It could be a woman; it could be a man — it just depends on the person.

I wanted to be a bohemian, I wanted to be a communist, I wanted to try all those things and they weren't going to let me. They said it was wrong, it was wicked. I wanted to wear all black. I even used shoe stain to paint my fingernails black, and that was seen as dangerous. I was seen as a threat. I wanted to be noticed, but once I was I didn't like it, because then it stopped me doing other things. Now I've found out that the more low-key and low-profile you are, the more you can get away with. There is only one way to beat the system and that's to join it.

I don't think I always knew what it was I was fighting. Just convention, I suppose. Being labelled, being forced into a certain path, having to do what was expected or, if you didn't conform, being cast out, punished. I don't think I've ever done anything really wrong. All my life it's been like I've had two lives going on. I've had one life in the underworld, outside society, and another little life on the inside. And the two just keep going parallel. Although I did everything I could to run away from my respectable upbringing, it stays with you.

I alienated myself from my parents, so that for about twenty years I never saw them. I feel so guilty about that, I find it difficult to talk to them or look them in the eye. They're very conservative and they lead their own lives. They know nothing about prostitution. They would just never ever hear of anything like that unless someone told them. I'd love to tell them, but they wouldn't understand. What's the use of telling them now they're in their eighties?

My sister is absolutely conventional too. The only thing she ever wanted to do was be a mother and bring up her children, which she's done very successfully. She's been my one strong thing to hang on to, though. She's been the only one who through all those years on the run I could keep contact with, and she stood by me all the way.

Life is a search. The whole of life is a search — there is never an end to it. You can't say, 'I know it all now. I've found what I want,' because you can always improve on that or enhance it. Every day is a surprise and I learn something new. When it comes to the real answer, it lies within, but you've got to look at everything else before you can see that. Prostitution is only one of many paths I have followed in my lifetime.

Working Girls

After I interviewed her, Lee went home and several days later wrote me a letter. In it she distilled the essence of her thoughts concerning her involvement in sex work. Those thoughts are included here in her own words and form an essential part of her story.

I became a prostitute at the age of twenty-two years after a bitter separation and custody battle over my four-year-old daughter. I lost custody because I did not have the financial means to fight for her or to support her. There were no benefits in those days and I refused to submit to the bondage of a violent marriage for economic support.

I had never thought of prostitution before this. The only prostitutes I knew of were those who hung around the hotels or walked the streets. I was pretty naive and a bit of a prude when I was approached by a businessman in a hotel lounge one day a few weeks after losing my custody battle. After talking a while he put a proposition to me that sounded like a way out of my hopeless situation, and a means of financial independence.

He knew several businessmen who would pay good money for sex if they had someone attractive and discreet to visit on a regular basis.

I thought long and seriously about this. Although I didn't particularly like men at that time, I saw a way to compensate and secretly revenge myself for all the pain and insults I had received from the men who were responsible for my situation. It wasn't long before I had set myself up in a city flat with a telephone and I told no one what I was doing.

I tried to adopt a professional attitude and made certain rules I felt would help my success and help me keep my self-esteem. The law against prostitution at that time was that girls were not allowed to solicit men and that two or more girls operating out of a flat established a brothel. As my clients rarely knew each other and only visited after making contact by telephone, and I had no other girl at my apartment, I figured I was pretty safe from the law. There was no law against men following, soliciting or paying girls.

I had no drunks and no boy-friends to hand my hard-earned (or easy-earned) cash to; all the clients were regular; I practised a high degree of cleanliness, which meant regular doctor's check-ups; and no advertising in public by way of dress or manner of speech.

It took me some time to get used to asking for money, but accepting money absolved me from enjoying sex for its own sake. I could not see why it was illegal to do something for money that was okay to do for free. Far from being humiliated by the offers of money, it gave me a feeling of power and compensated in some way for having to live a secret life.

I invented personalities and different characters for my clients and fulfilled all my own fantasies at their expense. Sometimes a man fell in love with me and wanted to save me or take me away from it all. They all asked the same questions. 'What's a nice girl like you doing this for?' 'I'm in it for the money,' I'd say. 'Do you enjoy it?' they sometimes asked. 'Only when I have to,' I would reply.

Every girl has to have a line where she stops and that limit is her own personal choice. There is no connection between sex and love and you must always keep something back for yourself. I refused to practise anal sex or to indulge in oral sex or unhealthy perversions. I would not allow men to sleep the night or become involved with me personally in any way.

I 'persuaded' the clients to wear condoms, and as most of them were married and 'couldn't afford to take risks', they did. I took no drugs, ate good food and had plenty of sleep.

I had no qualms of conscience. The act of intercourse was nothing sacred; about as satisfying as a good sneeze. Disillusionment had made me see sex as a mechanical force which required no depth of feeling or mutual obligations, with no moral issues involved. I was free to sell my company to a limited number of men and chose to do that rather than sell my integrity and independence to one man who would try and control me and take over my life.

My clients were all nice people — witty, intelligent and thoughtful. Most were middle-aged married businessmen. For a lot of them it was their funny way of being faithful to their wives, and some came regularly every week.

I became close to some of my clients — not serious relationships, more like relaxed friendships. They discussed business, their hang-ups and marital problems — and I sought financial advice.

Some of the men were skilled lovers and others were quick and easy. A few had psychological problems and required tenderness and understanding. I became interested in psycho-sexual techniques and was secretly pleased when I could prevent premature ejaculation or alternatively could help a man speed things up.

Some men came just for a cuddle and a talk while I listened — a bit like counselling. I felt like a social worker giving myself over to a higher cause. I took a pride in myself and what I was doing. My work was a needed service, but I had to be objective and remember that I was fulfilling a need. I think the secret of my success was that I treated the man as my equal and not as the inferior sex. I made him feel like a king.

From a feminist perspective, I believe that prostitution can be an honourable profession. There is no need to feel ashamed about taking control of your own body and making a successful career and lots of money from it. The word prostitute actually means to 'misuse'. I prefer to call myself a courtesan, a mistress or a paramour — and nowadays a sex therapist. I never misused or abused the power God gave me as a woman. I neither cheapened the sexual act nor romanticised sex. I allowed no feelings of sin or remorse. I kept my soul chaste with healthy thoughts and my spiritual virginity intact.

I finished my career with a tidy bank balance and the experience to be the best wife in the world to any man who deserves me.

'Girls that do it for money are bad, but girls that do it to oblige are worse.'

In recent years Lee has had what she calls a 'second chance' at having children and now spends her time enjoying them and bringing them up 'to the best of my ability'. She still pursues her interests in music and art, and grows herbs in the coastal city where she now lives. Her secret ambition, she says, is to write a novel.

VICTORIA

Victoria was thirty-six and had two teenage children when she first began doing escort work. Since then she has built up a regular clientele in the Dunedin area. I spoke to her shortly after she had been beaten by a client who attempted to rape her at knifepoint.

I was brought up in a post-Victorian professional family, within an unusual and very tight type of religious, orthodox, Protestant faith, which had a lot of influence on my life. When I was little my father was professionally employed in a rural area, but later decided to move us into town for a better education.

I was the oldest child and considered artistic and rebellious. I don't know how academic I was at school. There were things I excelled in and others that I just couldn't be bothered with. I started training to be a nurse, but left that without finishing when I married. I married young, and truly believe that I did love as much as an eighteen-year-old woman can love. I was married for thirteen years and had four children during that time. I had times of working and not working when my children were young, but the jobs I did were very much in the way of bringing in money for extras. At one stage I worked for two and a half years in a hamburger bar in the centre of Dunedin, being in sole charge of it from midnight until eight in the morning. That way I could go home just as the children were getting up. I'd get home, do some housework, make their beds and get them off to school, then take half a sleeping tablet to get some sleep before they got home again. I always wanted to be there when they needed me. Sometimes I'd be so tired, though, that I'd try to get a couple more hours of sleep in the evening, after they'd had their baths and tea and gone off to bed. I worked really hard, but got very little pay or thanks for it.

About a year before I left my husband I bought a little retail business of my own. I guess I was looking for lots of things at the time, and I started feeling like our marriage was inadequate. I didn't figure out until several years later that what I was going through was an emotional breakdown. I didn't go to therapy — I just got through it.

I left him but kept my business going. He'd been a good man, and I knew that I was breaking his heart and I never charged him any maintenance or anything. I let the children stay on there while I got myself together. I thought the trauma from the marriage break-up was enough for them to handle, and it was easier for them to still have their own bedrooms and backyard and local school.

Eventually my husband and I talked about how important it was to each of us that the children not be separated from each other and that they should be able to choose where they wanted to live. Gradually they drifted over to me, and although he helped me out in little ways, like with school uniforms and things, I was the one carrying the financial burden of it all.

I kept my business going until I knew I had to get out of that, but by this stage I had moved from a flat into a house, a small, modest house but a house I called home. I had a mortgage and was terrified of trying to manage on an ordinary wage, and I thought there wasn't anything else I could do other than prostitution. And the more I thought about it, the more I thought — why not?

I didn't really know anything about it, but I started working in Dunedin initially by ringing the numbers in the trade personal column. I rang the women who advertised there and said I was looking for work and would be grateful if they could give me some, for a fee. So I'd get occasional jobs from them which were basically the midnight drunks and the undesirables or the people they were sick of. I was still grateful for that, though, because it was money coming in.

VICTORIA

I can remember my first client. He was great. He'd obviously had a few drinks, and I think I was surprised about the fact that he was humane. He seemed to strike me almost immediately as being a person who would rather just sit and talk to me. He was a lonely person. I went to his home, and I felt really nervous. I hadn't told the woman I was paying the agency fee to that I'd never done this before.

At first I thought I was earning too much money for the time I spent with them. After a while I realised that actually doing it was no difficulty. I could see that it was a lucrative proposition; I could see that I could handle it; and I thought that it would be better to go into it privately.

When I first started and walked up to the hotel doors, I did feel really nervous. I used to think, 'What will they think of me? Will I be good enough?' One advantage I had was that I knew how to mix with people from lots of different backgrounds, because I'd come from a professional family, married into the working class, and was also artistic and cared about the bums of the earth and all that sort of thing. By the time I got into this work I had a pretty good ability at sussing people out.

I was very aware of my age when I started — I was thirty-six. Then I realised that the cream of the clientele were mature, and the mature woman was really what they were looking for. I suppose there's a certain type of clientele who are looking for a bit of sex on the side, and the younger the better. And maybe most middle-aged and older men dream and fantasise about younger women. But when it comes to actually *being* with one, in my experience anyway, I found they preferred the fact that I was more mature. They felt less inhibited with me. They wanted someone who would be as discreet as possible. Most of all I think they wanted substitute wives — someone they could talk to. My impression is that the average New Zealander is quite moral in the sense that they don't want someone walking through that door who's the same age as their daughter.

The average age of my clientele is between forty and sixty, although obviously I've had both younger and older men. The oldest, the best and the most appreciative is seventy-eight years old. When I told him I was going to be interviewed, he said, 'Well, you tell that lady that I think the world of you.' He'd been faithful to his wife all their marriage, and then he contacted me through my advertisement in the paper, three months after she died.

He's the type with a tendency towards wanting to be monogamous. In a sense I've becomes his 'wife'. It's not that we live together, because he knows that's not allowed, but in every way that he wants to revere, respect and love a woman and put her on a pedestal, that's how he treats me. Sometimes that feels wonderful. This man is thirty-seven years older than me, and I know his affection for me is genuine and it's comfortable and friendly. Other times I find it exhausting because it often feels like all the hype that goes with a seventeen-year-old who's being constantly demanding. He also has that chauvinist male streak in him, which means that the more he gets, the more he wants, and sometimes I feel really drained and exhausted. And then I feel guilty because he has been such a genuine friend and he's been so good to me.

Over the last three years he's seen me twice a week, and of course I make money out of it — it's quite lucrative. He thinks the obstacle to our getting married is the fact that I am so much younger than him, but I tell him, 'As much as I love you, I'm not in love with you the way you are, or think you are, with me.' And with our ages being so different, I'm still a girl to him. I've become his surrogate wife — I've taught him how to cook, I've washed his curtains, I've sewn buttons on his shirt.

I haven't said this to him, but to marry him would be like a fate worse than death. He just wants to take me over and possess me. To an outsider it probably sounds very flattering and very nice to be loved that way by someone who's no potential threat to you, but it is incredibly exhausting. I've got to notice the fact that he polished the brass plug in the bathroom before I got there, or he's got no reason to live. I've got to notice that he's dusted the ledges; I've got to notice that he put the crystal ashtray out for me; and I've got to notice that he put out his best china cup just in case I wanted a cup of tea. Occasionally I've lost myself and been vicious, and then I've had to listen for the next eighteen months to how much I've hurt him. As far as a business situation goes, though, I'm lucky. I've hit the jackpot. But it's still very difficult.

With my own clients I feel I have to adopt a professional attitude and separate my personal life from them. In my private life I've had love from men and I've had good sex and I don't think I could do what I do if I hadn't been privately loved as much as I have been. I've also had a lot of nastiness and a lot of violence in my private life. There was a terrible incident recently where a client attempted to rape me at knifepoint, which I may use coincidentally as a valid reason for stopping what I'm doing.

My clients typically treat me with respect and I wouldn't have it any other way. After the ordeal I went through recently I had a rest for a couple of days and then a client rang me. He's just a darling ordinary little man who paid me as normal and sat me down on the couch and brought out a little box for me, all gift-wrapped. 'It's a present for you,' he said. After all I'd just gone through, I felt like bursting into tears on the spot. 'Why?' I asked, because I was honestly amazed. He said, 'Every time you come to see me, you bring me so much sympathy and understanding.' It was a lovely gilt ornament and it was so sweet of him, and it made me realise that you just can't judge all men from one nasty incident. But it was an extremely vicious and traumatic thing to go through, and he was only a young guy. He got a heavy sentence for it, and it was written up in the papers and everything. They used the word 'prostitute' and that made me feel terrible, because I hate that word.

I see myself more as a mistress, and as someone who can be confided in. I enjoy the respect I get from clients, and they're often amazed that I have some degree of intelligence, spiritual feeling and all the rest of it. They always seem to be gratified by the degree of understanding that I have, from having been married and having my own family.

A few have wanted to marry me. Generally I tell them I

appreciate the feelings they have for me and I don't want to hurt them, but I don't feel the same way. I tell them, 'You're very special to me,' but I also play myself down. I tell them that I'm a very difficult woman to live with, that they've only known me on a short-term basis, and so on. Or I try to steer them off the topic and ask about their children or their job. I prefer to avoid it rather than confront it, and if they're clever enough they respect the fact that I'm subtly telling them they've gone too far.

I've never become romantically involved with a client. There is one client whom I feel I have a particular friendship with, but I can't figure out whether it's because he's so pushy or because I feel something there. I've never forgotten that they're clients, but that could be because I've always had a relationship to deal with at home anyway. And I've always been grateful to have that, because it's so nice to have your own special man who's got nothing to do with your work.

In the time that I've been doing this I've had only two relationships, and they've both known what I do. I've got strong feelings about being monogamously faithful and these men know that. It does take extra effort to keep a relationship going when you work the way I do. I know a lot of women in my profession go home and they just haven't got the energy, but I've always been lucky in not having the sort of men who have thought, 'Well, she's been out doing it and it's turned me on and I want sex.' They've always been ready to put their arms around me and cuddle first, and for that I've been prepared, whether I want it or not, to make that extra effort. It must be painful for men to put up with it. It does create a very difficult problem in your personal relationships. Sometimes they've used it against me, then apologised and said it was just words and underneath they didn't mean it. What they say doesn't really hurt me — what hurts more is the fact that they *say* it to hurt me.

My work has never interfered with my own sex life. In the five years or so that I've been working I've probably had orgasms only about five times with clients. I prefer to have them with a man that I love, though, and I must admit I've always felt a bit guilty about having them with clients. I couldn't love them, because it would be like giving my soul away. People always talk about women giving their bodies away as if that was everything. I think it's giving your soul away which is the really precious thing.

My clients like the cuddles I give them and the fact that I'm a sensitive person. They like the little things I do after it's over. I suppose other women do them too. Like I don't jump out immediately — I let them lie there and I cuddle them, or I'll go and wipe them or do something nice for them, be maternal with them. There's got to be a subtlety, there's got to be a profession about the art of making love.

The need for sexual release can be desperate in men. I use my voice and my words from the moment they ring me up, in order to put them at ease. Some of them ring up initially just for a chat, to find out the details, the cost, how discreet it is, my age, things like that. Often they sound quite nervous. Some worry about the health aspects. Sometimes they feel guilty, as far as their wives go and about the morality of it all. Some men tell me it's the first time they've ever done anything like that. They even say they don't know if they've got the courage to go through with it. When they ask me if I should make up their minds for them, I say, 'It must be your decision.'

Some people have the impression that the men who ring prostitutes are sneaky men, but I feel that a lot of them respect and love their wives and they're just trying to find a way of coping with a situation in a way that doesn't threaten their marriage. They know I'm in business. It's a job to me, so I'm not going to tie them up emotionally. They are going to be able to have a clandestine sexual relationship, but also a clandestine, surrogate-type, intimate communication relationship with a woman that won't bring about any repercussions for them.

Most of my clients come to me as much for the talking as for the sex. These are men who are too old to understand that all of us occasionally need therapy and it doesn't mean we're screwed up. They're men who are so tied up and respected in their community, even perhaps with the church, that they feel that out of respect for everything they can't even talk to their family doctor about their problems. Perhaps because of the typical lack of status we women have, they feel they can tell me anything, and if they get something out of it, that's fine. I've been known to tell them that they're chauvinist bastards and I don't blame their wives at all, but I still give them love at the same time. I make them think. I'm not a feminist, although I admire the feminists who have done a lot for our society.

This work can be glamorous too. When I first started, I met a man who was an importer. He flew me up to Auckland for the Trades Fair and put me up in a hotel. That was a wee holiday for me, believe you me. Five days in a lovely hotel and all he wanted was for me to be there from half past seven at night. But it's really hard to sleep all night with a man you don't love. I had the days to myself, though.

It was the Mon Desir Hotel, over at Takapuna, and it had a bar where young musicians played. And to have a beach nearby was, to somebody from Dunedin, like being on a tropical island. To be able to walk along the sea and paddle at midnight in March and be warm was amazing. I was treated like an absolute queen. If anyone knew what capacity I was there in, they were too polite to say. There was one woman whom I would have loved to talk to, simply woman to woman, but I was in no position to because I was there as his little lady.

After that trip, though, I realised that I had really missed the boyfriend I had at that time, and he found it hard to handle my being away for that many days. And I learned something about being professional, which is that you don't spend all night with them. For that trip to Auckland I was flown up there and back and put up in the hotel and given the best of alcohol and everything and I came back with $1,500 on top of that, but I think I earned every cent of what I got. I didn't come back feeling refreshed, and I felt sad that it wasn't a holiday with someone I loved.

VICTORIA

Sometimes I'll walk into a home or a motel unit and find the men have gone to a lot of trouble to set just the right mood. They might have turned down the lights, and have pâtés or a cheeseboard and wine there for us to enjoy. Often it can be a really romantic little fling for them. I often felt more respected by my clients than I did in my private life.

Other men have asked me out to dinner. I've done it, sometimes, but the reason I haven't done it more often is probably because I've had a private lover. Mostly these men want one-to-one dinners, and they don't mind what they pay. Sometimes they have engagements where they want to take a partner, and usually I explain that it's a small city and there could be other people there who are superior to them in the firm or whatever, who may also have been with me. That usually stops them, because what they're trying to do is say, 'Look what I've got,' and keep hidden that it's paid for.

I'd quite like to do it more, because I like the idea of being with a man for an hour or two or three, at his expense, and then say, 'Ta ta, darling.' It must suit me to a certain extent. But I don't do it very often. I worry about my own man sitting at home, unable to afford to take me out. But that's not my fault — most of them live off me anyway!

When I started working my youngest child was about twelve or thirteen, and I told the children what I was going to do, but to keep quiet about it at that stage. I said that if their friends asked what I did, then they could say I was just buying and selling from home instead of through the shop. And no one thought twice about it. As they grew older, each one in their turn decided to tell their special friends and it was just accepted, it was just what their friend's mum did. I think kids at that age don't really care as long as they've got a home.

I suppose my children could see that I wasn't a married woman anyway and they probably thought, 'Well, what does it matter if Mum's going to bed with a few men and charging them for it?' And of course, doing this job meant I had much more time to spend at home. I think the children thought I was basically keeping lonely men happy, and although they realised as they grew older that there was a bit more to it than that, I think it also gave them, particularly my daughters, an idea of what actually does go on out there. How can I say if it's done them harm or not? I don't know. If any of them went into this sort of work, I'd feel disappointed. I don't think it's a job for any young girl and I'd feel sad about them doing it.

I've told my close friends what I do, and they love me and respect the difficulties of what I do. But it's not the same really as being able to speak to someone in the same business. I think it's a very lonely occupation for someone like me. Most women with alternatives to face like I had choose the DPB or get married again. It's for financial reasons that I do what I do, but I've always wanted to be independent anyway.

I think in terms of charging, though, I've done it all wrong. I've realised that most women charge a certain fee for their visit and their company, and then sex is on top of that. And the unwritten rule in the whole thing is that you only give it once. But a lot of men, and they're *not* gentlemen, will ring up and say to me, 'Well, what if I want to come three times?' And I generally say to them, 'Well, as much as you might like to think you can come three times in an hour, I'm sure you know as well as I do that's very difficult.'

The genuine ones are those that say, 'I have a premature ejaculation problem — would it matter if I came twice?' In some cases you advise them to masturbate earlier in the day; with others I say, 'I'm a professional, and if you decide you want to see me, remind me when you call up that you have that problem and we'll try and make it last as long as possible.' For some of them it's like the ultimate time, and it's good when they tell you that. The sad ones are those who come too soon and feel like wee boys and say, 'I've done it wrong.' Then I sit down and say to them, 'Does it really matter? You've got your release. This is how I will do it if you see me again.' Business acumen comes in there.

One of the benefits about working in Dunedin is that you can be choosy. Up north there's just so many more women working. I assure my clients that I'm no prude but when it comes to work, cleanliness is important and therefore anal sex is out for me — just in case there's a risk of bisexuality or whatever. I don't tell them it's also because I've got piles in there and it hurts.

Another kinky thing they ask for is golden showers. I think a lot of them don't even know the difference between the holes it comes out of — it just excites them, maybe because it's hot and warm and wet. Occasionally I've been intrigued with it from a psychological point of view, but this is the sort of job where you've got to live and let live.

What the vast majority of my clients want is normal sex. Sometimes they come not for their own personal satisfaction, but because they feel inadequate in their own sexual relationship and want to improve it. They often ask what turns me on, because they're eager to learn how to please the woman in their life. I tell them it's irrelevant what I like — they need to ask *her* what she likes. And I remind them that it's my profession and I'm not here to be satisfied. But I can easily end up as a sexual counsellor.

One thing I've found to be pretty important, when you operate the way I do, is to have two telephones, one for the house and a separate business number. Also, by having a jackpoint system, I can shut myself off even to the dearest and nearest of my clients without them even knowing. They just think I'm really popular or I'm having a social night out. It doesn't sound like I've taken the phone off the hook because I can't be bothered with them. And whenever I feel like having time off, I do that.

I advertise that I'm available certain times of the day, but some people try to ring me an hour or so before that. It's like a garage sale — you're bound to ring early because you want those bargains. If I feel I need to pay a bill, or I'm so hyped up that another job won't matter, then I can take that call and do it, but I don't feel obligated to do so outside of the hours I've specified.

The phone calls can come virtually any time of day, from

8 a.m. right through until 5.30 a.m. A lot of the calls are enquiries from men asking what services I provide. Often they want to see me within the next half-hour, or as soon as possible. Other men will ring when they're in town and have lots of other things to do, and we have to sort out a time to fit around that.

Most of my jobs seem to be in the afternoon. I've done as much work in the afternoon as I've done in the evenings anyway, and sometimes even gone out at eight in the morning. I often think it's ridiculous that we're called 'ladies of the night', because we all know that men have their hardest hard-ons in the morning.

Other clients may have really busy days because of the work they're in, and often the men who are here for business are in a motel and they just want to sit and drink and unwind after work. They want a nice relaxing sleep, and I'm like a sedative to them.

Mostly I spend an hour with them. My original price was $100, now it's $130, although I never put my price up to men I've already set a price to. The reason it's gone up is because of taxi fares and advertising costs. More often than not I go to motels or hotels rather than private houses. Some motel-owners rent rooms out for a couple of hours at a time — why not let a room out for $25 when it's sitting empty?

This work *is* lucrative. I would say that I have been one of the best-paid women in this country. I must have been. But I've wasted it and shared it and thrown it around so I've got less than I should have now, and that's the truth. I suppose I didn't go into it to make money, really. I went into it to have a reasonable standard of living, to survive.

One thing that has affected my attitude to the business has been AIDS. When I started I hadn't heard of AIDS. I suppose ninety-nine per cent of the time I used a condom, but occasionally, for a man with a problem or an old man who I felt couldn't possibly give any venereal problems, I made an exception. The moment I heard about AIDS, I realised without anybody warning me the precautions I had to take. I could see that the risks didn't just apply to a promiscuous person or a homosexual but even to an old man who had had a blood transfusion years before.

The majority of men do seem to be still quite ignorant in that regard. Yet, at the same time, the type of clientele I have anyway have said that the reason they call me instead of picking up a lady in the bar is because they know I'm clean. They know I've got to be or otherwise I wouldn't be operating.

I like to think what I'm doing can have some effect on the crime rate. That's not what I'm doing it for, but maybe I help keep men off the streets who would otherwise molest somebody. Maybe I'm keeping things down so there's less domestic violence in the home and fewer grumpy men going into businesses and giving their staff a hard time.

I like to think that the particular incident of violence I recently experienced is out of the ordinary. I wouldn't want to go through that more than once. I'd never met him before I went to his motel. But now that it's over, I feel somehow my experience gave me the ability to handle it. It's by far the worst thing I've gone through, and I hope it's just an extreme one-off case. There's only two other situations where I've experienced any violence at all and then only to very slight degrees. I've never done a self-defence course or anything like that — I'm too old. I'm hopeless — if I aimed for their balls I'd probably hit their knees and get killed!

I can't say I've got over it yet, though, and I can't say that I ever will. I haven't analysed how it's affected me. It may be no different from a scar later on — just one that takes eighteen years to heal instead of three. I know I'll never forget it, but I'm a survivor.

The police were brilliant to me when I was beaten up. It was the second case I've had where they've been quite humane, they've been understanding, they've been respectful, they've been helpful. The other incident was where a man died on top of me. He had a massive cardiac arrest and died. It was all quite traumatic, it was sad, and I felt guilty. I felt that I had to make a decision in a split second — should I possibly give him the help of resuscitation, or should I run? I decided to call the ambulance and wait until they arrived.

We were in a flat he owned at the time, and there was no way I could have been a passer-by or anything like that. He was a reputable man from out of town, wealthy, married, and now he was lying there dead, with no clothes on. Next thing, from this clandestine little relationship between the two of us, there were ten people in the room — ambulance crew, the doctor, the police, the undertaker. There was an inquest and so on, but I was kept out of it all. I don't know what the family knew. I worried about that as well, and about his wife — would she have wanted to know?

He'd been a regular client of mine for five or six years. I'd see him once every six or seven weeks when he came to town. He was a farmer, and not much of a talker — one of those men who spend most of their time out on the hills with nobody to talk to. The last thing he said to me was, 'darling'.

I may decide to leave the job, but to be honest I've wanted to do that for a long time. It's so emotionally draining. You can look at people like Joan Collins and ask how their husbands coped with the woman they loved making love on screen, or pretending to make love on screen, for all the world to see. I don't see that as being any different to what I'm doing. It's an act.

It's also an act that requires more than an act, because often the person you're doing the act with needs more than that. When I go out to these people, often they're very ugly or they've got very little going for them. Sometimes they may be very badly physically deformed, or disfigured from burns —some of them look so bad they'd make the Phantom of the Opera look like an angel! I'd rather deal with a person who looks like that, though, than some handsome, suave man who's full of arrogance. All I can do is find something I can love in that person, whether it be the way they express a particular value or their depth of sincerity or whatever.

VICTORIA

It's not a case of ever being physically revolted by any of them, because I never ever feel physically turned on by any of them either. I've got that detachment. It's quite pathetic how grateful they are, but the way I see it, they've got as much right to sexual fulfilment as anybody else. It's important because if a person has one problem, it can set up a whole chain of others. They might start off physically disfigured but end up alcoholic or impotent or whatever if nobody understands them.

So with all my clients I have to appear to be turned on, whether they're beautiful or ugly. I make them feel like they're the only one in the world for that little moment, that they're the most special man I've ever met. It's not just a con, because I do feel that everybody's special. I don't think I could do this if I didn't love people. But I also think some people couldn't do it if they didn't hate people.

What I get out of this job is mental stimulation. If they get that too, that's their bonus, but it's mine as well. You don't need to have sexual satisfaction to have a tremendous feeling of job success. I've had situations where they've paid and said, 'I really enjoyed the sex with you, but I have to say that your company was just as good.' I've had that said to me many times. And it's not because it's a fuck — it's because I'm giving them cuddly sex.

I'd hate it to be printed that sex was a game, and yet it's true. It's been said by some men that a prostitute makes the best wife when she settles down. Maybe it's because we're all women who love to be touched, or some of us love too much, and we're so grateful to them for respecting our minds that we give them a surrogate form of love.

I'm like a jack of all trades now and a master of none. I can walk into a place and find a man there who's really proud of how he built up a ball-bearing factory. Now how the hell do you talk to a person about a ball-bearing factory? But I find a way, and I like the challenge of that.

I love the challenge of meeting new people. I use the first five minutes to find out whether they're basically a person who wants to talk or listen, and sometimes I find it really exhausting when they're a person who wants to listen. But I've got a wealth of things that I can talk about. Well, not a wealth, but enough. I can talk about being in business myself. Being married, separated, de facto — the whole thing. Being professionally brought up, being down in the dumps. Children would be probably the most common subject. So we talk about whatever they want to talk about, and talking puts them at ease.

Sometimes I've ended up staying a wee bit longer just because I'm enjoying talking to them. Sometimes I feel uneasy about that because I've always got to worry about the man at home, if we go over time. But occasionally, when I'm just thinking about me, I think, 'To hell with the man at home. I'm enjoying myself and it's not the sex, it's the conversation.'

One reason men come to us is because it's naughty, and men love that side of it. Some men ask you to talk 'dirty' to them, and I've always found that hard. I've always enjoyed sex, so I don't find the words associated with it 'dirty'. To them it's a naughty thing, but to me it just degrades what I find beautiful.

I'm not sure I want to see prostitution legalised, though. It could become so controlled that it would become like any other job with limited wages, and I don't think that, given the lack of status any prostitute's going to have, she should be lower paid. I think it deserves as much respect as the best-paid counsellor ever, and the best job involving risk that could ever be considered.

Prostitutes are women who obviously care about their bodies and their clients. I can't see how a woman who's basically doing it because she's a junkie or something like that is ever going to get a man who doesn't deserve to die along with her. I know that's a hard attitude, but that's what I feel. A refined man is going to be very careful about the way he chooses a prostitute. He's going to respect her cleanliness and her rules, just as he has to do with a marriage. I'd like to see prostitution respected by men and women and happily married couples and everybody else. If only those married women knew how good we were, on their behalf, to their husbands, how much we said for them that they can't say.

VICTORIA

Most men, apart from fanatics and strongly ignorant moral groups, aren't against us. Our biggest enemies are women. Yet, if they only knew it, we're women just like them. We're mothers, we're housekeepers, we're women who love men — in fact, we care about these men so much that we give ourselves to them and then send them back to their wives.

I don't see myself as supporting men; I like to think I'm supporting society. When I speak to a man who's been bereaved, I spend a lot of time listening to his respect for his wife and his pride in his children, and I love and honour his respect for that woman.

When he tells me about his frustrations with a woman, and asks me if I think he's wrong to feel that way, I tell him, 'I can't say if you're right or wrong, but why don't you take her flowers more often? Why don't you ask *her* what she wants?' I try to educate them. And those women should know that I'm not promiscuous — I am monogamous. And if I could have my way I would prefer to have one man and look after him and love him. I don't think I'm any different from them at all.

What I do doesn't threaten the family; it supports it. I definitely uphold and respect the family. It could be said that I'm doing it for business reasons, but there are too many times when the man's come to me and said, 'I'm glad you helped me. We only talked, and I might not see you again, but it helped. You know, you should be a counsellor.' I don't want these people to consider my relationship with them could be anything other than a step towards something better. It's true that I've had the worst and I've had the best, but what am I supposed to tell them — a lie? What pride can anybody have in earning money unless they've got some element of truth and morality in it?

Since being interviewed, Victoria decided to leave the sex-work industry. For eight months she did all she could to get a straight job, going for numerous interviews and producing good character references. When that proved unsuccessful, she went back into escort work again. More of her clients now seem to be local men, so she has a little flat in central Dunedin that she uses for work. This arrangement also allows her to keep her private life separate, and she plans to keep working but in a less pressured way so she can spend more time with family and friends. She pays tax on her income from sex work, and is financially secure enough now to be working not for daily survival but to provide herself with some retirement security.

GLORIA

Gloria is in her mid-thirties and began working in Wellington from the age of sixteen, as well as spending a lot of time on the ships. Later she worked in parlours in Australia before returning to New Zealand to raise her daughter, and in recent years has obtained financial support from various 'sugar daddies'.

I was born in Taranaki and grew up around that area. I came from a broken family and when I was about twelve was sent off to boarding school, but at thirteen I had a nervous breakdown and went into a psychiatric unit. From that point on I had no education. I spent three years in that place before I tricked my way out and went to live in Wellington, where my mother was living.

I lived in Vivian Street with her and got a job in Murdoch's icing sugar factory round the corner in Taranaki Street. I used to work there from 8 a.m. to 4.30 p.m. and then from 5 to 10 p.m. I worked in a dairy/hamburger joint before going to work in a strip club. I started working at the club after I'd been downtown to buy a marquisette watch out of my first pay, and I'd met Zorba when I was walking past there. He invited me in, threw a hula skirt around me, put me on stage and there it began.

I worked in the club from 10 p.m. to 2 a.m. Mondays to Wednesdays, and then until 4 a.m. on Thursdays, Fridays and Saturdays. I was still sixteen when I started there, and I was getting $24 a week. After work we'd go to Ali Baba's to hear live music. Later it was called the Cave, then the Sunset, then the Tokyo Bar. We might only get there ten minutes before it closed, but we would get up and boogie and then go on to someone's place to party. The band and the staff from Ali Baba's would usually come too and we'd party right through until Sunday evening. And we'd go to the Bistro sometimes, or the Downtown Club, where Quincey Conserve used to play.

I ended up working in the clubs for eight years. I wasn't only stripping though. I used to be a sound technician and organise the show, the music, the lights, everything like that. Sometimes I'd serve and waitress as well.

The clubs were always full then, even on Mondays and Tuesdays. Mostly it was middle-aged men who came — there were no hoons around in those days. There was no protection racket or anything like that — the girls just looked after themselves. Everybody knew everybody, and if you were broke you just asked your mate. I never knew anyone to walk the streets in those days. Some girls cracked it with men from the club, but nobody really needed to. I was getting paid and everything was cheap and I lived at home, which made it even cheaper. After a few years my mother moved out and my brother and I took over the flat. Then he went off to Auckland and I kept it on, and that was the first time I'd been on my own since getting out of hospital.

I spent a lot of time with the girls from the Purple Onion too. It was another striptease club, a pokey little dive, and the girls from there were real hard case. They lived in a little bach, no electricity or anything like that. The girls all had lots of stories to tell. If I'm honest, they never used to crack it then — they used to roll it. They would roll clients. There were a lot of kinky men round in those days who would hide their money in their clothing, sometimes even stitch it in. And the 'rules' were that if you got it without being detected, it was yours; but if you got caught, you weren't allowed to try again.

Another girl and I used to go down to the ships too. There was no such thing as prostitution on those ships then, and the girls would never go down empty-pocketed. Sometimes we'd go down there about lunchtime and the bar would be open with cheap booze, and you'd meet up with the seamen. For years I went on board and ate and drank with them, but I always went home again because by this time I was in a de facto relationship and I had a baby.

There were girls who virtually lived on the ships and travelled round the coast with them. They didn't live there for nothing, though. While the boys were all in the bar, the girls would be over the side painting the ship or cooking sometimes. But as long as the jobs were done, the girls could spend weeks at a time on them. When I split up, I did coast for a while, but not for long. I'm not one for leaving home.

The girls used to go around as a group often, and then when the ship went deep sea they'd all come home together. The seamen always had a kitty — a big jar on the bar that the guys put all their 'shrapnel' in. And that was for the girls who ringbolted, to pay the fares for them to get home again. Sometimes it would be enough to fly them home, or they might hitch or bus and have money for a drink on the way.

Even now, if I go to Wellington and there's an ACT or Blue Star ship in port, or any I've been on in previous years, I'll go on board and take my child with me. And we'll laugh and drink and eat. I won't necessarily go to bed with any of them, but if there is someone I've been with before, I'll stick to him. And you get the odd flutter doing that. It's a lot harder coasting now, but I reckon I could get from here to Australia okay if I really wanted, and my daughter with me too. There's not much risk of getting caught, or much of a penalty, so it's worth taking a chance, isn't it?

It never bothered me that some of the girls cracked it. I knew one girl from the Manawatu who was forced to go on the game or she got beaten up. She lived with this guy who in mid-winter would turn her out there in a very thin jersey and a skirt, and even if it was pouring with rain, he'd say, 'You get out there.' She made thousands of dollars for him. But he used to beat her with a baseball bat if she got too cold and went into the pub for a drink. He'd stabbed her and everything. She'd work day and night for him, and he used to buy cars and then get drunk and smash them up. She used to be plucked by the police quite frequently, although in the end they just used to check up to see if she was all right. I told her to get rid of that guy. It took her about three years to do it, though; not until she found out he'd got another woman pregnant. So she left and got a straight job and is now working as tea lady on a construction site.

I never ended up cracking it myself when I was on the scene. I had a lot of sugar daddies instead, though. Living off sugar daddies was something that just happened to me when I was in Australia. I'd gone to Aussie because I'd had another child and my relationship had broken up. I was really broken-hearted, so the only cure was to get out. I was seven years in Aussie, and I lived with the queens in a one-bedroomed place in Melbourne. They were all cracking it on the street and I worked in a knock shop. It had scrub baths and massage rooms, and I was pregnant and on heroin and in a bit of a state. I never went as far as having sex with them. I ended up managing four parlours there, but they're not like the parlours here. These were all run-down houses, often with no electricity or heating.

I'd do the straight massages and the bubble baths. I used to sell my breasts and do body massages. That could be very tantalising for the men, who'd end up pulling themselves off and they'd have to pay me to be there. I wouldn't have sex, though, because over there they didn't use condoms, or not often. A lot of the girls did oral sex and ended up with the jack in the mouth and throat, by which I mean VD. There seemed to be a lot of VD over there.

I also did a lot of golden showers and whippings. It was a lot of money for B and D — $150 for a hiding even then. I'd give them a good hiding for that. Some would bring their own horse-whips along. Others liked to have your stiletto shoes stamped and prodded into their bodies. I used to do all that rather than sex.

A lot of the girls wouldn't do B and D — they'd rather fuck, or charge him extra for different positions — some girls used to make a lot of money letting them do it doggy way. Golden showers involved weeing all over them. I don't know why, whether it was the heat of the urine or what it was. It was the men in suits working in high positions who paid the biggest and had the kinkiest requests, like judges, lawyers, all those types. Maybe because they travelled overseas and had seen a lot more and had a fantasy overseas. But the fantasy didn't end there — it got bigger and bigger, and then it is very hard to find someone to fulfil it.

I found a lot of men like to be slaves, or rather, like to be *your* slave. And they would come to your home and do your washing and ironing and whatever, and if they didn't do it quickly enough you would whip them, berate them, burn them . . . they'd pay to be my slave, and once they'd done all the work they would jack themselves off and that was it — they were gone again. When you're talking about B and D, you're talking about a lot of money — $400 or $500 a session. I was a big money puller in Aussie, but I never had to sell my hole. Sex to me is so private, so personal.

I'd do private shows though, where groups like rugby or darts clubs would pay the parlour when they wanted a lesbian act or whatever. Once they wanted a B and D show put on by two of us, and I was the one who bloody well got tied up and got the whip. I clouted her afterwards. But she really had to whip me — it had to be real. I was brave enough to take it, and at least she didn't open any wounds or anything.

I used to do a lot of lesbian acts for them. My girlfriend and I used to go and see this man who would pay us to screw his wife, and he would sit in a big rocking chair pulling himself off the whole time, just watching.

God, men are kinky! They really are.

When I was in Australia, I needed really big money because of my habit. I'd been tasting quite a bit while I was in Wellington before I went over. A lot of drugs had come on to the scene in the year and a half or so before the Bistro came down. Lots of pills, lots of heroin, and in those days we were snorting it, because we were none the wiser. I couldn't handle snorting. I burned my nose and my throat and everything, so I reverted to intravenous — hitting up.

I needed the money, so that's why I got into the B and D. A lot of men come to parlours because they're looking for their fantasies. So I was doing them a service. They'd have to ask me, tell me what they wanted, and if they were kinky they had to supply everything. I ruled the roost.

Some of them wanted needles through their nipples, some liked having a bloody peg stuck up their backsides. Some of it was real filthy, real animal stuff. Some wanted just to completely expose themselves to me or dress up in my clothes, my fishnets, whatever. It was up to them, and their fantasies could change. They might want to be a slave today, then next week they might want to be clawed to pieces, or whipped. And they wouldn't be happy until you'd drawn blood.

It was when I was in Australia that I first started having sugar daddies. I had two of them running at the same time. If I said I wanted to fly to New Zealand for a visit, one would buy the plane ticket and the other would give me the spending money, or one would ask, 'How much did Dimitri give you?' and then he'd give me a couple of hundred more. Or if one got me a big diamond ring, the other would get me a bigger one. They'd each try to outdo the other.

I was horrible to the Greek one. I used to do nothing for him, except demand to live a life of luxury. I was so mean. Sometimes he would give me $1,000 and then sleep with me, but I wouldn't give him any sex. Or one day I might take all his pay off him except for $10, and then the next day I'd take that $10 as well. Other times I might let him have sex with me. I never took any cash and went to bed with him. In fact, I have never taken cash and gone to bed with anyone. But I might take it a week beforehand and then say, 'I owe you.' You see, men would always fall in love with me. I reckon I was the one who got the most out of it all, though, because I kept my independence and I had my own place and a car and I was still supporting a $300-a-day habit.

I didn't kick that until I came back to New Zealand. I'd been away about eight years then, and I flew back into Wellington. I saw that the Bistro had gone and the whole scene had changed and moved straight on up the line. After about three months my daughter, Lisa, and I moved further north to Marsden Point. We got a cheap house there, no refrigerator or washing machine or anything, but we had a roof over our heads. And I had a job as a tea lady there. It was actually Lisa's godfather, Desmond, who'd been one of my Australian sugar daddies, who helped me get out of the drug scene. He wanted to stabilise me and to stabilise her, and I was able to bring her up with Desmond as my right-hand man, and Dimitri as my left-hand man. So I've had it really good.

The sugar daddy I've got now I've had for five years. He lives in Wellington and banks about $100 in my account every week. He's always trying to get me to live in Wellington, but I told him I'd just go straight back on the drug scene, so I prefer to live in a smaller town. We do a lot of talking on the phone, though.

He still works but he's pretty wealthy because he was left a lot of land. He was married, but his family has grown up and deserted him and he never hears from them. He has his own house and apartment there and everything. What he gets from me is sex whenever I'm down in Wellington. But when I go down there I go out a lot too, and he pays for me to go out without him. I tell him, 'I don't go out at home, and besides, I need someone to look after Lisa.' I may only get down to Wellington once a month, but it doesn't stop him from putting money in my account each week. So that money is going into my savings plan to buy a house. With him putting money in every week like that, two years means $10,000, a nice deposit. So I'll keep this arrangement going until Lisa finishes school.

He wants to marry me. They all want to marry me. But I have a family, and no man could ever replace the children's father so far as I'm concerned. Lisa's the youngest, and I tell him she must be independent of me before I could think about marriage, so if he is prepared to hang in there, so be it. What can you do when a man just keeps putting money in your bank?

WORKING GIRLS

When I first met him I was as pissed as a chook marching up Cuba Street. I was really out of it and I'd lost my bearings, so I bowled up to him and asked him where the taxi stand was. What was worse was that I dropped some pills on the street as well. He asked where I was staying, and I said I knew how to get there but I didn't know the exact address. He helped me along, then invited me to his place. He put me to bed and while I slept he cooked food, then woke me up and fed me in bed. Next day, when I was ready to leave to go back home, he disappeared into the back bedroom and came out with a diamond ring worth nearly $7,000 and just flipped it on my finger. And then he came out with this big fur coat and gave it to me. Well, I knew then he was a sugar daddy. It happened just like that.

I actually feel sorry for him. I certainly don't feel lust. He's at the age now, about fifty-five, where when he has a few drinks he reverts to being like a child. He's really very lonely, and when I'm there all he can do is bicker. He finds nothing nice and nothing pleasant ever seems to happen in his life, but he won't do anything to change it. Instead he just uses me to off-load on. I let him burble on and on, because he needs to.

I don't love him, but he's certainly in love with me. And if it wasn't me, then someone else would be getting it all. He's an alcoholic and can't sleep unless he's got a drink. But as long as he's doing things for me, he's happy. He washes my clothes, irons them, hangs them up. He makes me a sandwich or pours me a drink or runs baths for me, and he's so happy just to have someone to fuss over. Occasionally he'll come up here to see me. Maybe only once a year, but that's enough. When I go to Wellington, I try and stay just two days with him; otherwise he drains all the energy from me.

I've got my own lover whom I've had for the last six years, since I came back from Australia. He lives in the same town and has his own apartment — we tried living together, but it didn't work. Not when I'm working and he's staying at home. I couldn't handle that, so I sent him and his cases out the door. We have a good relationship. We may not see each other for a month sometimes, but sometimes I'll go down and take a chance that he'll be there. Our relationship is purely sex.

I have other lovers too. I've had a relationship with a woman for the last year, and they all know about each other. The women I get involved with aren't as important — mostly it's just lust. They're my fantasy. The woman I've been with for the last year came to me through my back door. She just walked in and climbed into my bed, so I thought, 'Oh well, fair enough.' I was actually raped by a woman when I was about eleven or twelve, just before I went into the psychiatric unit, and again when I was about eighteen in a toilet in the Bistro. I think that's maybe where the fantasy came from.

Work-wise I'm doing voluntary work here, cooking at a hostel. I had to do something because I was getting pretty bored at home. When I came back down after Marsden Point, I had a couple of different cleaning jobs and then worked as a shop assistant for a while. After I finished I needed something to fill my time rather than just sleeping and smoking dope all day. Now I'm working really hard in a voluntary capacity and hope I may be on the payroll there very soon.

I wouldn't ever work in a parlour. There's none in this town anyway. My phone number is similar to that for the local sauna. Once I had a joker ring up from the hotel asking for a lady, so I said, 'I'm sorry, darling, you've got the wrong number.' I gave him the right number, but I felt really stink. There are a lot of pensioners here who would go with a lot of the old women who prostitute themselves — I think $5 for a tickle is the going rate. There is also an escort agency here. But I don't need it. I've got a sugar daddy who looks after me well. I've got an income from Aussie that does me well. And I've got voluntary work out there which keeps me out of mischief. So who needs it?

Gloria was unable to be contacted before this book was published. It appears that she has recently married a well-off man and gone to live elsewhere in the North Island.

HILARY

Hilary is in her late twenties and first began working in an Auckland massage parlour when she was sixteen. Since then she has worked in a variety of establishments, and she and her lesbian partner have also run their own parlour in K Road.

I grew up in a large New Zealand city and came from a very split family. I lived with my mother and my stepfather, and my father before that, for part of the time, and I was brought up by an aunt and uncle the rest of the time. So some of my growing up was done in the country. I think that's why I was never given stereotyped images or hang-ups about things. In the country everything happens around you, so it's not talked about. So I was never brought up to believe that being gay was bad, or being a prostitute was bad, or screwing around was particularly bad — *except* in my mother's eyes. But then she was very religious and that was her personal choice — she only got religious after her second divorce, might I add.

I had a very good sex education. I knew how not to get pregnant. I knew all about abortion and everything else by the time I was fourteen. I cut my teeth on books like *The First Sex* and *Our Bodies, Our Selves* and other great feminist publications, because my mother was a feminist.

I had a very good basic education. The fact that I chose not to follow it through any further at that time was my decision, much to the upset of my family. I left home after a large disagreement with my mother over my moral standards, mainly the lack of them in her eyes. She was divorced for the second time by this stage and was living by herself. I moved out and went to live with my boyfriend, but after about ten months I got very fed up with being used as somebody's punching bag and moved on.

I had met an artist in the meantime, who used to come around to the fabric shop where I was working, and we got on very well. When he found out what my situation was he offered me a place at his house, no strings attached. I was far too old for him anyway. He liked them in school uniforms.

There used to be some pretty wild parties and things like that going on there, with lots of screwing around and 'experimentation'. At that time, about 1981, I was working a forty-hour week. I was actually in charge of a shop and setting up the window displays and everything else, and I was getting paid a lofty $72 per week. It was chronic, slave labour. The unions would have had a fit, but at that age you aren't aware of things like unions.

Anyway, Evan turned around to me one day and said, 'Look, you're getting paid lousy money and you screw around like crazy. Why the hell don't you get paid for it?' And of course me, being me, thought, 'What a good idea!' and that's how I became a prostitute. How corny can you get? Greed — the greatest motivator of all.

I was sixteen at the time, and in many ways I was probably a very ruthless child. I didn't feel things like love or empathy. I'd just come out of a relationship of ten months of being bashed up, and I think that had probably gotten rid of most of my inner feelings about 'the humanity of man' and all that kind of shit. I'd never been a particularly emotional child anyway. With my parents getting divorced left, right and centre every five minutes, emotions were a thing you learned to put away in a dark little closet and turn the key on. So by the time I hit sixteen I was as tough as nails. Although in many ways I'd had a very good childhood. I can honestly say that as a child I don't think I ever got hit, not even as punishment.

Anyway, Evan had the contacts and that's how I started working in parlours. The arty-crafty set and the nightclub set and the parlour set have always hung out together. They're the only people with the cash flows to be able to afford these kinds of expensive hobbies, and they can afford to be out at obscure hours because they don't have ordinary jobs to get up to in the morning.

I began working at Archimedes bath house, which in those days wasn't the tip it's become over the years. They paid us $2.14 an hour, which was the minimum wage then, plus whatever we made out of the clients. So in those days we were actually paying taxes, as legitimate masseuses, and had IRD numbers and put in PAYEs and all those sorts of things. Nowadays, though, most parlours don't pay the girls anything — it all comes from extras.

Back then, I was making more money than I could shake a stick at, and I managed to spend as much as I earned. You inherit the ability to spend money with the job. It's like going into town and seeing a pair of shoes you like and you don't know which colour to get — so you buy both.

When I started I had no expectations at all. I think that was half the trouble. If I'd had some expectations or standards, in terms of my own morality or whatever, then it would probably have been a lot easier. I was just wild — there's no other word for it. I drank far too much. I think Steve, who ran the parlour, and myself used to go through a bottle of vodka a night between the two of us, and that wasn't what I was drinking before or after work.

After three or four months at the bath house, I went to work at the Nordic. Originally, I think that place had been intended to be some kind of gentlemen's retreat, but they'd had trouble with the cops over that concept. Now they operated as a kind of 'academy of massage', and they did actually teach massage. My side of the business was like a sideline — they had a few girls available because people kept asking for them.

While I was working there I met a guy, a client, and he and I got on very well as people. At that time I think I had probably emotionally and mentally had enough of the work, without realising it. We were both into doing our own thing and enjoying ourselves. It was a really drifty time, and I ended up stopping working. So I only had a short spell of being a working girl then. I very much had the attitude that it was just a good laugh and now it was time to move on to something else. I was never doing it for any serious reasons. I didn't have a drug habit; I didn't have a boyfriend with a drug habit; I didn't have children to support, or any of the other multitude of reasons. For me, it had just been a bit of a laugh.

Anyway, I lived with this guy for a while, but we ended up having a massive argument, which on the face of it was really quite ludicrous. He went to Australia for a job interview and ended up on a very short shortlist for it, and I looked at my bank account and thought, 'Hey, shit, I've got no money, I'll go back to work for a few weeks,' and ended up working in a house out in the suburbs. It never occurred to me that he might want to take me with him.

He came back from his interview to find I was back working. The argument was about my working. So I turned around to him and basically said, 'Well, can you honestly say that you were celibate all the time you were in Australia?' And he goes, 'Well, no,' and I said, 'Well then, neither was I, and I was getting paid for it, so which one of us was stupid?' He couldn't relate to that kind of thinking at all. It was like he was saying, 'It's okay for the gander, it's certainly not okay for the goose,' whereas I was into total freedom of expression, personality, whatever. So I left. Like next day.

I went to live with Tricia, who ran the house in the suburbs. She asked me what I was going to do and I said, 'Look, honestly, I don't know. I'm getting on for seventeen, I have no job qualifications. I honestly don't know.' She said, 'Well, do you want to work?' I replied, 'No, not really. I think I've had enough of it.' And she said, 'Well, I know somebody who is very lonely and needs somebody to look after him. Would you be interested in meeting him?' So I said, 'Oh yes, what the hell.' And that's how I met my dear friend Uncle Benjamin. He was in his fifties or sixties and I was about seventeen. It was almost indecent really, but we lived together for two and a half years.

Tricia felt sorry for him because she and he had been very old friends for many years. His most recent lady had left and he was in a bit of a doldrum about the whole thing. She'd been there under a similar arrangement to me. Anyway, he was looking for someone to brighten his life up a wee bit, and I needed someone to support mine, so we became kindred spirits. We went to dinner first off and found out that we actually got on very well as people. I drifted over to his place and didn't move again. That was me entirely then. I would sort of drift and stop — there was no conscious decision made.

And from then on I had an extremely comfortable level of living. I was getting tottled round in a Mercedes Benz car; we had a three-storey town house with swimming pool and spa, both heated. I was getting an extremely cushy existence for a seventeen-year-old. I had pocket money to spend. I was never short of anything. I was certainly getting my money's worth. So was he. It was a mutual using situation.

What did he expect from me? Me, really. *I* was expected. God, it makes me sound like somebody's pet poodle! I had to look good, behave well, not say 'fuck' in public, and if I did have affairs, be very discreet about them.

He wanted somebody he could take out. His various business interests involved him in a lot of socialising, and he wanted someone to take out who wasn't going to get blind drunk and make a fool of themselves. And I'd been quite well brought up. I did know how to use the right knife and fork for the right occasions. You could take me to a decent restaurant and I wouldn't drink the finger-bowl water. And besides that, I looked good — I had very good dress sense.

At that age I was very malleable. In many ways he did take the rough edges off, but basically I had total freedom to do whatever the hell I liked. He'd give me $100 a week just to fritter around, but everything I needed he'd pay for. And then, when we went overseas, he'd spend quite a lot of money on me, especially in the jewellery shops.

We went somewhere at least once or twice a year, Fiji, Noumea, Hong Kong, Australia. It was his time to get away from it all, and my time to be splurged upon. It was a very good economic relationship really. And I really did care very much for him. It was just that one morning I woke up and thought, 'My God, I'm bored.' And so off into the sunset I went, much to his disgust. He still keeps asking me if I want to come back. I must have left an indelible impression on that one.

I did actually come to love him, although I think there is a big difference between loving someone and being in love with somebody. Being in love is when you don't mind being up at six in the morning to cook them breakfast before they go to work, or pulling out their dirty socks from under the bed where they've stuffed them. That fades. But loving someone is a very warm, caring thing. I don't think you ever stop loving someone.

By the time I left Uncle Benjamin I'd been introduced to a friend of his called Laura, whom he still hasn't really forgiven to this day. I'd decided I was bored with being straight and I would much rather go back to being gay. It just hadn't been economically viable up until that point. I mean, how many wealthy women do you meet who can afford to support you? I reckon I was probably gay from the time I was fourteen. But I didn't really know what it was. Nobody had ever told me. Therefore there was no comprehension that perhaps this wasn't normal. So I had lesbian experiences when I was quite young. There was a lot of partying going on in those days anyway, with everything being pretty much a free for all. The eighties was the era of orgies and group sex — that was before herpes and AIDS. Screwing around wasn't a problem then. There was room for lesbian sex when I was with Uncle Benjamin, too. We even lived in a *menage à trois* there for a stage.

And then I met Laura. I'd been straight — well, straightish. I went over to Australia later to see Laura and floated around the gay scene with her, and we ended up living together. She freaked out when I turned up — she's not the sort of person who's used to people turning up on her doorstep.

We spent a couple of years in Australia, and I worked as a

waitress over there. But when we came back to New Zealand I was basically informed that I was overqualified to be a waitress. So I floated around some of the people I knew who were in the nightclub scene.

Then I ran into Damion, and he needed somebody to answer the phones. And I'm actually a qualified telephonist/receptionist — although I hated doing it and my instincts told me there was no way in hell that I would ever do that for a living. Being stuck in an office with the same people, day in and day out, working nine to five, would be like living death. Anyway, I started working for Damion, but although he and I get on well socially, we couldn't work together. He treats everybody as if they're an idiot and a slut to boot, so we had a minor disagreement and I told him where to shove his job.

Meanwhile, Laura had also picked up some work around his company, because this guy was running escort agencies, strip clubs, a video parlour, and doing strip-a-grams and fantasy phonecalls. He picked up another massage parlour and offered it to Laura to run.

She came home and asked if I wanted to work with her, so I asked where it was, thinking to myself, 'Not K Road, not K Road, please not K Road,' and she says 'K Road!' So I said, 'Oh, that's nice,' thinking to myself how we couldn't have got in the worse end of town if we'd tried. But there we were, so we went and did it.

First off we walked in and got rid of everybody. The parlour had a bad name and was doing something like $400 in a week's take. That means you know the girls are either no good, or fiddling the till, or so zonked out of their minds that they don't know what's happening. So you get rid of them. We ended up with some very good crew working for us. Probably because we were women and were inclined to be a little more easy-going than the men. But also because I think we were used to dealing with people who'd come to work stoned or junked up to the eyeballs, or who wouldn't bother turning up at all. Yet we had some really lovely girls working for us, too.

When we moved in there were syringes all over the flaming

place and booze bottles tucked behind pot plants, and it was absolutely filthy. Drugs are a problem wherever you have prostitution. After a certain time working you get to the stage where you need to be off your face before you can face a client. But of course drugs are addictive. Whenever I'd get to that stage, I'd quit. I'm too fond of myself and I've seen the side effects and the damage they can cause. We tried to run a drug-free parlour. We had the odd junkie, but you don't mind junkies who are in control.

Laura and I managed the place; we didn't work there ourselves. You can't work *and* run a place. You can't keep your eye on things when you're up in a room for an hour. And it doesn't matter how trustworthy your staff are, because for every one who's trustworthy you can find one who isn't.

We had a very good relationship with the police at that place because they knew we were trying to keep it as drug-free as possible and they knew we didn't employ known drug addicts. The police want to be able to see that there aren't girls sliding out of the windows drugged to the eyeballs. They want something that people can walk past and say, 'Oh, it's a massage parlour — isn't that nice, dear?' Their whole job is basically not to eradicate prostitution or massage parlours, it's to eradicate the idiots that fuck it up.

Prostitution is actually legal in this country, but soliciting isn't. How you can have one without the other is a mystery I haven't quite managed to fathom. But those laws came in when the people making the laws were the ones who were using the prostitutes, and they needed to be able to protect their own ends. So you have a crazy law which makes it illegal for the girls to solicit the guys, but not the other way round.

Laura and I ran the parlour together for about four or five months, then I had another big argument with Damion and left, and she kept it on. I reckoned if I was going to be pissing around working the kinds of hours we were, I might as well be back on the game. I always said jokingly when I left the first time that if ever I went back it would be out of economic necessity. Mind you, my idea of economic necessity is when I can no longer afford to buy $400 pairs of shoes!

I decided I didn't want to work in Auckland, though; partly because I knew everybody, and partly because the place really is such a sleaze. Working in Auckland then for me would have felt like shitting on my own doorstep.

So I moved cities and went to work at Edward's place. I'd known about it for years because Edward was an old friend of Tricia's. I'd heard that Edward's was a house rather than a parlour, and you could live in, and all of that suited me. Saved me the problem of trying to find accommodation in a new city and all the associated problems. This was one of the few old-style houses left, if not the only one, since by then Flora had died.

I had known Flora McKenzie a little and had even worked a few days in her house. Places like that are remnants of a past age. The prices were a remnant of that time too! But it was good — everything was organised for you at Flora's. People didn't come in casually. It was appointments only. And you'd phone up in the morning and be told you had X amount of bookings for the day.

When I knew Flora she was practically in her eighties and living on whisky and milk. She'd be sober in the morning, but by the end of the afternoon she'd be getting quite slurred. And it was then that she would come out with the most outrageous stories. I think those people who have a few skeletons in their closets from Flora's place would have 40,000 fits if they realised she may have chatted about them in the afternoons.

Basically she had very good clients, having come from a very good family herself. In her younger days all the important people went there, but when I went it was nearly the end of an era. Still good people, though, and you never got hassles at her place. At Christmas time the Vice Squad even used to come round for drinkie-poos with her.

Flora was probably New Zealand's only real madam. She came from a very good family but was a social rebel at a time when it wasn't considered normal, like it is today. She had a great sense of humour, and could be totally uncouth and rude to her clients. She wouldn't tolerate any shit from the girls either, any more than she did from the clients, so it was a very fair system.

All the money side was handled by the madam. The guys used to give her the money, and she'd give the girls their share later. You could still earn as much as in a parlour, or more, because you were going through a lot more people there. Especially when you're new. But that's true everywhere.

You see, clients fall into three different categories. You have your regulars, who are like a life-blood system. You need regulars for when the days are rotten, because you can rely on them to turn up. They're also the biggest hassles, though, because they are usually emotionally attached and can drive you up the wall. They can be very demanding on your time. Sex gets to a stage with a regular client where it's only a very minimal part of the relationship, because you are basically a life-support system to them. You become a mother and a wife and a confessor all rolled into one. But it's part of the job, it's what you're getting paid to be — sympathetic.

Most of these regular clients tend to be in their forties and fifties, married, with kids, although the kids may have left home by now. They're people who have communication problems in their relationships with their wives, either in bed or out of it.

So the relationship one has with regulars is like being a surrogate wife. The problem with regulars is that they often want to please you in bed too, so the idea is to train them very early on. You set down very definite rules — this is what we are here for, this is why we are doing it, this is what I do, this is what you do, all that sort of thing. And you have to be very ruthless and blunt, otherwise you end up with the situation where they want to make you happy. And they'll spend hours trying and you can understand why their wives aren't interested in sex any more!

So those clients are regulars of one *person*. But you can also get clients who are regulars of a *place*. They go to one parlour exclusively because there's something about it that appeals to them. They're usually people who need to feel secure — usually your business types. They really do have this idea that they're slightly more important than they are.

In some ways they're the most demanding of all, because they feel they have some sort of personal say in how the place is run. They're the ones most likely to complain to the owner. These guys go through every girl and know everybody intimately. Sometimes they'll get used by the management to suss out new girls.

There's also a third group of clients, who are a totally floating population and will go anywhere where they think there may be a new girl in town working. They don't have any loyalty to either one place or one girl. Usually they are oncers. A large portion of your floating population is from the Chinese business sector, and they like their girls young and new.

Those are your three basic client categories.

When I moved down to Wellington, I went to live in Edward's house. Two other girls were also living there at the time, as well as Edward himself. The house is really his own private hobby, in many ways. It's been going for twenty or so years, and it gives him company on tap. It's full of reproduction antiques. He's made a habit of collecting all sorts of things which he stored away, so it felt like living in a bad-taste party sometimes. The house had large rooms for hostessing both up and downstairs. I think the original idea was to keep the peasants below and the upper crust above, but it didn't always work out like that.

Some girls took their clients back to their rooms because these doubled as work rooms. I was very fortunate. The first room I lived in had a four-poster bed in it, but it was a walkway to other rooms, so I couldn't take clients there. The second room I had was like a bedsit, with its own kitchenette, and the only time I ever used that for clients was for people who were worth a bit of a fuss. Usually I'd entertain people in that room but not actually have sex in it.

HILARY

Originally, Edward used to get the guys to pay on an honesty-box system. But those were the good old days when you could rely on honesty. Now a client gives the girl the money directly, and she gives Edward his share later, so the system is completely reversed.

You earn a lot less working in a place like his, but you do have a lot more freedom. If somebody comes in that you can't stand, you can turn around to Edward and say, 'Look, he's a real prize pain and I don't want to do him.' It's a lot harder to do that in a massage parlour. You also don't have to worry about the Vice Squad so much, since you know virtually everyone who goes there.

I'd like to say you get a much better clientele at Edward's, and to some extent that's true. There used to be a lot of top businessmen, politicians, Olympic athletes — the upper crust. But three-piece suits can get as drunk as anybody else, and they're just as bloody objectionable. And so even at Edward's you'd get the odd drunken pain in the ass, and towards the end of my time there they were turning up more often.

I lived in there for eighteen months, although I was still living with Laura at the same time. We had a commuting relationship, and besides, I really needed to get away every fortnight or so.

Edward's was different from Flora's in that the girls had to do more of the entertaining of clients themselves. At Flora's you didn't entertain the clients — you just screwed them. You'd chat away, but it was very much Flora who was the focal point, and they all came to pay homage to her. It was probably like that originally with Edward too.

I found, with living there and everything, that I had no time out. And I could end up working very long hours. Like, I might not get up until 11 a.m. but then not get to bed until 3 or 4 a.m., and I would have been at work all that time. But sometimes we'd say to him, 'Okay, Edward, it's very quiet tonight. If there are no clients here by ten o'clock we're going out,' and we'd all piss off and leave him.

So because it was a twenty-four-hour business, I made it

very clear from the day I arrived that I would be going every fortnight for a few days off. Laura was up in Auckland to begin with, then later she moved south, and I'd fly off to see her. It was easier than having her come and see me. Where would she have stayed? It's very hard to find a spare room in a brothel!

Personally I think it's probably easier being a lesbian and a working girl than being heterosexual. Most of my regular clients knew I was living with a woman. That meant they were a little less inclined to push — like they wouldn't want my phone number and stuff like that.

I didn't tell my ordinary clients, but my regulars all knew and just accepted it. The only problem could be if they reacted like, 'My God, she hasn't had a real man.' Men still do have that attitude, even in this day and age, when confronted with lesbianism. You've got to admire their arrogance really, don't you?

So the first thing you learn as a prostitute is how to fake an orgasm. In the old days people would have sex and as far as the guys were concerned, it was all about them enjoying themselves. You would never have got this 'I want to please you' crap, whereas nowadays every single person wants to bloody do it. Ever tried having eleven people in a row all wanting to please you? Believe me, faking is a very easy alternative by comparison. And it makes them feel better. Let's face it — half of the thing in this job is to make other people feel better.

Essentially you're there as a service industry. It doesn't matter whether you're a waitress or a prostitute or a typist — you're still doing things for other people. A secretary uses her hands, and that's considered quite nice and normal. A prostitute uses another part of her anatomy, and 'oohh!'

Most of the clients at Edward's wanted straight sex, but I also had a lovely collection of whips which used to frighten the living hell out of people. I probably only used them twice in all the time I was there. And that was at their request. Mind you, I do remember one guy who was particularly objectionable. I threatened him that if he didn't behave I'd get the whips out.

HILARY

He said, 'Go on then,' so I did. He was quite drunk at the time, and I don't think he was very aware of what was happening. The whip I used left very nasty welts, and when he went to get up next morning he must have suddenly twigged what had happened. His wife was lying there next to him, so he had to slide out of bed and back his way into the bathroom to grab a towel!

My relationship with Laura was certainly affected by my going back working. I'd go to see her, but I would have been socialising with people all the time I'd been away, being nice to people whom I normally wouldn't give the time of day to, and so when I got there I was totally anti-social. All I wanted to do was stay in bed. It would take me about a week to wind down. Whereas she hadn't really been out anywhere much while I was away. I certainly wasn't the easiest person to live with during that time.

I left Edward's because I got to the stage where I thought I would probably kill somebody. I was constantly listening to all these people's little whinges and problems, and the constant dramatics that come from living in such a place, and I figured that for the amount of hassles I was starting to get compared with the returns, it just wasn't worth it any more. I had earned enough to pay off what I had gone in there to do, like buying furniture for the house and stuff like that. I'd gone back purely for financial reasons, and felt totally ruthless about that.

When I'd started at Edward's the money had been bloody good. But then the slump hit, there was the stock-market crash, AIDS hit, and everything came all at once. Especially in Wellington, which is like a business town anyway. And our clients were affected. You see, when I first went to Edward's, I was earning over two grand a week. But when I left I was probably down to about $1,300, sometimes less.

Effectively it was Edward who set the prices. The girls used to charge more sometimes — if you really didn't like a client you'd charge them more. Edward used to take a commission — seventy/thirty split, with him getting thirty per cent of the money. That changed when the prices went up, at last. The trouble with people like him is that they don't like putting up the prices because it offends the regular clients. I'll never forget one guy actually said to one of the girls that since he'd been coming for so many years, he thought he should get a discount. She turned around to him and said, '*I* give *you* a discount? I wouldn't give you the time of day if you weren't paying me for it.'

Some weeks there you might only make $700–800, and that's lousy money. I can't survive on $800 a week. There was always rent to Edward, which was about $100 a week, and doctor's and chemist's fees. A packet of condoms can cost $15–20, and Edward didn't supply those. He didn't even like the girls using condoms. This is something I've noticed about private houses. Most of them don't encourage the girls to use condoms; in fact, most actively discourage it. I had regular checks, but that was my personal choice. It wasn't made mandatory by the management at all.

My doctor thought I was paranoid. She'd say to me, 'Look, Hilary, you practise safe sex and what have you. You know your chances of actually catching something are a lot less than the average woman's out there. In a year and a half of coming here you've had absolutely nothing, which is more than I can say for most of my ordinary women patients. Most people catch at least one thing at some time.' I was staggered by that comment, actually.

When I left Edward's, I went down south to live with Laura. I thought I wouldn't mind going to university. I felt I'd have to learn how to use the English language again. I'd used my body for so many bloody years that when I came back to school I had difficulty writing my name. But that's what I'm doing — sixth form courses to reground myself again. So far I'm doing very well. I got nearly full marks for my last essay.

Now I'm getting older, I've learned responsibility. It's hideous. Now I look at clothes and think I can't afford them and don't buy them. That's the worst. It's the withdrawal symptoms. No more shopping days.

HILARY

I've still got a heap of clothes from before, of course. But I really don't think this high school is ready for me to turn up in $500 evening cocktail dresses! That's what I usually chose to wear up at Edward's. However, that doesn't always work. I remember one night I'd been shopping with my kid sister and I burst in to Edward's wearing my favourite rugby jersey and jeans and with my hair tied back. I must have looked about sixteen. I got whisked away immediately and it was like that for the rest of the evening. I didn't even get a chance to change or unpack my shopping or anything.

Now, however, is the first time probably that I've never been involved with the sex industry. Even when I was living with Uncle Benjamin I still had ties with it. This is the first time in my life that I've got absolutely nothing to do with the sex industry. I don't really miss it. At this moment in my life I'm not bored. I don't have time to be bored. My whole life is doing domestics, cooking bloody dinners, doing flaming homework. I find it humorous that at age twenty-five I've finally started to do homework — I never did any at school!

And I try to get to bed early enough so I can wake up at seven the next morning. I find the idea of me getting up at seven in the morning quite humorous. That's been a big change. Bloody near killed me for the first week, it did!

One thing I do feel strongly about is that other people should get their heads out of the sand and try to be helpful rather than obstructive. This especially applies to feminists, who, despite trying to change social barriers and people's concepts of women, have still adopted this good girl/bad girl policy when it comes to their cousins, the prostitutes. It's ridiculous. I mean, we're women too. And we, if anything, need more support than any other group, because we don't have unions, we don't have health schemes. If you get sick and you're off work, you don't earn money — it's as simple as that.

Also, not all prostitutes are junkies. We're not all forced into it. This is something else that really gets up my nose. The image of poor women being coerced into becoming workers really annoys me. Most prostitutes do it by choice. I'm talking about this country, not overseas. If they *are* forced, it's through economic necessity, in which case you can blame the Government for not providing childcare, or for giving out benefits that are totally impossible to live and raise a family on.

Here's feminism trying to change the face of women in the world, and they've still got incredible hang-ups and stereotypes themselves. What gives them the right to say what they're doing is the right way of going about it? If they want to be helpful, then by all means let them be helpful, but they needn't tell us we're wrong. If feminists really want to help, they could get stuck into a few things like improving the girls' working conditions. They could set up support systems so that when the girls retire they can have counselling and anything else they need. Maybe they could set up some sort of counselling for girls who are currently working too. Working girls often don't have anywhere to go except to each other. That's why they're such a closely knit bunch. They have to be.

There are a lot of things that working girls need. They need better working conditions. They need medical insurance. They need unions to stop themselves being exploited. And they *are* being bloody exploited by the bosses, especially in some of the major centres, where you've got the bosses actually charging them for the towels and charging them for each client they take through, regardless of whether they make any money from him or not. Law change also is needed urgently. It's so one-eyed at the moment. It protects the client and gets the prostitute every time.

When I interviewed Hilary she described herself as 'a retired masseuse'. However, she added that it was very hard to ever get out of the sex industry completely, because 'New Zealand's too small for anyone to have a secret life in!' Since then she and Laura have packed up and moved to Australia.

GENEVIEVE

I talked to Genevieve in the chapel of Arohata Women's Prison two years ago while she was serving her first prison sentence. She has worked since she was sixteen in massage parlours, escort agencies and on the streets.

I was one of ten children, with a Maori father and a Pakeha mother. We used to live out in the suburbs of a large city where my parents were involved in the Mormon Church. When I was sixteen I got a job doing massages in a local bath house. It was straight massages only, no prostitution, and we could do them while topless, nude or fully clothed. I tried it and I liked it. For every massage I did I'd get $10 commission, maybe more depending on the kind of massage. I was earning anything up to $200 or $300 a week, which was good money then.

The clientele were good. They'd come in knowing they would get a decent massage, and you'd be busy doing clients one after the other all the way through from ten o'clock until your shift finished, or you could work double shifts and earn even more. I worked there for about eight months, then my girlfriend went into town to work.

We thought all parlours were the same, but she came back and showed me all this money she'd just earned. She said it was from massaging, she didn't tell me the extra bits. So I figured if the money was that good in town I'd go in there to work. I chucked my job at the bath house and went to a parlour called the Monte Carlo.

On my first night this codger offered me something like $30 for a hand job, and I said, 'I beg your pardon, I don't do anything like that,' to which he replied, 'Well, what the hell are you working in a place like this for?'

I really got a shock. My girlfriend hadn't told me what went on in those rooms. I went out and told the boss this guy had just offered me $30 for a hand job and he looked at me and laughed. I finished there that night, gave it away and went home. I kept watching my girlfriend bringing home all this money, though, and I thought about it. After about a month I went back in and gave it another go. My first crack was $50, and from then on I never looked back.

I can still remember that first client. As soon as I saw the money on the table, I looked at it and I looked at him and I thought, 'Oh yes, this could be easy.' I jumped on the bed, closed my eyes and away he went. It was all over within two seconds. He jumped off and said, 'That was an easy $50,' then asked if I'd done it before. I told him, 'Actually you're my first one.' I always kept that client, for the whole two years I worked there.

I got to know him quite well. He used to take me out to dinner or to other places, and if I was broke he'd give me money. He wasn't a boyfriend, though, he was still just a client. He used to come in on a Friday night and ask if I'd had my tea break. Usually I'd say 'No, would you like to take me out to tea?' We'd go out for tea, then go looking around town, and he might buy me clothes or something, and that would be it. He'd drop me back at the parlour, and I wouldn't see him again until the following week. Some weeks, though, he might just come in, pay me my money, have his crack and go. He was a married man and loved his wife, but he didn't have a very good sex life with her.

That very first time, when he asked me if I'd 'cracked it' before, I didn't even know what that meant. There was an older lady at that parlour, about thirty-seven or thirty-eight, who had been doing it for a long time and she took me through the whole run. She showed me what to do and how to do it and how to be polite. I never ever lost that. For weeks I used to work with that woman, and do all the same shifts she did. I even went out with her and we talked a lot. We need those older women to learn from. They can tell us so much about how to do it, how to read a guy's mind, and what their actions mean. You know, some of them have been out there fifteen or sixteen years and they're still learning themselves, just like I'm still learning.

The first guy I did, he was between forty and forty-five. I had some really young ones, like seventeen-year-old virgins, right up to blooming seventy-year-olds. One old codger I had was eighty-two. He couldn't get it in, but he gave it a damned good go, I must admit!

A lot of what goes on with clients is acting. You have to act out a role all the time, build their egos, fake orgasms if you have to, tell them how nice it feels, how great they are — all that crap. Many of the guys may have been married for years, but they still don't know how to make women feel good. I used to tell them, and show them how to massage, all that sort of stuff.

We sometimes get women coming to the parlour because they want a woman to do them. It happens reasonably often. I've done quite a few women in my time. Most of these women are married, usually forty and over, and I don't know if they're lesbians or not. They might end up becoming one. Or they'll stay married but keep coming back to the parlour and get a female companion on the side.

When I was in the parlours it was a treat to have women coming in as clients. A lot of the other girls felt the same. They were nicer, less demanding, and so much more pleasant that we'd give them longer. Sometimes we'd even end up being given a massage in return, and might even get off on it sexually. A lot of the women in the parlours have lesbian relationships anyway. You just get so sick of working with men all the time that to have a woman touch you feels really nice. But you have to be very careful in that respect. Lesson number one is that you don't get sexually involved with other workers.

Anyway, while you're working it's almost impossible to keep a relationship going. You spend all day practising how to be switched off, so it's impossible to turn on later, especially to a man. And if you're involved with a man, he's likely to give you heaps. If you piss them off at all, they turn around and say, 'Well you're only trash anyway, a hooker, nothing but a little whore.' Women who are trying to develop a career don't need that sort of shit! It's easier not to have relationships at all while you're working.

I was married when I was a hooker. By seventeen I was married and had already had two children. I adopted the first one out, but then had two other children to my first marriage. I couldn't handle working and being married, though. Our marriage was a good one, to begin with, but he couldn't handle me being in a parlour, which is pretty understandable. It was pretty hard when we broke up. The children were just babies, and we'd bought our own home and everything, but I don't think he could handle me earning all that money either.

So I left town altogether and took off down south to live. I went to work in another parlour and that's where I met my second husband. He owned the parlour, but I worked for him for about a year before I really got to know him. Then we started going out together and we invested in another parlour and got into the business world. I ran one and he ran the other.

I kept working as well. I bought us everything, in fact. Cars, the lot. It was all out of my working money. It makes me sick every time I talk about him. As soon as we got married he started laying into me, beating me up all the time. But if it wasn't for my 'art' he'd have ended up bankrupt. The marriage only bloody lasted fourteen months and in that time I'd had another child. I left him, walked out and left him with everything — house, cars, child, the lot.

I got into street work after that. I worked on the streets in Wellington for three years or so. There comes a time when you get sick of massaging. You can't be bothered having to be nice to clients. Out on the streets you don't have to make conversation to get your money. The streets are a different ball game altogether!

GENEVIEVE

The guy thinks it's cheaper on the streets. It's still $80 for straight sex, but in the parlours they'd have to pay a $40 cover charge on top of that. It's just like going to the grocery store and if the price is $2.99 instead of $3.00, they think wow, it's a bargain. It's just the human mind.

You find out on the streets that the girls mainly work down one street and the queens will work down the other end or around the corner. But the queens stay with the queens and the girls with the girls, so the clients know who are girls and who are not.

Out on the street you get mostly businessmen as clients. They want a quick job. Usually they take us somewhere away from Marion Street. There are quiet little spots all around Wellington that we can use. Or they take us back to their motel or to their homes or whatever. I reckon you get more pleasant people out on the street.

There's a lot more choice out on the streets, for the guys as well as us. If he doesn't like the look of you, he can just drive on by and look somewhere else. And if you don't like the look of him, you can wave him goodbye. You've got all the freedom in the world to say no.

It's important to suss clients out first, and you've only got five minutes to get it right. We suss them out mainly by looking at them really well, talking to them, smelling their breath to see if they've been drinking. I very rarely go with anyone who's been drinking, unless he happens to be someone I know. If I'd never seen the guy before, I'd hesitate, or maybe just give a hand job or start playing with him right there, in Marion Street, rather than go off somewhere. It's dark enough there that you can do that, and the other girls are close by if he acts up.

So far I've been lucky. I can't say I've ever been really frightened by anyone, because I use my mouth a lot. Guys come round sometimes with bottles in their hands and try hassling us, but for myself I can't say I've ever been scared out on the street. If you show your fear I think you're more likely to have something happen to you.

Escorts can be a lot worse, though. You don't know who's going to be at the other end until you get there, and that can be quite freaky. A lot of the clients don't like that either — they'd rather see who they're getting first. I tried the ships as well. We just used to get a car-load of us together and drive up to Auckland when the Japanese boats were in. We'd stay up there for a month, live like slobs, earn heaps and come back home. Or we might follow the boats down to Napier, maybe even go down to Lyttelton. But we weren't shippies — we drove ourselves down there.

What the guys are looking for doesn't change no matter where you work. But it's not just sex. When I worked at the Monte Carlo I used to do body rubs all the time. That's where you put slime all over their bodies, front and back. There's no sex involved usually — it's more like a titillator, and they get it off on their own.

You'd also get guys coming in wearing nappies — the nappy men. They often shave themselves and everything. While you give them their massage they wear their nappies, and when they piss in them you have to smack them on the backside for being naughty boys. I had one bloke who came to me wearing nappies who told me he'd worn nappies until he was four. Usually mothers spank kids for wetting and try to potty-train them, but the way he was talking, his mother didn't ever do that. And he wanted to know what it felt like to be disciplined in that respect. You can laugh about it, but then you've got to try not only to be a hooker but to understand what they're going through. The more times you see them, the more times you can understand them, and the more you can understand this stupid world.

I had one client nobody else would do. He'd come into the parlour and shit in a potty in front of me. Then he wanted me to put gloves on and rub his shit all over his face and body. He'd just stand there and be degraded. He wanted to be really put down, called a real messy pig, an animal. He'd get off on that, and after he came he'd have a shower, get cleaned up and pay me $500. I must admit I felt sick when I did it. But that was his fantasy and he was prepared to pay heaps for it, so why not?

The men who ask for the strangest things are often high-class businessmen. Just like the guys who want to be disciplined are often from private boys' schools where they used to be caned. They must have got off on it, because now they come and beg to be hit, or whipped until they bleed. I can't get into it, but some of the girls have made heaps from it.

But really there are hundreds of reasons why a man might come looking for a hooker. He could be lonely. He might not have a lady, or he may look so ugly and repulsive that he can't get a woman. Or he might be looking for companionship, even five minutes or so might make him happy. If a guy really enjoys you and he's rich enough, he may come back two or three times a week. But you always charge that client the same price, no less, no more. Even if he goes out and buys you a watch, you still charge him. It's part of being a professional.

One client even offered me money. He fell in love with me, that one. Because I had car trouble at the time he said, 'I'll pay for it.' It came to $1,500, but he was still willing to pay for it. So you know what I did? I took it, and charged him for sex on top of that! He asked for nothing back.

The most important thing you can give a client is affection. I can relate to clients and be nice as pie because it's only for half an hour, maybe an hour. I'll be thinking about how I'm going to spend that money or what I'll do next day, all sorts of things. Sometimes it can be mind-wrecking, though. It could play on your mind if you didn't forget it.

There are some things I won't do or can't let clients do to me. I don't have anal sex, and I refuse to do blow jobs. If they want anal sex they might as well go to a guy for it, and if they want blow jobs they might as well go to a queen. Those are the only things I refuse to do.

I don't mind if they touch me or fondle me, but kissing is completely out of the question. I just can't bring myself to kiss every Tom, Dick and Harry. To me, kissing is something you do with a partner and it means a lot to me. It means you're in love with someone. It's something you do for only one person, not for ten thousand men.

I've never got anything out of it sexually. But then I can never come with a man anyway, that's something that's been taken out of me. My father sexually abused me when I was thirteen. I was raped, ripped to smithereens, and from that day onwards I never ever saw my father again. If I did, I'd blow his brains out. I could never ever forgive him for what he did to me.

I told my mother, but she couldn't handle the situation. There were ten of us kids, all under eighteen. It happened one day right out of the blue. It was during the afternoon and I was in bed and had just got my first period. I didn't know what to do about it, and my father came in and said, 'I'll show you how to use these tampons. You'll have to learn how to put them in.' Mum was out working, and I didn't know anything about things like that. He said to me, 'Didn't your mother tell you anything about this?' then started tampering around with me. One thing led to another and I got uncomfortable and told him, 'If you don't get out of here, I think you're being rude, bloody rude.' He said, 'If you don't lie down I'll do something even more drastic to you,' and he did.

I'd never seen my father like that before. I find now that I don't relate to very many Maori people. He was a Maori, you see, and my mother was a Pakeha. If Maori clients come in I refuse to do them. I don't know whether it's their force or their roughness. It's not their colour as such — it's just that when my father did that he destroyed all my respect.

I've had a lot of treatment since then and I am snapping out of it, but you know, it hit me when I was twenty-five that my father actually raped me. It didn't really dawn on me for years that that's what it was — he raped me.

After that you could say that in some respects I wanted everything out of men. I wanted to take, take, take, everything a man had. If it was their money, I didn't care how long it took me to get it, as long as I got every cent they owed me.

And I've never ever orgasmed, right from the word go. Ever

GENEVIEVE

since my father had sex with me, I've never been able to orgasm with anybody. Sometimes it's different with women, if they use their fingers, but if I'm entered at all I can't. I've never been able to have an orgasm with my husband or my boyfriend — that's been taken away from me.

It's been easy switching myself off from clients because of all that. And you have to switch off, sex-wise I mean. You still talk to them and everything, but you don't *feel* anything. That's where the acting comes in. I pretend I'm getting off so they hurry up and come. Sometimes I ask them if they'd mind hurrying up, and they might even jump off without coming themselves, because they're so chuffed to think they've pleased you. Getting their egos up is just as important as anything else.

I make them wear condoms for everything, though. I have VD checks every few weeks too, and I've had three AIDS tests, all of which were negative. But then I've got a sympathetic family doctor, and he encourages me to do that sort of thing because he's pleased to see a careful hooker.

When I'm hooking I find there's something new to experience every day. It's like a learning process, with all the girls and all the clients. A lot of it, though, is to do with what I can get out of men. Whenever a client comes in, it is dollar signs I see. I don't care about the person. I just care about the amount of money that's staring at me and about the amount of time it will take to earn it. Beyond that, who gives a damn?

Genevieve was very willing to be interviewed for this book, she said, because she has often felt like writing down her own life story. Since then she has been released from prison and her current whereabouts are unknown.

ALEXANDRA

Alexandra was nearly seventeen when she began working in massage parlours. After four years she left and went to study at university.

I grew up in a professional family and spent much of my early childhood living overseas. I returned to New Zealand to go to boarding school and university, but left very rebelliously at the end of the fifth form and got a job.

I think I had actually decided that I would end up in the sex industry for a long time before I did. I would end up in situations where I would think, 'I might as well have been paid for that.' I didn't go looking for opportunities to do so, but knew I was capable.

I'd started sleeping with a lot of people from the age of fourteen onwards. Sometimes I would think to myself, 'I don't really want to do this,' but I would do it anyway and then think, 'Oh, why did I bother?'

When I was nearly seventeen, I had a flatmate move in who had a regular job. The rest of us in the flat worked nights in various hotel and restaurant jobs, and Stephanie was the only one with a daytime job. But after a while she started coming home as late as us at night. We got talking and I asked her, 'Where are you going every night?' She told me a big confidential story about how she was a receptionist at a parlour, but then realised I wasn't knocked over by what she was saying and told me she was working. I was just conversationally interested, and she asked if I wanted to go along one night, so I agreed.

One Sunday night, after I'd done a dayshift in the hotel, I went home, got in the bath, dressed up and went along. When I got there I realised I was actually expected. There had been a bit of a misunderstanding, because she'd just said, 'A friend of mine's coming in,' and they thought I wanted to work so they put my name up on the board. I thought, 'Well, here I am,' and I stayed.

I ended up staying at the Las Vegas a long time. I knew nothing about the logistics of working, although I had talked to her about it. I'd had visions of all sorts of really dangerous, nasty things happening, and the bosses manipulating you to work for them — like you see on TV. She'd explained it wasn't like that, and it wasn't.

The guys who ran this parlour were fairly nice — I'd stop and talk to them if I saw them in the street, even now. It would have been fine if I'd said no that first night. It wasn't very busy and there were three of us on. We were just sitting around talking when someone came in, and they said I should go first in case they got busy later and I was left on my own and had no choice. I was still going over how you do it with them. I didn't feel I knew enough, so somebody else did him and I took the next one. It wasn't very busy that night and I took home only about $150–200, but that was money I hadn't anticipated having at the time. The hardest part of it was all the conversational niceties. Actually having sex itself wasn't hard, probably because it wasn't all that different from the way I'd been living before then.

I didn't go back again for another three or four weeks because of my job, and for the first year I worked I kept my job and just worked two or three nights a week, often starting after work at eleven. I did that partly because I was scared about getting too involved, and I tended to keep myself a little separate from the other women working there.

After a while Stephanie gave up her job and stayed there full-time. I think the man I was seeing, John, had twigged about her, and then after a year or so he found out about me and got really aggressive. She and I would come home together smelling like we'd just got out of the shower, and one night there was a big confrontation scene. I admitted it and he got really violent. It shouldn't have had any bearing whatsoever on his life, because I was still only seventeen and you don't have deep, heavy relationships at that age — I was simply a person he knew. But he had a drug problem, and I said I would stop working if he stopped drugs, and he agreed. But then after about two or three months I met him one night and he was just bouncing up and down in the trees, totally out of it, so I got really angry and said I might as well go back to the parlours.

I felt really let down. The fact that he had been so violent had shown me that perhaps he really did care about me. I'd made a decision to stop work for him. But now I thought I might as well go back. I just went on reception at first, and later started working again. He was getting more and more uptight about it, but then one week I gave up my regular job and began working there full-time, doing five shifts a week.

I became really anti-social and started drinking a lot and would go to work drunk all the time. I don't think that it was because of the work, though — it was from being around him and his drugs and everything else.

He was uptight about me working, and wanted us to live together, so I moved out from my flat and we went and lived together. I kept on working, and I was also doing some escort work at the same time. That had started by accident really, when I was flatting — people used to ring Stephanie and after a while I realised why, so if she wasn't there I'd offer to do them.

The two guys who ran the parlour had employed a manager by now, and he was one of those thick as two bricks, kind-hearted but with a massive ego, bullshit sort of people. One night he had one of the girls up for something. I got really pissed off and started arguing with him on her side, and it ended up with the two of us walking out.

We left feeling indignantly righteous and on quite a high, and went and got something to eat. Then I said I had better start looking for a job, and we tried to think where I could possibly work. Despite the fact that I had been working at least eighteen months or so by then, it had all been at this one place. I decided to try Cleopatra's, because I'd heard there was a lot of money going through there at that time, and I walked up there straight away, still in my street clothes.

I had an interview with the woman who was managing the place. By then I was eighteen so I was legally allowed to work in a parlour. She asked if I had tattoos or anything, then said I could start on Monday, but she'd only let me have three shifts per week, which didn't impress me.

I started there and found I was earning less money than ever. I didn't like it either, probably because it was so controlled. At least at the Las Vegas, even though it was a lot sleazier, you were in control of yourself, and the place had no hold on you. The first night I went to Cleopatra's, though, I was given a list of rules to read about the dos and don'ts of working there, fines for lateness, all that sort of thing.

I started switching off quite a lot then. Asking clients how they had their coffee then forgetting what they'd said. Instead of being totally busy and charming and all the rest of it, I'd go blank. It put me under pressure, since I knew the regulars would think nothing of complaining. The indignity of being fired from a massage parlour would be terrible — that's like the real bottom of the line.

So working there wasn't a lot of fun, and I began thinking I would give it up, but I didn't know what else I could do. I was still living with John, and he was still seriously into drugs, and when I'd get home he would either be very violent or just really mentally aggressive. I was trying to be sensible enough for two people, but it was hard. If the phone rang and it was anything to do with work, he'd get really violent and abusive because I'd dared to let them intrude into our home. Whereas it wasn't a home at all by that point — it was pretty horrid. And by now I was scared of not being able to get back into proper work, so I knew I was quite trapped.

What I didn't realise by this time was that quite a few people knew I was working. One night a man came up to Cleopatra's and sat on the couch waiting and watching, only I couldn't see him because there were screens up. Then I was told I had a client waiting in a room and I walked in. He was somebody I knew — not all that well, but I'd met him when I was in the third form and he was seeing a seventh former at my school. I'd seen him round occasionally since then too. He was about twenty-seven by now, and I remember walking in and getting a real fright.

Normally if that happened, you weren't obliged to do anything about it and you could just walk out. But I was terrified because I wanted to know what he was doing there. He came over and said, 'I came up here because I heard you were here.' And I said, 'Well, so what? *Why* are you here?' And he said, 'Becaue I've always wanted to go to bed with you.' He went on, 'I can remember when you were thirteen and you would be in your school uniform and I always used to think you were really cute.' And then he said, 'Well, come on, you're here now,' so I went through with it and had sex with him, and he didn't pay me. Why should he? What could I do? He was pretty much implying, 'You know you'd better, otherwise . . .' What I should have done was just left the room and sent somebody else in. Anyway, I made him write out a cheque first, which is what you always do with people you're not sure about, we had sex and then he ripped up the cheque, said, 'That's really great,' and left. I just felt like the absolute pits, the worst, the bottom — and that was my last night. I didn't go back.

I went home and I was shaking the rest of the night. And because I don't take drugs, I was fully aware of all these things fuzzing around in my head. I got somebody to ring up for me to say I wasn't coming back, and I didn't know what to do, so I did nothing for a week. But then somehow he got my number and started ringing me at home.

The more he rang up, the more violent John would get, so I packed my pack, got on a train, got off up north and hitch-hiked around the country for two months and spent all the money. Because I didn't want that money. And I only came back to Wellington when it was virtually all gone.

I told John before I left, 'I don't want anything; I don't want to live with you any more,' and he was all upset. I don't know whether it's peculiar to people with drug problems or whether it's just him, but he would be really violent and grossly nasty one minute and then later on he'd be all tears, telling me he was sorry and he didn't mean it. I told him, 'I want a holiday anyway,' and I knew I had to get out of there. So I just went.

It was quite hard for the first month because I still had this horrible feeling inside and I couldn't talk to people to begin with. I was feeling dead, just totally dead. It was just a horrible feeling that things had gone over my head, that all the control stuff I'd been going on about was now gone.

I came back home and felt pretty on to it when John and I met each other at the railway station. While I'd gone he'd got himself sorted out at Aspell House. He'd actually started seeing a counsellor when I was still working. I'd arranged for him to go, partly because of the drugs but more because of the violence. It was dangerous for me. It wasn't just that I was being beaten up, but he'd start throwing knives around and stuff. In the end I got him to see somebody. It ended up being quite demoralising, though, since during his sessions he would patiently explain to the counsellor that it was my working that was contributing to his problems.

Anyway, when I got back we went home to our house, bought some furniture and rugs and painted the walls. I got a part-time job for a while in a quiet place, then a couple of months later I took on a job in a hotel where I knew nobody. I worked there right up until last year. I'd only ever done one outcall to that hotel, but he turned out to be an American who was a regular guest there. When I saw him next I just acted like a total blank. Somebody else recognised me, too, but didn't say anything for ages, although rumours did fly through the place at one stage.

Once I saw a woman I knew from working in the hotel. I don't think she saw me, though. She was in this horrible situation, because a lot of the staff were standing there watching. I started to walk over to talk to her, but a taxi pulled up and she got in. Everyone was saying to me, 'What were you doing that for?' and when I said I was going to speak to her, they said 'Why?' They were smirking and carrying on, and it made me really resent people who hadn't had anything to do with it and were just displaying their ignorance.

I was working really horrendous hours often, not just to earn money but to keep busy. John was earning good money too, and we did all the right things, like replacing all our old cheap furniture with good furniture, and buying a proper car.

But then one night I got home from work and he wasn't there. I thought he'd stayed out after work for a drink, which still was a worry, since now that he wasn't using drugs, supposedly, he was drinking a lot. But he didn't come home that night or the next day, and after about five days I knew what he was doing — getting smashed again.

So I left him. I found a flat on my own and moved out. I didn't take much with me because I didn't want to leave too big a hole for him in that place. I felt pretty scared. I had actually done something — it wasn't an accident. This time I had made a move — it was a deliberate action. And in a sense I'd destroyed my brick walls. Now I had to start again, and I didn't know if I could even manage it financially. I'd also decided I wanted to go to university, and it was nearly time for that to start, and that was all pretty scary too.

For the first year I didn't have a phone — partly because of the money but also because I didn't want John ringing up. He was coming around quite often, and sometimes he'd be out of it and get abusive. I'd really worry about him disturbing the neighbours, so I'd let him in. I started feeling quite defeated because I still couldn't get things to be the way I wanted them.

It was during this time that John had a serious accident which ended up with him in hospital for some time. I was obviously really horrified at what was happening to him, but in some ways I was also really relieved, because at least he was out of my hair. So I found I could visit him really positively and have a good time with him. We probably got on better when he was in hospital than we had for about a year. And I was able to go to varsity during the day and study at night and visit the hospital once a day, and it was great.

When he came out of hospital he went to stay with someone I knew, but he'd still come around to my place sometimes. I felt like I had to let him in. Then after about three months he left for overseas, and it felt like this huge weight being lifted off me. Everything was just very clear. But it was also really lonely.

It was around then that I started having lunch with Steven. I'd met him through the hotel and he used to drive me home at night. Both of us were students and feeling sorry for ourselves because we had to work so hard, and we started having lunch with each other once a week.

We sometimes talked about prostitution but very casually, acting as if this knowledge we had about it had just fallen into our laps. Then one day he said he wanted to be straight with me, and told me that his partner used to work. So I told him I had too. He didn't react, and that was great, because now there was actually someone I could talk to about it — there was somebody I didn't feel I was deceiving.

Apart from the people I knew when I'd been working, he was the first person I'd talked about it with. For years I'd pretended that it hadn't happened. One of my friends knew, but for whatever reason we never mentioned it. The only person who ever did bring it up was John. That was when he was in a bad temper, and would tell me I was just a whore, so how dare I be judgemental about him.

So Steven was the first person I talked about it with, and that felt okay because mostly we talked about his partner and how he felt about her working. After some time we started having a relationship, and it was at this point his partner went back to work. He came and stayed with me for about four or five months. We were going to go away together, but he went overseas and met up with her again. They got back together for a while, until she met a new sugar daddy, who's been flying her around the world ever since.

I think what was really important about Steven was that somebody wanted me because of the way I was. Enough time had passed and I could look at it all without getting paranoid. Besides, I was now on my way to achieving something for myself. I realised I'm no different than anybody else. All the negative things you think about yourself are not of your own devising — they're things that the people around you make you feel. Coming to university and managing all that made me feel like an okay person — well, almost.

Talking about working had been the first step. I still felt quite distanced from it at that point, however, and it wasn't until after Steven left me that I really ended up feeling less distanced. I was able to talk about it now in relation to me. Most importantly, I could talk about it with myself. I stopped having to make up for a space of time that's chronologically missing from my existence. I started being more social, and that was largely due to Steven and getting confidence. In some ways I resent the fact that I couldn't have done it on my own.

Then it was Christmas, he had left and I was feeling totally distraught. I thought about going back to work but decided it wasn't worth it. It had taken me four years to make a rational choice to do something for myself, and three of those years had been absolute hell. I was scared that if I'd gone back to work for the holidays, I'd have to repeat those four years again. All I wanted was enough money for the fees, but I didn't do it.

When I was working I used to feel nothing, but after a while it got to me. It had all become so mechanical, even the conversation, and the more repetitive it got, the more stressed I became. You start feeling like you've got something wrong with your mind, but then you just drink some more and that's okay for a while. It makes you a very fragile kind of person, or what other people call imbalanced, but that's because you're trying to balance out so many things. When you're out shopping you're trying to be like any normal person, and when you're at home with your partner you're trying to be twice as normal, and when you're at work you try to be something else again, so of course you're imbalanced.

I used to feel superior to the clients — they were the stupid ones, going and spending all this money. I used to think about them going out and buying sex, rather than me selling my body.

I would never kiss anybody. Somebody else said once that kissing was reserved for special people. I never looked at it like that — I just didn't want anyone spitting in my mouth. I'm not adverse to kissing, but I'm not going to kiss strangers. One might ask what's the difference between that and fucking strangers, but it is different.

I think if I went back to work now it would be different. It would still have detrimental effects, because it does for everybody, but I wouldn't spend two years at home not going outdoors and another two years being really scared of meeting people. I wouldn't take on other people's social constructions about it and think I was just the world's biggest drop-out — I know I could go back to work and quit and it wouldn't have that effect. It's not something I'm planning to do, though — only if things got right over my head, but I'd make sure I had explored every possible alternative first.

Alexandra is now in her mid-twenties and is about to commence her second university degree. She plays an active role in NZPC, which she sees as an essential support system for sex-industry workers. Through her work with the collective she hopes to be able to assist women in the industry to build up the confidence necessary to combat the abuse and stigmatising they so often receive from the rest of society.

BRIDGET

Bridget is now twenty and has worked on and off as a sex worker for the last five years. During this time she has tried massage parlour work but generally prefers to work the streets.

The first five or six years of my life were spent in Wellington, and then we moved to a rural area. I spent a lot of years living in the bush, and it was often quite a heavy scene. I was brought up around drugs, so that I was used to coming home from primary school and seeing people with needles in their arms, or finding my mother OD'd on the floor. From a very young age I ended up seeing what I shouldn't really have seen as a child.

My mother was an addict, on and off, and she was quite nutty as well. Also, she didn't actually want kids. Now I'm not putting that on her — it's just pretty hard *not* to take it personally when your mother says, 'I didn't really want kids.' But I also understand that from her point of view she was in a rut. She was in a marriage that was just disastrous. She'd been in really violent relationships and had felt pressured to get married.

She had two of us, my younger sister and me, and although we moved away from Wellington and my father, I've always seen a lot of him. Both my sister and I left home early because we just couldn't cope living with her. I left when I was about fourteen, and was very lucky because I had people in Auckland I could stay with, so I didn't end up in institutions or anything.

I sometimes look at myself now at twenty, and it's hard not to feel disgusted with myself. Because I saw so many horrific things when I was younger, I promised myself that I would never ever become a junkie, or have a habit, or be a prostitute.

BRIDGET

I woke up one morning about a year ago and it hit me that I have done everything I vowed I wouldn't. And it happened so slowly that by the time I realised, it was too late. I find you can actually slip into drugs, prostitution and all those things, and it's very hard to get out once you're in there.

I first got into prostitution in a casual sort of way when I was in Wellington. Now and then I'd turn a few tricks, or do a crack here and there, and not a single friend of mine knew about it. If the opportunity came up, I'd take it. I would have been about fourteen or fifteen at the time, and if I was walking home from a movie or something, I might get offered a crack. So it almost started by accident, and then I realised I could go out there and make money doing it.

My first experience of sex would have been when I was a little girl aged about seven or eight. That wasn't through choice. It was by my mother's boyfriend, when we were living in the bush. He told me that she had told him to do it. Though I don't believe that now, as a child I did. So I always had a lot of resentment towards her from a very young age. I don't know how often it happened, but it went on steadily.

I have never slept with a male by choice in my life. Never. It's either been rape or prostitution. Prostitution is a choice, I suppose, but money is exchanged. I would never sleep with a man unless he paid me.

When I was thirteen I was sexually molested and had to go to court over that. Then about two years ago I was raped by a taxi driver. And I've been raped in parlours. It seems it doesn't matter where you go. I've never laid charges against any of them, because of what happened to me when I went to court the first time. They stood the man up there in front of me and asked me, with the courtroom full of people, what happened. I was only thirteen years old. After that I felt that if anything ever happened to me, there was no way I would go to the police again, because in some ways I found that more damaging than the abuse.

In the scene I'm in now, you don't go to the police anyway — you go to someone else and get them to fix it up. It's an unspoken rule in the drugs and prostitution scene that you don't go the police. If someone hurt me badly now, there are people around who just wouldn't let that go. So the taxi driver, for example, got done over.

When I was about thirteen I got taken on to a ship by someone else, but I wasn't going there to work. That was my first look at the scene on the ships, and I was just there for a rage. I knew a lot of the girls, though, and it just sort of started that one of the girls would set me up with a Jap or something, or we'd go night-clubbing where the Japs went.

To me the ship scene is the heaviest of all the prostitution scenes. For a start, there's a lot of crooks on the ships, and it's easier to get ripped off. It's not so much the guys that you'll get trouble from — that's not where the shit is. It's with the girls. There are all sorts of rules and codes. When the boat comes in, generally you try to get your Jap straight away, and he's yours. If another girl's got her Jap and he comes and starts talking to me, or I approach him, look out!

Sometimes you can spend days on the boat, like one big party. Other times the men want to get off the ship, so you'll go to a nightclub. A lot of them, after sailing at sea so long, like to go and stay in a home for a few days, so they might go back to the girl's place.

Most of the girls I knew were into the Japs because they pay the best. Some of the girls end up marrying the guys. You look at all their kids and you realise there are very few European babies — they're all Japanese or Korean and that. I know of one woman who went to Japan and lived with her Jap over there.

Out of all the areas, the boats would be the best place to earn big money, although it's only seasonal. It's not so much that the prices for sex are higher; rather, the Japanese are so much more generous. It's a cultural thing too. Because they love kids and the family atmosphere, they'll be really keen to stay on shore. It's different from the streets or parlours. There's much more involvement, and you spend much more time with them. Some girls will go on board and offer sex for $100, but

BRIDGET

the guys who come and stay on land give money in other ways, for food and stuff.

I only dabbled in the ship scene, though. I never got fully into it.

When I was about fifteen I left school and went up to Auckland to do a design course. I needed to get out of Wellington because I felt like that scene was all around me. I was also seeing one of the offenders who had abused me around the place all the time, and I knew I had to get out for a while. So I went up to Auckland, and for a whole year I was really good. I just did my course and didn't touch drugs at all, apart from marijuana, but I don't consider that a drug.

I don't know how I first got into drugs. It was when I was still at school and going on the ships. Working girls are often junkies or drug addicts, and it becomes a really vicious circle. You start taking drugs because what you're doing is so torturous, but eventually you get a habit — then you have to work to keep your habit going.

I don't think I've ever been a really bad junkie, but I have had habits. I used to take heaps of speed. Then I had a really bad habit on Valium, and I would have people coming around with cards of them every day for me. In the end I was actually quite messy on that stuff, and they were very hard to pull myself off. I wouldn't usually be sticking to one drug, though. I would take whatever went down my throat, whatever I could swallow. Then I got into needles, which is another of those things I'd always said I'd never do.

I still use drugs now, but I don't have a habit. I can control it, and if I have a little binge, I know when enough is enough and I pull myself out straight away. I've taken myself off the needle for about two weeks now, which is really good for me. But that's because I know my limits.

After that year in Auckland I came back to Wellington and I was all right for a while. I was living with my lover and she was completely straight — she was a devout Christian. She didn't like drugs, which was probably good for me. But she was both a lesbian *and* a Christian, and was incredibly mixed up about it.

I lived with her for about a year. When I broke up with her I got back into drugs again. It wasn't because I was devastated about breaking up — it was more like having all this freedom to do whatever I wanted, so I slipped back into the scene and started working the streets.

I didn't work on the streets very long, probably only about four or five months, because everybody kept telling me I should be in a parlour. They said parlours were safer, but I always felt safer on the streets because I knew all the girls and the queens and they looked after me. The grotty part about the streets was the clients. You get a lot of perverted or kinky guys who are just really horrible, gross, revolting men.

I wouldn't do a lot of what they asked, because it was a bit sick. In the prostitution area I've always stuck to straight sex or whatever. I've never been into bondage, and I won't do fantasy — I won't do things like that for my own sanity. There's no way, for instance, that a man could pay me thousands of dollars to act like a little girl for him. I find that one of the sickest things you can do to a girl, but I don't condemn other working girls for doing that.

Some nights I'll be working on the street and I'll get a client who'll want sex and I'll say, 'No — I'm not doing sex tonight.' They look at me and say, 'Well, what are you doing out here then?' I might have my period or something and wouldn't mind doing hand jobs or blow jobs, but nothing else. You can't afford to be too picky, because realistically speaking a lot of them are jerks. But keeping that power to say no is really important.

I used to feel safe on the streets. I have so many people around me there and some of them are good friends. The last time I was raped was in a parlour, not on the streets. Because of what happened to me as a child, I couldn't do anything. I froze, I was paralysed. So I don't blame the parlour, because I couldn't yell or scream or do anything. Afterwards I quit.

Each girl operates on the street in her own personal way.

BRIDGET

I'm quite shy for a start, so if a car is hovering around, I don't usually approach them. It's silly, because you do lose clients, but one thing I've never been good at is approaching cars. Once I'm in the car it's all right. I know how to chat and talk to them then.

You get some clients who only want to go with a girl, and other guys prefer queens, and some will go with both. It's quite competitive on the street. You're all standing there trying to look your best. But it only really gets catty and nasty if you try to hone in on someone else's regular client.

It can be awkward knowing where to take clients. A lot of the work was just in the car, on the front seat — I'm talking about hand jobs and oral, which are very easy to do in a car. If you do sex, it's sometimes with guys who are staying in motels or you can rent a cheap room at a lodge or motel nearby.

The police come round a lot when you're out on the street. They'll round up everybody and get their names and addresses. I don't know why they waste their time. What's the point? I've never been arrested. You've just got to be careful and spot who the undercover cops are. They're no good, though, because they may as well be in uniform. I can spot them for miles. I look at them and laugh and think, 'God, it's embarrassing!'

I was really reluctant to go into parlours. People just started saying to me, 'There's no need for you to be on the streets. You don't have convictions and it's real dangerous on the streets —there's no reason why you can't work in a parlour.' I just didn't think parlour work would suit me. I had to be rostered on certain days; I couldn't just call up and see whether I could come in or not. That's fair enough from the parlour's point of view, but it was taking away my freedom. You don't have much choice in a parlour. They'll walk in and say, 'So this is Bridget,' and you take him off. You can't really stand there and say, 'Oh no, he looks horrible. I don't want to do him.' You have a boss, someone you have to answer to, and you have rules that you have to follow.

I only worked a few weeks in a parlour. Ended up storming

out. I went back on the streets, but there was pressure from everyone for me not to be working the streets. Another friend of mine asked me to come and look at the parlour where she worked, and I ended up taking a job there. I've only recently left there. I had a really bad fight with the boss. They were treating the girls like dogs.

One night when we were all working the boss came in behind one of the girls, clipped her across the head and said, 'Sit like a lady.' No one was allowed to knit or read or anything — I'm not saying you should do all those things in parlours, but they were just treating us like animals. It was disgusting.

Then about a week ago one of the girls had an outcall and the boss made her walk to it. I felt disgusted that they would make a girl walk around the streets in high-heeled shoes and a tight leather skirt at two in the morning. That's totally unprofessional. In the end the girl made the receptionist walk her there. In the morning I approached the boss about it politely and said I didn't think it was right, but he just started yelling at me. I kept on saying, 'Would you please stop yelling? I'm trying to talk to you here.' In the end I started yelling back at him and it got quite nasty. Then his bottom line came, 'Well, remember who you work for.' I stormed out. I said, 'Okay, you don't want to listen to me, so I'm not going to bother,' and I left. I've been for an interview with another parlour, a really nice one, but it's got a waiting list. They'll roster me on for one shift and have me on call in the meantime until they've got more vacancies.

I keep on asking myself why I'm looking for another parlour job. Mostly I've found the attitude of the bosses really bad. After I left that last parlour, apparently the guy sat there calling me a scrubber and saying how he should have punched me. The treatment in parlours is just so shocking. Most know they can get away with it because they've got girls there who aren't supposed to be working because they've got convictions or they're from another country.

Some bosses try to put it on the girls too. That's never happened to me, but I've heard of girls applying for jobs in parlours

BRIDGET

and being tested, checked out, by the boss. It's that power thing again.

There's another thing — they can pay me as much money in the world as they like, but I wouldn't crack it without a condom. I'm doing voluntary work with NZPC/WIDE and the needle-exchange programme now, and it's almost totally conflicting in some ways. I'm working in a job for the prevention of AIDS, and yet I'm still a prostitute. But the two do tie up, and they're very important. I'm glad I can work with the collective because I know that I can work and be safe, and I can tell other people about that too.

I see the prostitution side of it as a job, and what I do is shut my mind off a lot of the time. It can be a bit risky sometimes, because I'll be lying there with this look on my face which says, 'Oh God, hurry up would ya?' and I'll forget I'm in a room with mirrors, then suddenly realise that they can actually see me looking like that. You can't just lie there with a tortured look on your face. It's not very good for business. So you've actually got to pretend.

The guys who want to make *me* feel good are the most annoying. So you fake a moan here and a groan there and pretend you're really loving it. I always think, 'If only they knew what was going through my head!' I hate the line they use on you, 'So why do you do this job?' I always say, 'Well why do you think? — for the money.' They think you're there because you're a slut and you like being on your back all day.

I haven't met a woman who, if she had the choice of getting that much money doing something else, wouldn't take it. The money is so seductive. Once you're in there it's hard to pull out, because you get used to having $1,000 or more a week. Where else can a young woman get that much money in a job?

The more you get, the more you spend. A proportion of it goes on drugs and on your bills. I've tried to start saving, but I never get that far. It's good to know that if you see something new you can just go and buy it. I love that feeling when I've got money.

I've always thought that this is something I'm just going to do for a short time to get some money together. But I've had so many girls say to me, five or ten years later, that they're still doing it and they only started to get some quick money. I'd love to be able to sell my art and design work, and I think it's a waste to be in this job if you have other talents.

I still have my pride about me. If it came to having to work at NZPC/WIDE or in prostitution, I'd prefer to work with NZPC/WIDE, even if it was for a tiny amount of money in comparison, because that's where my heart is. I'd rather do something constructive. Prostitution doesn't go anywhere. You do it, you get older, then what are you doing to do? Once women start hitting their forties, where do they go?

I don't see any need to tie up my own relationships with prostitution. I still see it as a job. The woman I'm involved with now I've been with for about a year and a half, and that's working quite well.

I was about fifteen or sixteen when I decided I would never sleep with a man unless he paid me. I made that choice when I first started having relationships with women. My mother is a lesbian now as well, and while there was no pressure on me to be a lesbian, it meant I could be one and be comfortable.

It's a disadvantage to be both a lesbian and a prostitute, in the sense that I actually hate sleeping with men. I still really like guys as friends, but I find them sexually repulsive. Yet in another way it also works to my advantage because I can go home and leave work completely behind, because I'll be going home to a woman.

I'm always open and honest with my girlfriend about what I do and how much money I make each day. I just see it as our money. She knows I'm only doing it for the money, so it's not as though I'm cheating or doing it behind her back. It's just a job.

Sometimes clients ask for lesbian acts. I sort of feel in two minds about that, although I have done doubles. Because I'm a lesbian I'd much rather be paid to sleep with a woman, and yet at the same time my feminist views come into it. For them to sit and watch me make love with a woman is for them to enter into my personal life. I enjoy it more sexually, but I'm not overly keen to mix my personal and my working life.

I've never ever been paid by a woman. I know of women who have, though. I don't think I could ever take money off a woman just to sleep with her. I wouldn't feel right about it. But that's also part of keeping my personal life and my working life separate.

I'm not open about working to people like my parents, or to my dyke friends. I know they wouldn't feel comfortable about it. They'd harass me or nag me. They'd see it as really lowering myself. And I don't want to have to go out and justify myself to people all the time. You get enough bullshit in this job as it is.

This sort of work has changed me. It makes you hard because you have to get used to blocking so much in your head. I find I have more of a barrier around me now than when I started. It definitely affects my personal life. I can cut it in the sense that I can go home and everything, but I'm less trusting of people generally. If a guy says hello to me, I think, 'What the fuck do you want?'

It's also opened my eyes in a lot of ways as well. At one point in my life I was quite a radical feminist and very anti-prostitution. I used to think it wasn't worth pleasing a man for any amount of money, but that's what I'm doing. I still have a lot of feminist views, but I'm not as extreme as I used to be. I still see prostitution as total exploitation, but unfortunately the money's there. And that's the bottom line for me at this point in my life — I need the money.

I know some women think they're the ones exploiting men. I don't, because I still think that no matter how much they're going to pay me, it's not enough. They could pay me all the money in the world, but it's still not enough for what I'm giving them. I'm giving them my body. They can't have my mind, although they always want it.

There are a lot of costs in this job, but since I've been working I've been so much more assertive, it's unbelievable. I've learned to cope on my own and not get ripped off.

Everyone deserves a choice, and if you want to go into prostitution it should be a choice. If you go into prostitution because you're desperate for money, I don't really think that's much of a choice. Ultimately I don't think it is a choice for most women, because there's always other reasons behind why they do it.

I feel I've got other choices and other skills, but I'm addicted to the money now. It's the most seductive thing I've ever come across.

In recent months Bridget has tried to stop 'working', for, she says, the sake of her sanity. She now has a straight job doing basic art and design, and is much happier but much poorer. She says she doesn't know how long it will last, with her income having been reduced to about one-third of what it was, but it's a positive step for her to be taking at this point in her life. It gives her a good feeling about herself and some sense of direction for the future.

DESNA

Desna identifies as a half-caste Maori woman who became involved in the ship scene when she was fifteen, and began working as a prostitute on shore a couple of years later. She is now in her mid-thirties and, after a long break from the sex industry, has recently done some escort work for a Wellington agency.

I was adopted by my grandparents when I was two weeks old and grew up with them in a very religious household. My grandfather was like an evangelist, and I can remember attending a lot of different churches, all Protestant. We had Bible class meetings every Wednesday, and of course Sundays were taken up with church. Other evenings were normally spent reading the Bible and all the rest of it. However, it didn't do a heck of a lot to stop me!

A lot of my childhood was a real big contradiction. Even though I grew up in a religious household of 'love thy neighbour' and all the rest of it, by the same token they used to thrash me something chronic. If I appeared today with the marks I used to have on me then, they'd be sent to jail, no two ways about it.

On top of that, I was molested a lot as a child from when I was five years old by two of my cousins, and by a friend of my adopted brother who was in the navy, and by one of my brothers. I can also remember this dirty old man. I was quite small and I went to a Maori marae with my grandparents. I've got a memory of being down near fences, like a cattle yard. This old fellow came up to me and kept trying to drag me over into the bushes. I was absolutely terrified. I didn't know what the hell was going on, and what he exposed to me didn't look that healthy at all. I didn't want anything to do with it, much less touch it — yuk! So I can remember taking off back up to where the main group of people were and hiding behind my grandfather. I never told anybody about any of it — I was too scared to.

I got the same as what most young molested kids get — 'If you tell anybody . . .' and all kinds of threats. I'm holding a bit of a grudge about it still, because just a few years ago I was talking to one of my sisters-in-law and she was telling me how many years ago they were all sitting around the kitchen table discussing how I had been molested as a child. If they knew, why the hell didn't they do something about it? Probably the biggest damage that it did to me was generating my sex life at an age far too early for me to deal with. And I think that's been a contributing factor to what I became later on. I probably rebelled against it, because here you've got this wonderful dear old man preaching the gospel while his family's coming in through the back door helping themselves to the kids.

When I was eleven years old my mother took me back home. I found that really hard because there were three sisters after me who had all been part and parcel of this particular family, ever since the day they were born. I was apart from them because they thought my grandparents had spoilt me rotten. And they thought I'd been spoilt because I was the baby in my adopted family.

They took me down to the Social Welfare building in Auckland. They all had a discussion and then I was told, 'You're going home because your grandparents are getting too old to look after you.' I stormed out of the office and shot downstairs to the car, crying, and found my grandfather out there crying his eyes out. So then I realised that my grandparents hadn't said that — somebody else had.

When my mother took me down to Palmerston North with her I started running away a lot. I just wasn't happy there. If I did something wrong, I got a belt. And if one of my other three sisters did something wrong, I also got a belt, because I was the eldest in that family and should have stopped them from doing it.

DESNA

I used to hitch-hike all the way back up to Auckland from Palmerston North, just to get away. On one trip I got pack-raped by about twelve guys in Ngaruawahia. They weren't gang guys — just your normal average, nice, Mr Maori New Zealanders. Anyway, after I'd hitched up there about two or three times, they realised I wasn't going to stay put. On one of these jaunts, when I was still eleven years old, I got picked up and thrown in a girls' home. I kept running away from there too, so they shut me up in the boys' home, because it had cells. Then they shipped me back to a girls' home in Palmerston North, so I ran away again, back up to Auckland.

I was being picked up for all kinds of little petty nuisance things, like car conversion, shoplifting, and of course, absconding. There was no understanding there for me at the time. They decided I was Kingslea material and put me down there when I was still twelve, and I got out exactly twenty-five months later to the day. They kept me there until I was fifteen because they knew I wouldn't go to school once I got out.

They had a school room set up there, but we did all our work through correspondence. My first year there I just kept ploughing through the work and I was sending in assignments so fast it wasn't funny. All I got for my efforts was: 'Slow down — you're going too fast.' So I stopped. There was no recognition — nothing. So a lot of my creativity was killed then.

When I turned fifteen I went back to Palmerston North. My sister got me a job there as a toll operator. But I couldn't settle down there. I had already lived by then — I'd been molested, I'd had a sex life, I'd been drinking, I'd been locked up . . . On top of that, I came out of Kingslea extremely changed. When I went in there, I was one of the youngest, if not *the* youngest, they'd had. My grandfather would send down parcels for me; there might be cakes of soap and lollies in it, and there would always be a letter and at the end he would make the statement, 'I hope you share these with your friends.' So I did, and I ended up getting used and abused a lot. I stopped giving, which in turn upset a few people. For six months thirty girls gave me sheer hell.

WORKING GIRLS

My life was a misery. I was thirteen years old. I had nobody I could turn to. I was getting my things stolen, I was getting my property destroyed, I was being verbally abused — you name it, I was wearing it. So after six months I had had it. I was at the end of my tether, and if I'd had a knife at the time I would have slit my throat. I went to the superintendent and asked her to put me in the security block. She decided that wasn't fair, since I hadn't done anything wrong, so she locked the main ringleader up instead. At lunchtime that girl's mate came up and hit me, and I exploded. I just went berserk, and I swore black and blue that nobody would ever walk all over me again. And they haven't. That's why I'm so bolshie now. Thirty girls taught me how to be.

Back in Palmerston North I met up with one of the other girls from Kingslea. I was fifteen, she was eighteen, and I was completely under her influence. All of a sudden I wasn't turning up for work — in the middle of the night she'd say, 'Hey, let's go to New Plymouth,' and we'd pack up and go. I parted company with her after about two or three years because we both ended up going into Arohata together.

When I first went into Arohata, at fifteen years of age, everybody else was older and the majority were ship girls. They'd been picked up mainly for ringbolting around the coast, or being in the wharf area. It was ridiculous. There were people out there slitting other people's throats, yet they were arresting these girls just because they were down on a ship. Once they got on the ships these girls were well behaved, they didn't get up to any mischief, and the boys kept them all in line — otherwise off the ship they went.

To me ship life was magic. Here I was at fifteen listening to somebody tell me stories that included every single part of the world. Not only were these girls travelling up and down the coast, but the guys were flying them here and there, and bringing them back presents from overseas.

So when I got out my friend Mary and I ended up going up to New Plymouth. That's where I went on my first ship, the

Otaki. We went to a pub and, as luck would have it, a whole pile of Pommie seamen came in. We started talking to these guys in the pub, and I ended up pairing off with one of them, a guy called Ron. I saw him off and on over a period of about three or four years and through about three or four different ships.

Next night he came back in, and came back to the motel Mary and I were staying at. That was the only time I went with him, but a couple of nights later I met another Pommie seaman off the *Otaki*, went down to his ship and ended up sailing with him from New Plymouth to Auckland. I thought it was a perfect opportunity to get up there and see my grandparents.

I was green. I didn't know when I could come and go on the ship, and really I should have stayed on board until night-time. But as soon as they'd hooked the phone up on the ship, I was ringing my grandparents. I wanted to go ashore and see them, but I got picked up.

A lot of the Pommie seamen loved New Zealand. All the ships that came down here were chock-a-block full of crewmen, and we used to have a brilliant time. We would do jaunts inland because this was a foreign country to them. We didn't usually bother with the nightclubs because the bar on the ship would stay open longer than any club and the booze was four times cheaper. If you had three or four Pommie ships in at the same time, you had a party and a half! We used to go on all kinds of Scandinavian ships too — Danish, Swedish, Norwegian, and there were Germans, Spaniards, Greeks, Mexicans. They were all merchant ships, with all kinds of cargo on board.

I remember one ship was loaded up with alcohol bound for all the high-class restaurants of Europe. It was Christmas time, so we got all this alcohol up out of the hold and we partied and partied. Probably the best Christmases I've ever had were on the ships.

It was funny — you could tell the seamen that had been down here a number of times. Most of them wanted to take a greenstone tiki home. They'd been told about the superstition around greenstone and knew the only way to obtain one safely was for one of the Maori girls to buy one for them. So they picked up bits and pieces of information about New Zealand and we, as the girls, basically lived around the entire world. Their normal conversation would include India or Japan or Russia or wherever they'd been, and we were included in all that. When they left, you were getting mail from all over the world.

You had the same sorts of relationships with these guys as you do with onshore, girlfriend/boyfriend-type relationships. The guy I was engaged to for two years — he was a New Zealander but used to ship out here with a UK line.

Then there was a German guy, Hans. He stood six foot two, blond — if Hitler had seen this guy he would have told him, 'You're a true Aryan.' He couldn't speak a word of English, but he and I communicated for about four or five trips together.

The terminology for partnering up with somebody then was called being 'boxed off'. If somebody walked up to you and said, 'What are you doing?' and I said, 'Oh, I'm boxed off on the *Medic*', then they would immediately know I had a guy on the *Medic* and that while he was in port I was taken.

The girls never bothered with local guys. Hell's teeth — they just didn't compare. The Kiwi male could not have stood up to the competition at all, not in any shape, form or fashion. They're not as clued up because they haven't travelled as much. They're certainly not as sexually aware.

The Japanese are the ones that were really responsible for the word prostitution creeping into the ship scene. Japanese men were obviously used to paying for it anyway. They have their own bath houses in Japan, and they're used to women being in a subservient role. Geisha girls are highly paid women, but let's face it — all they are really is just extra-painted prostitutes. They make a nice cup of tea — so what? Sooner or later they've got to take their knickers off, don't they?

The girls on the ships were predominantly Maori then. Everybody made a sort of community effort. In the mornings when the guys turned to, the girls would get up and clean up the cabins, help mop down the alleyways, clean out the bar, help in the mess. If one girl was caught lagging, she would basically be sent to Coventry. Girls who came down on the ships and were dirty and didn't climb in the shower on a daily basis got the word from the others first. Then, if they didn't do something about it, they got thrown in the shower and scrubbed down. We were all very much clean people, and we kept the guys clean too.

There were no condoms then or anything. AIDS wasn't heard of, so it wasn't a problem. Syphilis was the biggest problem, but gonorrhoea was the mainstay, and everybody used to wipe it out with a good round of antibiotics. If any guys came into port and they'd picked up something overseas, we heard about it. Everybody was expected to say whether they had a dose. It wasn't a big sin as long as you told people you had it and you were doing something about it. If a guy had a dose and he tried to box off with a female anyway, they'd beat the snot out of him. Same with females — she'd just get kicked all the way down the gangway. So there was very much an honour code where diseases were concerned.

Diseases weren't a problem, but pregnancy was of course another thing. That's where my eldest son came from. Yugoslav, he was. I remember his father, Djordj — a hard name to get your tongue around!

There was about a year and a half of my life where it was just off one ship and on to another. I didn't have to worry about money; I was supported as I went; it was a live-in situation. If you want to call it prostitution, you will have to call every wife in New Zealand a prostitute, because you were considered the guy's missus. You were certainly treated that way, and if anybody threatened you in any way, he and all his mates would be there having a go.

Girls were ringbolting then to Holland, the UK, certainly backwards and forwards across the Tasman, like a taxi service. I knew girls who might climb on a ship just to go and visit mother! Other girls got picked up — the Panama Canal was the worst place for getting caught. I only went around New Zealand.

Because I lived on the ships for so long with those guys, I was part of their daily conversation and I never felt a need to go overseas. I know exactly what it's like to live inside a Pommie home, or a German home, or a Norwegian, or a Spanish, or a Greek — I don't have to go to their countries to see it.

The ship was divided into segments, so that girls who went with the crew didn't go with any of the officers. The best captain I ever came across was on the *Canopic*. Once when I was about seven or eight months pregnant, I went down to Lyttelton with this other girl and we were on the ship when the police came on board. They wanted to know who we were, what we were doing there, what our address was, and all the rest of it. The captain came down and told the police to get off the ship. When the police said to him, 'We'd like to question these girls, we'll take them off here,' he said, 'No you won't. You're on my ship, you're on British soil, get off.' He immediately rang the shipping agent and told him to send passes down for us, then said to the police, 'If I catch you laying one hand on any of my guests, I'll have you.' So he kicked the police off.

Not all captains were like that. This particular one was because he had common sense and a lot of brains. He quickly realised that with his guys being at sea for months at a time, they could get scratchy and cranky. And when these guys hit shore, they were looking for wine, women and song. The captain figured, why not let the females come on board — then the guys will get up in the morning and do their day's work because they know there's going to be a female waiting there for them at the end of the day. So he was quite supportive.

One trip all the boys came down with the flu, so the girls got out and did all the work. We even painted the ship — I was seven or eight months pregnant and there is a photo of me in a pair of grey overalls with ten foot worth of stomach sticking out the front of me, paintbrush in hand!

The officers had their own round of females. We didn't pay that much attention to where they found their women, because they didn't socialise with the crew a great deal. They realised that the girls who preferred the seamen and the stewards wouldn't go with an officer. It was kind of like trying to get a girl who is used to going out with somebody who wears jeans and leather jackets to go out with a yuppie in a suit and collar and tie — it just didn't happen.

I only went with one or two officers along the line. I can remember I went with the captain once. He was Greek, and another girl and I were selected, if you please, and presented to him. It was like, 'Which one would you like, the cherry one or a nice bit of lime?' I felt quite good when I was selected. He paid me for that — that's the only time I prostituted on a ship. He wanted to do some kinky things to me, like sit on the floor with my legs apart so he could roll things up into my fanny, like putting in golf. I didn't actually let him get that far, because he was weird and quite aggressive with it, so I ripped him off and left the ship.

I was on the ships for about seven years, which is a fairly good length of time to be a ship girl. There were mothers and daughters and all sorts. One woman had five children to five different fathers, and these kids looked almost five different colours.

As ship girls we definitely thought we had it better than the prostitutes. We certainly thought we were better than prostitutes, and now that I've gone back recently and done a bit of escorting, I can see why. All prostitutes cater to basically are dirty old men, or men that have got kinky habits, or men that are so small in their anatomy that they're too embarrassed to try and produce it in a normal situation. But for us, we were getting a taste of the world.

I must have been about seventeen or eighteen when I first got into prostitution. My clients were all shore-side based — that's what Kiwi males were for. I got into it because the other girls I was flatting with were ship girls and also hookers on the side. More often than not, the ship guys would take care of your needs, but there was the odd occasion where you had to make money, or the earn was such that you would be stupid to turn it down. In those days, and remember we are going back, fifteen, sixteen, seventeen years, an all-night booking with one customer brought in $300 — that was a lot of money. That would be the equivalent of a hooker being able to pick up $900 for an all-nighter now.

It basically started for me when one or two clients popping around to the flat spotted me and asked the other girls, 'Who's that?' And if they fancied you and you weren't into it, you would say no until the offer got so high you said yes. I can remember the first guy I went with there. A right dirty old man. I felt absolutely disgusted and I bathed for about two or three hours afterwards — I only said yes because I was flat broke at the time and needed the money.

I only really needed to crack it then one night a week. I picked up clients either through my flatmates or down at the Great Northern, which was my favourite drinking hole at the time. I picked up a couple of out-of-towners there, like guys from out in the suburbs who were looking for a little bit on the side as far away from home as possible without actually leaving town.

When I was eighteen or nineteen I had reasonably good looks, very noticeable looks in fact, so I had the power of choice. I decided which ones I wanted to take on and which ones I didn't. I had one guy, though, who was just a dirty old man, nothing more, nothing less, and he would see me two or three times a week.

They wanted a variety of things. One client I never ever had sex with in all the time that I saw him. All he wanted to do, for $50, was have me tie him up with a silk cord, tie his hands behind his back and his hands to his feet, and then ridicule him. I didn't even have to undress. Then I'd jack him off for thirty seconds, and he'd say, 'Thank you — see you next week.' Sometimes he didn't even require jacking off. He was a taxi driver, self-employed, and after he'd gotten all this out of his system he was just Mr Ordinary Joe Bloggs — you'd swear that he'd just stopped round for tea and sticky buns and same time next week, then?

DESNA

I only had about four or five regular clients, and that's all I needed, that's how I did my money. My particular clients wanted to believe that what they were doing had nothing to do with prostitution, so you could quite easily go out for a meal and talk a lot and the actual act of sex would be all of five minutes, on account of that's all they could manage anyway.

These guys have got their own insecurities. If they're doing sneaky things behind their wife's back, like visiting sauna parlours or visiting hookers, then they've got problems, believe you me. They're obviously not talking to their wives, and they're certainly not getting at home what they're getting in the parlours and in the private homes of prostitutes. So you get a lot of talking.

Ship girls were just so liberated — I think that's what made me so appealing to my clients. I'd been 'trained' in bed, for want of a better term, by guys from all around the world, so I was pretty clued up in the sack. And we ship girls were more liberal about sex. We were able to discuss it, so we were a novelty. The ship guys didn't know about my clients, because when they were in port you were just down on the ship with them. And the clients had to accept that. I was in amongst a particular group who were all ship girls and we swapped clients round. When one of us got sick of the silly or kinky habits of one, she'd pass him on to someone else who would extract as much cash from him as she could until *she* got sick of him.

We never had any hassles from clients. We were all fairly street-wise ladies and we could see aggression coming a mile away. We were naturally suspicious of Kiwi males to begin with. We didn't like them. None of them could perform well in bed. So it wasn't like there was some big turn-on for us in any way.

Once you had to start doing it for money, you had to switch off. You immediately lost the power of choice. The act of having sex with somebody wasn't something that you'd chosen to do. What was paramount in your mind was making a dollar. This was the only way of doing it, so you had to tolerate the situation to get the dollar, and that's basically how you looked at it. And you'd just switch yourself off.

When I was escorting recently, though, I had an absolute pearler one night. I just couldn't believe this guy. He had it all. He'd split up from his wife, he had his own home, he had nice, long blond hair all swept back, extremely good-looking, a design architect, everything together. Apparently he couldn't be bothered with all the bullshit of going out, trying to find a suitable female, making friends, trying to chat her up and maybe, just maybe, a date or two away, he might get into her knickers.

When the *Hertford* came in, I had Don. Don was gorgeous. He and his cabin mate Charlie, and my flatmate, a tiny little Australian girl we called Shrimp, and me all piled up to Colin's place. He was the big drug dealer in Auckland at the time, dealing lots of dope and acid. Colin's house was crowded when we took those guys in, and we were dressed exactly the way the guys were, which was very unusual. All four of us had on patchwork-denim-type suits, waist jackets, pants and long midi coats — very trendy outfits which weren't available in New Zealand at the time. After that I took a couple more seamen up there, mainly because these guys smoked and Colin was getting hold of really good smoke at the time. The boys would take him up a dozen overseas beer, so there was a wee bit of trading going on, which also helped make me popular.

So when the ships started flagging away I became more involved with the shore side, and that's when I met Marty, my daughter's father. He was a junkie, he was doing smack and he was requiring $1,300 a week to do it. So I got tied up more and more into a heavy drug scene. At first I was introduced to snorting morphine and then snorting smack, and then the smack started coming in rock form — brown rocks and pink rocks. You couldn't really snort those, you had to crush them down. So while you were crushing them, why not heat them and stick them in the needle? Marty gave me my first taste and after that I was shot to shit. I was a junkie for the next couple of years.

I stopped cracking it when I met Marty. He's an only child of extremely wealthy parents, and when I got pregnant I was basically taken under the family wing. My daughter was really ill when she was born, and I went through a bad guilt complex about giving her a habit. I'd stopped using needles as soon as I knew I was pregnant, but from time to time I had to swallow Doloxene, otherwise I was in agony. It was enough to affect her and she was in Karitane for the first six months. I felt so guilty.

By now I'd already been inside a few times. I got picked up in Napier for ringbolting once, and got a month in Arohata for that. I had a small remand in Mount Eden when I was a junkie, but they managed to get me out on bail after they'd talked about sending me to Carrington because I looked so sick. All of this happened with Marty. When we were in Auckland we got busted. He'd already been busted for Class A, so when they found the fix and the smack, fortunately not much of it, I just said they were mine. Since I hadn't been up on any drugs charges at that particular point in time, I wore that one. Then when we moved to Palmerston North I got done for cultivation, possession, and possession for supply.

After the baby and everything I had bills piling up and I didn't know which way to turn. So I became a professional burglar. I had a guy in Palmerston North who used to set up jobs for me. He'd find out where all the goodies were, give me the address and tell me what to do. I'd make a bit of money, he'd make a lot of money, and everybody was happy.

Then he found out about a Dutch guy, from a banking family, who had brought this old coin collection out to New Zealand with him. It had gold krugerrands in it, but when we went round and did the burg we couldn't find them, but we did find the coin collection so we loaded that up. There was a little wee plastic bag with this old dog-eared-looking coin in it, and we were tossing this around and found a little piece of paper that read 400 BC, so we were going, 'Hey, wouldn't you like to know what this coin could tell you? It must have been in a few orgies and Roman bath houses!'. We found out afterwards, after I'd been done for it, that it was for real — the only one of its kind in the world.

WORKING GIRLS

The cop knew we were looking for the gold — he told me later that we'd walked straight past a box with half a million dollars worth of gold krugerrands and family heirlooms in it. But this cop caught us on circumstantial stuff and managed to put it together and tie us in with it nice and tightly. He told me he had us under surveillance because they needed to track that coin collection down — it was worth too much money.

I went away for two years after that. At the same time I got done for another burglary, and that had a wounding with intent charge with it too. I actually regretted that one badly. I had no business being in that guy's home. He and his wife had gone to bed early with no intention of hurting or upsetting anyone else, and I walked straight into his world and I shat on it and nearly broke his neck in the process.

Life changed for me after that. I got into prison, and I was twenty-five or twenty-six, and I looked around and I thought, 'I'm too old for this, I'm sick and tired of it.' I'd just had a gutsful. On top of that probably the police were responsible in some small measure for the change in me. I remember the day I got sentenced and all these charges were being read out, and I was being sentenced to two years on each one. I noticed that every cop around had zoomed in to watch the big female burglar break down. I immediately toughened up. I thought, 'Over my dead fucking body,' and when I got inside I was determined that I was going to get more out of the system than they were going to get out of me.

So I made use of the system. I used the education facilities, I learned to type and then I got into computers. One of the prison officers, Andrea, helped me change my outlook a lot too. She'd take me out on home leave and act as a buffer for me in the prison at times. I also met a man, Michael, who worked within the justice system, and he and I talked and communicated a lot, and then got together when I was released. He knew all about me, he'd read my files. But he set up a flat and the day I got out I took a taxi from Arohata to the railway station, where he picked me up and we lived together for several years without the Justice Department ever knowing.

Desna

Even though we split up, he's probably the only man that I've really, really loved, because he helped me find my self-respect. He taught me, for the first time in my life, what it was like to experience unselfish love. So what Andrea started, Michael finished, and the two of them together changed me. I had so much feeling for him that I wanted to get up and go to work and do the right thing.

I found it very hard when we did split up because he'd given me an extremely nice lifestyle. I had a job and an income, but I struggled for a long time.

Just over a year ago my sister was going through a really bad financial stage and got into prostitution for the first time. That got me back into escorting for a short while, just to make extra cash. I found escorting very tiring. I had to work at my job Monday to Friday, nine till five, and then escorting basically starts after the pubs shut. Sometimes you'd be lucky to get a call early in the evening, but that didn't happen often. Normally the Kiwi male likes to go out, get himself a belly full of Dutch courage and then, when he's good and drunk and thinks he's the world's best lover, he'll call up a female just so he can show her. So I'd end up awake until two or three in the morning and then have to get up at six to go to my normal job.

I found being a prostitute this time around probably a wee bit easier, because when I was younger condoms weren't really used. Now they're a necessity. I didn't really have to touch that part of the anatomy, much less wear the mess that came out of it. So he could just take the whole thing away with him and I didn't have to tolerate any of his residue. But at the same time I found it harder this time because, one, I'm almost thirty-five and they all like them at eighteen, and two, I could do with losing a stone or two and they like them nice and slim. It's very competitive out there.

I know one lady, about eighteen, who'd done this guy and said no way would she go back to him again. He was so full of himself. He started pushing her around and all the rest of it. Hell, I went and did him and he didn't push me around because I laid it straight on the line. When he got too carried away with himself I said, 'Listen, sweet. Never mind you criticising how I am or what I look like, because you're no fucking oil portrait, my dear, otherwise you wouldn't be calling an escort agency.'

You get very, very cynical when you're on the game. A lot of these guys are managers or they've got their own business premises — we're talking Mr Nice Guy here, who probably contributes at least $100 to Telethon every time it's on. And you see the other side of their nature — their kinky perversions or the stupid things they think and talk about. It's amazing, absolutely amazing. A lot of the guys have this stupid notion that once they've visited you two or three times, it's not the cash you're after, that you actually want them. But you're there for the cash.

I could take it up again if the situation called for it and if the buying public still considered me an option. As far as I'm concerned, it's a matter of survival. If I'm flat broke and what I have to do costs money, then I'll get my hands on that money the best way I know how. I'm not hurting anybody and all I'm doing is providing money for myself and a service for others.

For me personally, at this point in my life, it's not a good idea. It makes me feel cheap and nasty and sleazy. It's not the act of being a prostitute — it's the customers that you come across that make you feel that way. I did a customer one time, a highly professional man, who was absolutely gross. Despite that, I did him, but I nearly vomited when I got out of his place. I was so disgusted with myself that I cried for two or three hours, which isn't like me — I don't cry easy. I felt I had stooped so low because ordinarily a man that looked like that would never get within ten feet of touching me. He was such a bad buzz for me that I couldn't work for a week after I did him. And in fact, the next night I went and looked up my old boyfriend just because I wanted somebody nice to hold me.

He was a Maori too, and I've found that because of that early abuse, Maori clients just don't do anything for me. It's like where you come across somebody and immediately get pictures in your mind of something that happened years ago. Maybe it's not even that, it's just something so that I turn off, I can't switch on to them.

I think, too, it's worse now that I know that the adults in my family knew all the time but didn't do anything about it. Nobody in my family has ever tried to talk to me about it. Nobody never asked me, 'Desna, how did you feel about it? How's it affected you?' Because nobody in my family can deal with the answers.

Yet obviously it *has* affected me, and will for the rest of my life. I have had one or two medical problems since being molested which have never completely gone away and which have affected me through my whole life. I have a constant reminder of it all. Even when I want to forget, I can't. The system just has no idea what victims really do go through. I'm full of hurt and I always will be.

I've been through a lot of shit. I've had my life threatened, I've had knives at my throat, the works. Every time I see identikit pictures of rapists who are alleged to have attacked kids, or even females in general, I can almost feel my skin about to crawl. And then I get such a sense of anger. I know for a fact that if anybody broke into my flat, one of us would die, and I've got a sheer, bloody-minded determination that it won't be me.

People like me get forced into prostitution because there is no other option. All girls who get into it will have thought of every other possible option first. And some nights you'll want to go home and cry because you're disgusted with yourself, you're disgusted with the guys you've had to do for the evening, and you're disgusted with the whole world because nobody in it tried to help you.

Before I ever got into prostitution I actually did try to get straight jobs, but I had no qualifications and nobody would listen to me. Nobody wanted to know. Yet those are the same people who later turned around and said about me, 'Isn't it terrible what she's doing? I can't understand why she's acting like that.' But it was those pricks who made it so hard for me in the first place — how dare they!

What's made me so bitterly angry is that I was denied the right to say, 'I'm going to have sex when I decide and with whom I decide. *I'm* the one who's going to decide that.' I will always have a hatred for those guys for denying me what was mine — it wasn't theirs to take. And I'm never going to be able to regain that.

I'm thirty years down the track from first being molested and I'm still talking about it. It's still affecting me. Yet the guys who do this sort of thing get six months, two years, if you're lucky. And then they can just walk away — but we can't.

Sometimes I sit down and wonder, 'What could I have been now if I hadn't had the stress of being continually molested as a child?' All through my life I've had people say to me, 'Desna, you've got brains — you could use them.' What could I be doing now? Where could I have gone? What could life have been like for me, if those bastards hadn't got me?

Desna has been employed in the same industry for eight years now, during which time she has worked in a number of positions from the factory floor through to the office. She has also been studying for a professional qualification in her line of business and currently earns over $30,000 a year. Desna's position in the firm is one of trust — she turns over millions of dollars a year for her company. 'It's a bit radical from being a burglar,' she said, 'but it's all because somebody out there decided to give me a chance.'

Liz

Liz has worked in parlours and on the streets in Auckland since her late teens. She has also run her own rap parlour in K Road. When I spoke to her she was serving a prison sentence for a drugs-related offence.

I grew up in Auckland and have always lived around the central city. That's sort of my home base; I don't really like anywhere else.

When I was seventeen I started working in what I thought was a photo studio, but it turned out that extras were expected. The guys would come in and pay $15 for half an hour and $25 an hour to take photos of girls with a camera that actually had no film in it, and afterwards they could get extras with us if they wanted.

The photos began with us with our clothes on right through to being totally nude, and we could charge them extra money for different poses — it was actually quite lucrative. I hadn't realised extras were involved until I began working there. I'd already thought about cracking it, and decided no, but when I got there the money seemed all right so I got into it.

I worked a few months in the photo shop, then got a job in a rap parlour. I also got into escort work. It's good money, but I don't really like doing them. The guys who ring up for escorts are usually a lot shyer than the guys who come into parlours. I don't know why. Maybe they don't want to be seen going into a parlour, or think they'll get spied on or something. Being asked back to motels with them was okay. I don't like doing private houses though, because you never know what you're going to walk into.

Working Girls

The guys I had came from all different walks of life. I never had any important people, but I had a lot of rich people. I used to go to this house up some poncy street in Orakei. He was bloody rich that guy, and he was nice too. He just wanted straight sex usually. He'd had an accident, something to do with his muscles, and the doctor had told him that he had to have sex with more than one person, not just with his wife — I can't remember why. Anyway he found me and thought I was just grand. I lost touch with him just before I came inside. He would always give me a couple of hundred each time, sometimes three or four times a week. His wife didn't know all this. She'd kill him, I'm sure she would. He was the only client I actually liked.

I did parlours and escorts and the streets. Some girls are absolutely petrified to go on the street and think it's bad, but as far as I'm concerned it's really good because you're not working for anyone. My girlfriend and I decided to go on the street. We thought, 'Fuck the parlours! We can just pick guys up off the street and make our own money.'

Out on the streets we used to have our own corner. The queens used to hang around up the top of Queen Street, but it's different now. You can wander all over the place and no one will bother too much. If a guy wants you, he's just going to look for you and find you no matter where you stand.

I ran my own rap parlour for a few months. It was in K Road. The guy I used to work for in another rap parlour got this building just down from the Sheraton and asked if I wanted to lease it. It was only $200 a week because the building was coming down — in fact it's down now. I made heaps of money because of it being on that corner just by the Sheraton. Most of the girls who worked for me were off the streets. I used to work down there too if I wasn't too out of it. I used to charge the street girls $10 to come up and use the rooms. It worked out fine, until we got closed down by the Auckland Businessmen's Association. I think the Sheraton complained. The wives didn't like it. Couples would walk past and we would tell them how we catered for couples as well, and they got sick of it. So

LIZ

the Vice Squad came down heavy on us and closed us down.

It didn't really matter. I knew I was going to be closed down from the day I opened the parlour. But we lasted five or six months and it was a good money-maker. I used to make at least $500 a night; that was with me working as well, mind you. I didn't have a licence so I didn't give a fuck what anyone did — it was none of my business what they were into.

I used to get hassled by the police all the time. They pick us up on the streets — when we're working on the street there are coppers cruising around all the time. Mostly they just hassle us and they say, 'Well, you know if we come back here again and you're still on the same corner you'll be under arrest.' I just tell them, 'You're all full of bullshit.' They like to pick on us. I just stand there. I don't care.

I only got charged twice for prostitution, and each time I beat them at court, so I haven't got anything on my record. The first time they tried to do me I was standing on a corner with a girlfriend and these two Ds came along and started chatting us up. We decided we didn't want to do them because they were a bit funny, so my girlfriend said to them, 'If you want us two girls you can pay us fucking $600 each.' We were just joking, having them on, but they said, 'Right, you're under arrest.' So they did all the drama down at Central. When it came to court we both pleaded not guilty. Then we heard that the coppers had dropped that charge because they didn't want to go through the embarrassment — they knew what they'd done was entrapment.

The other time I got arrested I was up in K Road by myself. This copper got me in his van and started talking to me, and then he asked me how much everything was, so I told him. Next thing a couple of blue and whites come by and I'm told I'm under arrest for prostitution.

I pleaded not guilty to that one too. I got up in court and defended myself, made up a big bullshit story and won my case. My husband was in the courtroom and he leaped up and said, 'My wife's not a prostitute. Don't you dare suggest a thing. She was just waiting outside that parlour for me to pick her up.' I told the judge I thought the cop had asked me how much is sex, and I'd said I believed it was about $80, but I don't work in parlours so I wouldn't know. That was when I got arrested. I told the judge I *thought* that was how much it cost, but I only go there every now and then for a sauna and my husband picks me up afterwards, so I couldn't be done for that. The judge thought about it and said, 'It does look a bit like entrapment to me, but then of course it may not be. But I'll give you the benefit of the doubt. Not guilty.' The cop was furious, real furious — it was great!

Sometimes the coppers come along as clients when they're off duty. I wouldn't ever do them, though, because you can smell a cop coming, their whole attitude, everything about them. I've asked a couple of guys if they're policemen and they've said, 'Well yes, but I'm off duty.' I've still told them, 'Well I'm not fucking you — just go.' Some girls will go with them, but not that many. Chances are you'll crack it with them, then a couple of days later you'll get picked up for cannabis. They're going to arrest you in the end, so why do them any favours?

I don't think I'd ever go to the police for anything. I might if my girlfriend had been murdered or something, only *might*, though. I have my own ways of doing registration checks without having to go to the police. There's a traffic guy who's good. He is usually up K Road every night and he's quite a nice person. I'd get him to do it. I trust him to some extent, and he gets me off lots of driving things. He's still a member of the law, though. But he's only just a young guy, only just started, still human. As far as the coppers go — they suck!

Most of the guys I had as clients were wankers too. Not the sort of guys I'd want to know. I bumped into a couple afterwards but just didn't want to know them. It's really hard being nice to them all. You go in there and smile and act pleasant and all that sort of crap, but if they come on like arseholes, they deserve to be treated as arseholes.

LIZ

There are things you can do to get rid of a guy quicker. Fucking them well helps! I could never get into the talking stuff — 'You're the biggest, you're the best . . .' I'd start laughing if I ever tried that. Sometimes they'd want me to have an orgasm, so I'd pretend. I'd fake it if it was necessary to hurry them up. But I'm a bit cold with things like that. I don't think I was a very friendly person when I was working. I was only friendly enough to make my money and get what I wanted.

In some ways the job put me off men, but in other ways it didn't. I still like men, more than I like women, and I've got mainly men friends. I don't particularly like women. I think they're stupid. These days if I want sex I'll only go with my old man. I'm totally loyal to him. No other man does anything for me.

So I get the guys to pay for it. Preferably in cash too. If they pay by cheque, they often bounce, so I don't take cheques any more. In the parlours they might pay on Bankcard or something, but we have to pay to get them processed. So cash is best, and foreign money is a go. Don't get that many from overseas, though. The ones who do are the ship girls who go down to the boats. I know quite a few of the girls and they ask me to come along, but I usually can't be bothered. Besides, those guys, especially the Japanese, like you to stay the night with them. They pay real good, but I want it over and done with —it's easier.

A lot of the clients who come to parlours are out-of-towners. Probably sixty per cent or more are married men. I usually ask them if they're married just for my own curiosity. I don't know why they come to parlours, though. A few of them complain about their wives not liking sex. Usually they can't be bothered going and picking up a woman, getting her drunk or whatever, then trying to get her into bed. They'd rather just come and pay for it and get it over with and go home to their wives.

Some times of the year we were busier than others. School holidays were slack because they were at home with their families and had to pay out more money then on kids' outings.

Christmas was also slack. The end of the financial year was always quite busy for us, and international cricket and rugby games are always good, Whitbread yachts and all that sort of thing.

Clients want all sorts of services from us. A lot of it's just straight sex, but I still reckon that's a service. If there weren't people like us around, I don't know where they'd get it from. I wouldn't say that rape would go up, because there is heaps of rape around now. But if *I* wasn't there cracking it, there would be other people doing it.

Sometimes we get asked to do kinky stuff. I had one guy who used to like being tied up over a chair. He used to wank himself while you threw a vibrator up his bum. He'd paid well for it. He used to like to be whipped beforehand as well.

There are a lot of guys who get off on bondage. More so the business set than anybody else. They're always looking for something different. They don't just want the normal run of the mill screw. And they've always got the money to pay for it, because it's not cheap. It starts at about $150. I really enjoy whipping people — it's good fun. I whip them hard. So far I've never drawn blood, but I'd love to. I love doing nasty things to people, especially clients, buggers, sickos. I don't know why they deserve it but they do.

The guys who get into wearing ladies' knickers are a bit of humour, though. They just get off on dressing up in ladies clothes. They usually like a good whipping too, those sorts, but often want to have a fuck as well. There are not many people like that, though.

Some want golden showers and stuff. I get embarrassed, but I've done a few like that. It's good money. I can't understand who would want to get pissed on. The guys who ask for that are usually businessmen in their forties. I used to have one guy come in every Friday for that. He used to bring in a couple of bottles of really expensive wine and two of us would play with him and all that sort of shit, then do a two-girl act for him and then one of us used to piss on him. We'd get all we could out of him, several hundred, whatever he had on him.

LIZ

Not long ago my girlfriend and I charged a team of national sporting 'heroes' $600 to do a strip show and a lesbian act. We probably could have got extras afterwards, but we didn't stay because they were fucking animals. I ended up by whipping them because they were clawing at us and trying to get up on the stage. We'd been told there'd be about 300 people there at this stag party, so I took my husband along. He and his mate just bundled us out real quick. We didn't even stay for the whole time. Got the money, did a bit of a show, looked at them, thought, 'Christ!' and fucked off. They were the worst bunch of people I have ever come across.

I had done a few strips for a couple of shows before but not that often. I've done lots of two-girl acts in parlours and during escorts, with one guy or two guys maybe, but not a big bunch like that. And us the only females in the place.

When guys request a lesbian act, sometimes they just get off themselves watching it. Others want to join in too, in which case that's an extra. Everything's an extra. I don't really enjoy it all that much, but its all right if you have a girlfriend you like.

Some guys like it when you dress up as a schoolgirl. I used to wear a school uniform a lot when I was working, a little gym-slip, and my hair in pig-tails. I used to get a lot of work in my uniform, it was good. I think it was the age thing turned them on, looking so young. Some of them wanted me to keep the uniform on while they had sex, others just liked looking.

Lots of guys like leathers and garter belts and studs and all that sort of stuff. I was into all that. I used to wear suspenders and stockings and stuff like that. The more of a turn-on you look, the more money you're going to make. But I always had to be out of it to do any of this.

You meet a lot of guys who want to get married — I mean, married for money. People who want to stay in this country but couldn't otherwise — they're always a good earner. You either marry them or get someone else to marry them and they pay. I've never done it. I don't think it is worth it. I wouldn't do it unless it was about fifty grand. Most of the guys are from

India, mainly countries like that, curry-munchers, Fiji also, but mainly Indians.

Working like this does become a whole lifestyle thing. Sleeping lots of the day, working all night. I usually slept until lunchtime, then I'd get up, go shopping if I wanted. I used to get between $500 and two grand most weeks when I was working. It would depend how busy it was. If you were working five or six nights a week, you would have to be making at least $500 or it wouldn't be worth it.

Most of my money went on cars. I deal in cars, buy and sell a lot of them. I always used to make my money work for me, otherwise I'd just waste it. I didn't buy that much dope, as I always made my own. Much of the lifestyle is tied in with drugs. A lot of the girls have got old men and habits to support and they have to work. I've always been into the drugs. It just comes as part and parcel of it all. Maybe I know one or two people who just work, but they'd be rare these days.

I was already into drugs before I started working. I've always smoked dope, I've always dropped pills, and I've been sticking needles in my arms since I was sixteen, so really it didn't affect me, since I was always into it. But a lot of people start working to support their habits.

For me working was just good money. I could always afford to support my habit because I used to do other things. I've always sold dope. Cannabis isn't a very big earner these days, so mostly it's been hard drugs. I've been manufacturing drugs for a long time. Made heaps of money from homebake. I gave up work after a while because I didn't need to any more.

I was always out of it when I was working — on anything I could throw up my arm. If it wasn't speed, pills, downers and that, then I used to smoke heaps of dope, anything to be out of it. I felt nothing when I was working. The sex side of it was boring.

A lot of drugs used to get sold through the parlours. It's much harder now, because to get a licence you have to be completely straight, not one conviction, nor employ anyone who's

LIZ

got any involvement with criminals. But as far as I'm concerned, nearly all criminals have something to do with parlours because they're good places to sell things. It's easy to roll stuff there — not to the clients, you don't trust the clients, but to the girls. They've always got money to buy clothes with. Who wants to go out and pay $200 for a dress when you can get it for $50? I always go to parlours to sell things, like clothes from shoplifting. I used to go out daily on hoisting sprees. I love hoisting. You can earn more doing that than working.

The only way I coped with the job was by being out of it. I couldn't go to work straight, no way. It just gets really boring being screwed by ten different guys every night. All I could think of was the money or anything but them. It's the only way I could do it.

Sometimes it was quite risky. It can be risky on the street. There are a few guys you have to watch out for. One particular guy up K Road seems to do over everybody. He picks them up, beats them up, robs them and rapes them. That's how a mate of mine lost her teeth. He did it to me, he's done it to everyone I know. He looks just like a salesman, he's got a new Falcon and everything, but he's a real nutter.

He really freaked me out, that guy. He picked me up and I said to him, 'Let's go into the carpark.' He said no and locked all the doors with the internal locks, click, click, click, and I thought, 'Oh, fuck.' He drove right down to the wharves and just beat me up. He raped me for about half an hour and then kicked me out, taking all my money with him. I kept thinking, 'God, what's he going to do next? Stab me?' but he didn't. The security guard came along and I got him to take me back up K Road. I didn't go back to work that night, though — I felt buggered.

Some guys will pay you, then can't get it up and expect their money back. Although you've done your damnedest to get it up for them, they'll keep on insisting and call you a fucking bitch. I make a quick exit from the car. I'm pretty good at doing that now.

You get crazies coming into the parlours sometimes too. Usually you don't have that much hassle because there is always someone there who can hear you. The guys know that too, so they're not going to start trouble — it's just when you're in the car with them, by yourself, that you think, 'Oh yeah, well there's only me.'

I used to carry a blade with me all the time, but when you keep being searched it's not worth carrying any weapons. The police come and search you just about every night. Where I have my car parked there's a long iron bar, but that's not going to do me much good if I'm in another car.

Another on-the-job risk is AIDS, or catching a dose. Some of the clients used to bleat and carry on because they had to wear french letters, but I wouldn't do it without them. You may find that some of the girls in the parlours don't use them — they're grubby little chicks. The girls on the street are usually really clean. I don't care what people say about street girls. I know some people run us down and say we're nothing but shit, but really we're only out there because we don't want to work for anyone else.

When I met my old man I stopped working. I didn't think it was right to have a relationship and work at the same time. I couldn't get into it. It doesn't work, sexually or mentally. I wouldn't like my old man to be going out screwing other people, so why should I, even if I'm getting paid for it? He didn't want me to work anyway. And I was sort of sick of it by the time I met him. He thought it was great when I gave up. So I took a break for about five years.

I went back only because I had left him and I thought, 'Fuck you.' He kept on following me around, so I thought if I went back to work it would fix him, but it didn't. I started off working for a girlfriend in a parlour for about a month, and he was up there every day, so I thought, 'Oh, fuck it, I'll go on the street then, he'll hate that.' So I went out on the street and he'd be sitting in K Road all night waiting for me to finish. I couldn't get rid of him, and after a couple of months I thought I may as

LIZ

well go back with him again. I just kept on working. He still hated it. He used to come up K Road every night to see if I was all right, or I had to ring in a couple of times. After a while I decided I couldn't handle it any more, so I stopped working. Then I got sentenced to come inside.

A lot of the girls have got partners and stuff. Most of the ones I know are supporting their habits and their old men's habits. I wouldn't do that — he can support his own. In fact he doesn't have one any more. And he's got his own business now and is making heaps of money. So I'm not going back to work when I get out. I don't need to. Besides, I hate working. I can't stand all those different men, I think they're fucking wankers. All those different guys wanting to grope you all the time. I used to have about ten showers a night. It makes you feel dirty. I'm not ashamed of it, though. I don't think anybody that works is any worse than anyone else. I think everyone's equal. I just can't be bothered any more, although it *is* a good earner . . .

It's actually quite a respectable job, really. You still have to go to work every day and you've got to look nice. It doesn't matter what you do, you have to keep yourself looking good. When people asked me what I did, I might tell them, depending who it was, but really it's none of their business. Sometimes when I wouldn't tell people they'd spy on me up on the corner, and that was embarrassing. Friends of friends have done that, and friends of my family.

It doesn't worry me, though. I'm not ashamed of what I do. I told my grandparents what I was doing. They weren't particularly offended. They didn't like it, but they wouldn't be shocked at anything I did now. The way I see it, I was just selling a service, that's all. It was more like a business transaction than anything else. I didn't feel degraded by it.

When I get out I'll go straight back up to Auckland, home. My old man's not inside at the moment, so I'll go back. Don't know what I'll do, though. I have had straight jobs before, but nothing significant. I used to work in a shop. I was a tea lady once, and I've worked in a bar. If I get work release from here I'll have to take a straight job.

I don't want to work again anyway. Unless I could set up my own place, but then I'd just run it. I'd like to grab one of those old ferries and make it into a floating massage parlour, bar and everything. I've always had a fantasy about doing that, but I'd need a financial backer. I'd probably specialise in bondage if I set up my own place, have a special little chamber with shackles and manacles and all sorts of things.

Anyway, I'll get out of here soon, and I'll just take it from there. Don't know if I'll get back into the drugs or not. I'm not making them any more — that's what I ended up in here for. Actually, I don't know whether I will or not. It's pretty risky these days, and I'd hate to get caught again. This time I was lucky, fucking lucky.

I wanted to do some university work while I was in here, but they won't let me because it costs too much. I wanted to do individual and social psychology. I'm doing something else in psychology — it's not university, though, but I'll keep it up. That's the one thing I will do when I get out, because I don't know what else to do. I might get a job, but I hate working. I'd rather stay at home, or really not have the responsibility or commitment of having to get up every morning and go to work. These people that *work* — God, it's boring!

After Liz served her prison sentence, she went back up to Auckland for a while, then apparently ringbolted on a ship across the Tasman to live in Australia with her husband.

JASMINE

Jasmine was still at school when she became involved in sex work. She spent some years working in massage parlours in Dunedin before moving to Wellington.

I was born in Dunedin twenty-two years ago and grew up spending some time with my grandmother as well as living with my own family. My mother was a Catholic, and all of us children went to a little Catholic primary school, but I was the only one who attended a Catholic secondary school as well. It wasn't really a staunch family — mostly it was just restricted to mass on Sunday and grace before meals.

We were a lower-middle-class family — like we'd only just got out of the working class, but we had ambition. We certainly weren't poor by any standards, but I can remember when I was a kid always feeling that there was never enough money there. By the time I actually left my family, they'd got to upper middle class, and I think they'd forgotten about me.

The first time I left home was when I was fifteen. We lived some distance out of town, so I'd go and stay with friends in the centre of Dunedin for a couple of weeks, then come back for a shower and a change of clothes. It wasn't really leaving home so much as an extended holiday.

I was always a very slow learner when it came to sex. I was sexually abused by my uncle when I was seven or so, and that went on for a couple of years. I successfully blocked it out, though, until I was about thirteen. Then one day we'd been having a conversation at school about how nice it would be to have an older brother so he could bring his friends home. My friend said, 'No, I hate it when that happens because one of them keeps trying to feel me up behind the bike shed,' and I said, 'Yeah, my uncle used to do that to me when I was seven.' Then I stopped and thought, 'Where did that come from?' It wasn't until I made that remark that it all started coming back.

I never told anybody. He said the devil would get me if I told. It made me draw back a lot from boys later on. Also, I was not what you call classically good-looking. I had braces at the time and I cultivated a very loud and angry exterior towards boys.

I had my first boyfriend when I was fourteen. I think he was gay, actually, although that was never said. I met him in the park. He was about nineteen at the time, and I sort of got into drugs through him, just pills and stuff, because he was a supplier. We used to sleep together but not touch each other — I never really started touching boys until I was fifteen. I just couldn't see why anybody would want to bother.

I was at school fairly regularly until the end of the fifth form, then I virtually stopped going because it seemed totally irrelevant. I couldn't stand the people I was going to school with, or the teachers, or what I was being taught. I thought I shouldn't leave without UE, so in the sixth form I would go once or twice a week, but usually just to have a sleep. Then I moved back home, went to school more and got my UE.

The Catholic girls' school I was at was really weird — it conforms to all the stereotypes of Catholic girls' schools that you've ever heard. One girl at school who was two years below me was called 'a dollar eighty-three Bridget'. One night when a group of girls in my class were going to see a band play somewhere, she was $1.83 short of the ticket price. So she went up to the guy behind the desk and said, 'If I give you a blow job, will you give me $1.83 so I can get in?' There was a real thing at school about being a prostitute. It was like, 'We don't know what this is about, but it sounds really exciting.' There was one girl who used to give blow jobs behind the bus shelter to the guys from the local boys' school. But that was okay because she wasn't taking money for it.

JASMINE

When I was in the seventh form, four of us went away together and stayed in a cabin, and two of the girls had fucking contests on the top bunk, to see who could have the most guys over a twenty-four-hour period — no sleep on the bottom bunk, let me tell you! And these were like the top Latin and French class type girls too. The nuns never knew about all this.

When I was in the sixth form I came to the end of the list of people who were prepared to supply me with free drugs. I'd been getting around with this group for about two years and I started moaning about having no money. A woman I knew said, 'I know where you can make some money.' 'Oh yeah?' I said, 'How?' She said, 'I work in the parlours — come down with me.' I went down there and they said, 'Can you start tomorrow?' So I did.

I'll always remember that first night. I felt really fat, really horrible and unlovely. At that time I didn't have any hair at all; I'd shaved it off, and I looked about as mean as anyone with a face like mine can ever look.

I was so scared — I didn't know what to do, I didn't know what to say. You were supposed to ponce around in gorgeous lingerie, and everyone else was wearing these million-dollar outfits, but I'd just been down to an op shop and got myself an old nightie.

The first guy I had was a builder. I just sat there trying to massage him, shaking like a leaf. All I remember is that he didn't come. There was a knock on the door saying, 'Your time's up,' and I said, 'Oh, I'm very sorry but I've got to go now.' He said, 'But I haven't come yet!' and I said quickly, 'It's not my fault.' He walked out, and I threw up all over the carpet.

I usually worked about four shifts a week then. I was not one of the favourite girls, because I didn't try that hard. I was also a hustler, which is like the lowest form of life — I couldn't stand people touching me, but if I got a guy who'd say, 'Please let me touch your breasts,' I'd say, 'Okay, you can touch one for ten seconds, but it will cost you another $20, and it will be $30 to do the other tit as well.' It was surprising the number of guys that wanted kisses, so I'd sell those as well. You could make as much from selling various bits as you could from a hand job.

I never put the effort into dressing or behaviour. To be a favourite girl you had to look nice. You had to know how to get more money out of people, not just for you but for the parlour as well. Basically you had to be a hostess, and I couldn't fit into that. I wasn't interested in having them stay with me for another half-hour. They only had so much money, so my aim was to get what I could.

There were exceptions. There were some really nice guys, but I'd always think that probably they'd have a wife or little girlfriend somewhere, so what would be the point of getting screwed around by them? Besides, I don't think I'd trust a man who went to see a prostitute. That may sound like a double standard, but why can't they get their own girl?

I always wanted to do B and D, but nobody would ever let me. I didn't like these guys at all, and I couldn't think of anything better than hitting them. I did have one guy, our family lawyer actually, who used to get me to verbally abuse him and slap him, and he'd pay me extra for that.

I remember the one time I went out and bought myself a fabulous new camisole. It was white stretchy lace and I thought it was stunning, absolutely top of the range. The first night I wore it this guy came in and he must have been fourteen stone. My top was lying there and he decided to put it on. If I'd had any sense I would have thought, 'Hang on, this guy's a prick, but let's just work this through and try to get some more money out of this one,' but instead I screamed at him, 'You're stretching it, you're fucking stretching it!' The poor guy got very embarrassed, tore it off and ran away.

I had one client who was a Japanese sailor and he was being really horrible. He didn't know much English, but what he did know was very anti-women and he kept abusing me continually. I said to him, 'Look, I've had enough of this,' but he asked, 'What about sex?' So I said, 'No, I don't do that sort of thing.' He got really angry and tried to rape me. I kicked him off, but he pushed me backwards into a full-length mirror which shattered everywhere. Luckily I bounced off it, so that by the time the glass was breaking, I was about a foot away from it and moving fast. My feet and my legs were really badly cut, though. I stood there shaking, thinking, 'I don't need this shit.' And I left. That was the very last time I worked out of choice.

We always got hassles, because guys are always trying to get just that little bit more for that little bit less. Businessmen are the worst. You say to them, 'Look, you wouldn't sell *your* time short, so why should I?' and they'll sometimes respond to that sort of mentality.

When the clients came in they'd always turn their personal possessions over to the receptionist for safe keeping. Later, when they knew how much they wanted to spend with the woman, they'd go back and get it from their wallet. There was one businessman who used to come in and insist on keeping his wallet with him. He would always ask for me and then, when I got him into the room, he'd pull out his wallet and say, 'Somebody's been stealing from this while I've been in the shower.' Every time. He was continually five and ten bucks under what he should have had and he'd expect me to say, 'Oh dear, that's dreadful,' and do him for free or for whatever cash he had.

When I got into prostitution, it was because I wanted the money for drugs, but as soon as I started I thought, 'Right, this is it. I'm going to clean up my act.' I thought it was just so glamorous, like a touch of Las Vegas in my own little life. It got to the stage where I wasn't really doing it for money for drugs any more. I enjoyed being with the women I worked with. I enjoyed the feeling that we were a united front, and that the men coming in were what was disrupting us. I enjoyed sitting there talking with the women, then a guy would come in and you'd go off with him, but half an hour later you'd come back and rejoin the conversation — the guys were just peripheral.

I also did strip-a-grams. This other woman and I would go out to do them together. She was a bit older and a bit bigger than me, and felt a bit embarrassed about it, so I'd do them and she would provide the extras afterwards. It was fun — I really enjoyed that. It was a feeling of power to have these guys go, 'Oooh, wow,' as I moved down to my G-string. I did feel a bit silly, though. There's no way you can take all your clothes off and still be really serious. I felt like the nearest thing I'll ever get to being a movie star.

Mostly we went to rugby clubs, soccer clubs and other sports clubs. I can remember going to a squash team too — that was quite bizarre. Real men don't play squash! It was always that end of the scale — never businessmen or rich people. Anything from twenty to sixty or more guys might be there. I don't remember ever seeing any women there with the guys, apart from barmaids sometimes. After I'd done all the preliminary work, the other woman turned tricks with them. I refused to do anything sexual outside the parlour because I didn't think it was worth the risk. So I'd just stay there until she was ready to go. I'd be paid the entire strip-a-gram fee of $100, and she'd get the money from extras. Sometimes we'd get tips as well. For twenty minutes' work it's not bad. Then I'd sit round and drink the free drinks until she was ready to go. The guys would hassle me sometimes, but they were pretty easy to cope with.

Last year I met a guy in Wellington who had just bought a singing telegram business. He heard me tell another woman that I used to do strip-a-grams and he went, 'Oh really, how disgusting.' Later on, when there was just the two of us, he asked if I'd consider working for his new business. It was like, 'We'll put these strippers down, but it could still be worth a buck or two.' I just wanted to hit the bastard.

I don't think I could go back to doing them again anyway. I don't have that sort of confidence any more. When I was doing it before, I was still at school and working in the parlour, but I just got sick of it. I got sick of having to be nice to people. Also, I was using pretty heavily by that stage and losing a lot of credibility because of not being exactly reliable.

The other thing was that my hair had grown. It sounds bizarre, but I was getting an entirely different range of clients. When my head was shaved my clients were older businessmen. I don't think I had anybody under the age of forty, and they mainly wanted to be abused and sworn at and stuff like that. But then as soon as it started growing out and it got to about three or four inches long, suddenly I was no longer popular with that set. Now it was the younger guys, as if it was, 'She's a little bit prettier now so she could almost be a girlfriend.'

It was all of that, and the Japanese sailor man, which made it seem like the hassles were outweighing anything else. So I stopped. I was still in the sixth form and I started cleaning up my act drastically, and after about six months I gave up drugs.

I went to Otago University for two years, then I moved to Wellington in 1987 and found I needed money, really badly, just to pay the rent. I walked into the first parlour I saw and got a job. But it's horrible there — the scene is just so different. It's much slower and it's tackier. The receptionist was a bitch and let the clients choose which girls they wanted. I thought that was gross. It made me really angry, because it felt like a bloody meat market.

I also had another hassle, a couple of weeks after I started. Again it was with a Japanese sailor, so I'm not very well disposed towards Asian men now. I was only going to give him a hand job, then he decided he wanted a fuck, but offered me only $10 more. That's well under the price, so I said, 'No way.' He started getting abusive, but since his time was up I just walked out on him. The receptionist asked, 'What's all the hassle about?' so I told her, 'He's angry because I wouldn't screw him.' She turned round and said, 'Well, why wouldn't you? Get back in there and do it at once.' I was only there about a fortnight when I stopped — they do say it's a transitory industry!

Since then I've worked for an escort agency. That feels like, 'This isn't me — it's an illusion.' At the parlours they're after sex, but hopefully they'll do it in as nice a way as possible, so you get them in, you turn them over and you get them out. At an escort agency you can end up with them all night, going, 'Oh, that's so interesting — do tell me a bit more,' when you don't give a fuck. And for not much more money, sometimes for not even as much money. Plus you haven't got security, and that's something I'm really hung up about.

Mostly I was sent out to houses rather than hotels, and that's really scary. You don't know who's going to be there, and if it's his house then he knows where everything is and you don't. Some of these guys lived on their own, but a lot didn't. I remember one guy in particular was living in a very frilly house with a pink bedroom, dim lighting and women's clothes everywhere — I don't know where his wife was. Another place had kids' toys all over the floor and I wondered, 'My God, did your wife and kids just nip out to see Nana or something and you quickly got on the phone?'

None of these guys gave me hassles physically, but you still have to put up with so much more. At an escort agency they're selling so many hours of your time, so the man thinks he's got a right to your entire body. I find the guys who get escorts really sad. They're buying something that they consider real and it's actually just a lie. There's this whole illusion about a woman who's actually been paid for, clinging to his arm. There's a real difference too between what they're looking for and what they get. They have an image of the prostitute and they imagine what this woman will do for them, or how they'll feel with her, but I would say ninety per cent of them end up disappointed.

I didn't realise it at the time, but I was actually under age when I started working. I was only sixteen and I looked a young sixteen, but a mean fourteen. There was one guy in the Dunedin police who hated prostitutes. He was really sick. We would always be given taxi chits to get home from the parlour. Sometimes we might be waiting on the street for a lift and this guy would grab us and say, 'You owe me a freebie,' or 'Do you want your mum and dad to know you're doing this?' He'd also say,

'We can take away any chance you've got of working in a parlour again.' He did that to all the women who worked there at least once and we all had to go along with it.

I thought that if I didn't do what this cop wanted, I'd be out of the parlour, and I thought that because he was in his uniform, it must be okay. It felt like an official act. The parlour was in an older-style street with Chinese shops and gambling dens and there were lots of dark places. He'd just take us down an alley and have whatever he felt like.

He'd also come into the parlour to inspect the register every so often, and he'd walk around calling you by your real name, which is horrible. In front of the clients and everybody he'd say, 'Which one's Virginia? You call yourself Cassandra when you're working, do you?' It was a real power play.

About a year later, after I'd stopped working, I got raped in the street. I told a taxi driver and the police sent two *men* around to deal with it. I didn't get taken to hospital at all and it felt horrible. Another woman who was a 'nice girl' was raped as well, and the same guy confessed to doing both of them. I was scared that if I went to court and it came out that I'd worked as a prostitute, nobody would believe me.

I got hassled by the police at other times, not for being a prostitute but for being a junkie. I was always really careful never to have anything at the parlour that could even remotely be construed as a drug, not even aspirins. That was as much for the parlour management as me. I always tried to keep my arms covered or put plasters or make-up over any remaining marks, and I'd never go to work stoned, or maybe just a little bit but not much. You'd just be crazy to do that.

I once got caught up in this really funny set-up that I'd never heard of before, to do with the Mongrel Mob. It happened to one woman, Carol, but she never told me about it until later. This woman at the parlour, Miranda, suddenly got really friendly with me and said, 'You must come around and see me. Come around on your own at such and such a time and we'll have a smoke and a drink together.' I said, 'Okay, fine,' and then one night when I was staying at Carol's place,

I told her Miranda wanted me to go round. Carol said, 'Maybe I should come with you,' but I said, 'No, she said to come on my own.'

Carol insisted on walking round to this house with me. I walked in first and there were three Mongrel Mob guys sitting there. Patches. The works. Huge men. As soon as I walked in it was like 'Fresh meat!' and they raced up to try and get me. I thought, 'Oh shit.' Carol grabbed me and we took off down the street. They chased us, but we got away.

Later she told me what had happened to her and I was quite angry that she hadn't told me before. It was known as a Mongrel Mob set-up — you get a woman on her own to walk into a house where she'll be gang-raped, then later she's sent out to work for them, at conventions and stuff. She's literally their prisoner and slave. Carol got away, but it took her four or five days to get out.

We told everybody we knew about it, and we made sure Miranda got hers — she was paid a visit by some friends of mine. We also rang the police, anonymously, after another woman went missing, and asked them to look into it. I know they did an inquiry, but when we called back nobody would tell us what happened. We never saw that woman again — she'd been working with us and she just vanished. I didn't think she was the sort of woman to just move on without saying, and I knew she'd had a surprise invitation to visit people she didn't really know. I told her not to go, but she said, 'No, it will be fine. Things like that don't happen to me.'

I didn't tell the police myself. There's not a lot of joy to be had if you go in saying, 'Hey, I'm a prostitute — guess what happened to me?' They don't tend to take you seriously. It sounds as if there's more of a working relationship between the police and the parlours in Wellington now, but in Dunedin then, six years ago, it was a real fear/power relationship.

I still see prostitution as an option. It's something every woman has as an option. I've heard totally straight women say, 'Oh dear, I can't pay the gas bill — I'll go on the streets,' as a joke.

But it's always there, and it's certainly always at the back of my mind if I'm really broke.

I've never told many people about it, or many other men, because it's really only been in the last year or so that I've admitted to myself that it happened. Sure you tell some guys and they'll go, 'Really? Is that what you used to do?' and it's like they're thinking, 'I must remember that.' Some men are only interested in it from the men's perspective — like they'll ask, 'What's the longest one you've ever seen?'

My partner's reactions have been good. He's encouraged me to talk about it and write about it. On the other hand he's certainly not keen that I should ever do it again. For him it's just something that I used to do in Dunedin. I haven't told him I've done it in Wellington; that's possibly a bit too close. I haven't told my family at all. They're very middle-class, very respectable people and I don't think they'd cope with it. They'd just totally freak out.

One thing I made sure of when I was working was that every man that walked through that door had a condom on. Even if I was only going to massage him, he could still wear a condom, damn it. This was 1984, so you didn't have the AIDS thing and I never really thought about getting clap or anything. It was more of a psychological thing — I didn't want any of that nasty, messy stuff getting anywhere near me. He could just keep it all to himself.

I think you should be able to have advertisements for safe sex on the walls of saunas or whatever, and you can't really at the moment. Not until the law's changed. It should be decriminalised, so there's no law against soliciting for a start. If you decriminalised it, you wouldn't have a situation where people like that bitch of a receptionist could act the madonna over us.

There should still be some controls, though — like I think the age thing's really important! Weird, eh, given how young I was, but I could handle it whereas I don't know if other people could.

If women are going to do it, it's better that they work in a parlour and have that protection, so what I'd like to say is, 'If anybody wants to work as a prostitute, please do it in a parlour, because it really is the safest thing.' I have so much admiration for the women that work on the streets. I think they've got so much guts — I don't know how they do it.

I've slept with very few men outside my working life — I never saw the point of doing it lots of times if you didn't like it and you're not getting paid for it.

Men have got to realise that we're selling them a service. We're selling them our time and we need the money for it, so could they please stop fucking us around. It's attitudes that have to change more than anything. If only you could take the sleazy attitude off it and see it as just a business, just a job. That's all it is to me.

Jasmine is no longer working in the sex industry but still considers it to be an option that she could come back to in the future. She has just graduated from Victoria University and is now 'out to change the world!'

KATE

Kate and her partner both began working as escorts at the same time, while Kate was a university student. When I talked to her she had been working for only three months.

I grew up in the Wairarapa and lived there until I moved to Wellington to go to university when I was quite young. I had a couple of years at varsity, then dropped out and spent a while messing around being unemployed. Then I worked with intellectually handicapped people for about eighteen months, before going to Australia and working there for a while. After that I spent time travelling through Asia and Europe and then came back to varsity to complete my degree.

I was fourteen when I first had sex with a guy, although I had been pashing up boys since I was thirteen. I had always thought that I was probably bisexual, and in fact I had been quite open about that at high school. I hadn't done anything about it, though, because of being in a small town.

I'd always considered myself a feminist from the time I was thirteen or fourteen, and when I came to Wellington I started getting involved in feminist things around varsity. I got quite radical and angry, and a lot of the women I was hanging around with were lesbians and quite anti-heterosexual. They maintained that the only way you could be a proper feminist was to be a lesbian, and in some ways I feel that I was pushed into declaring myself a lesbian then. If I'd been in a freer environment I would probably have stuck with the idea of being a bisexual, which is what I've come back to in later years.

Because I was so politically involved, I got really involved in the lesbian community for the next three years or so, despite various doubts I had and still wondering if I was attracted to men. I felt as though I couldn't see any way out of that while I was still in Wellington, because too many other people I knew were political heavies and would have been pretty fucking awful to me had I gone with any men at that stage. I didn't know any heterosexual men then anyway — I just didn't meet them in my social grouping.

Initially I would have seen it as a contradiction in terms that a feminist could be a prostitute. It seemed to involve objectification and women selling their bodies and all that sort of thing. But I found out that some women I already knew were doing it, and then a close friend of mine who was a lesbian wanted to save some money to go overseas and she went and got a job working in a parlour. I was spending a lot of time around her at the time she was doing that, and I just got accustomed to the idea.

She talked about the work a lot. She wasn't enjoying it particularly, and I definitely had a sense that she was being forced into it because there was no other way that she could make that much money so quickly. I saw it as a possible option, and I had never seen that before. I came from a reasonably middle-class background where this sort of thing would never be considered. My mother would never dream in a million years that I was doing this.

So up until then I'd had the same view of prostitutes as most people do. A lot of people perceive prostitutes as some sort of alien breed — they all have needle scars up their arms, bleached hair, fishnet stockings and stilettos. And that was certainly how I felt for a long time until I started to know women who were prostitutes. After that I was aware that it was something I could do if ever I needed to. But I never thought I would.

I didn't know many prostitute women, but nearly all the ones I did know were lesbians and a lot were feminists too. I don't think they were really 'out' as prostitutes among the whole lesbian scene. The lesbian feminist ones were a small cluster who were earning money to go to Europe, and they had a wider group of friends around them who knew what they were doing. There were also others working who weren't as involved in feminist things — I suppose you'd call them 'gay women', if that's not too derogatory a term. Everybody knew they were prostitutes, but they probably wouldn't have been too acceptable around lesbian feminists, for their politics as much as anything else.

It was when I had run out of money that I decided to start working. I just couldn't cope with the wages here at the time, with having to clean someone's house for $8 an hour, or waitress for $6 an hour. I could have gone back to working with disabled people, but that's too stressful. I wasn't qualified to do anything else, and all the jobs were really grotty menial jobs with fucking appalling pay. I couldn't bring myself to do it, though. I had a real block about it, and my money got lower and lower and lower until it got down to almost nothing. My partner's friend had been doing it, and my partner started wondering if she should do it. I probably wouldn't have if she hadn't.

Penny's friend had been doing escorts, and essentially we both got into escort work because we knew somebody who was doing it. Penny and I talked about it a lot, then one weekend I didn't see her at all and when I rang her up she said she'd gone and done it on Saturday night.

It sounded really simple, really, really easy. It didn't sound any more complicated than picking someone up in a bar and going off and fucking them, which I've done a million times in my life. I don't necessarily see sex as some great sacrosanct thing where I have to be in love.

I was still trying to decide, because even though I had known people who had done it and I knew it wasn't the end of the world, in some ways it still seemed like a huge hurdle to get over. The idea of doing it was absolutely terrifying. It's almost as if I felt like I'd become a 'fallen woman', and why was I stooping to this? I arranged an interview with the woman from the escort agency, then the night before sat there thinking, 'Oh God, surely, you could go and find a job in a restaurant, surely you don't have to make yourself do this . . .' Then I woke up next morning and I thought, 'Oh no, it's not that big a deal really.'

The woman from the agency came around that day. I was always a bit terrified that someone would lay eyes on me and say, 'You're not pretty enough, you're too fat — we won't employ you.' But that wasn't an issue in the least. And the woman who interviewed me was very professional and organised and quite nice. She told me always to use a condom for everything, and talked with me about difficult situations that might arise and how to make sure I got the money and stuff like that.

I started work a couple of days later. I thought at the time I should have made it a bit earlier, because by then I was panicking, feeling like I didn't want to do it. I was living in a big household in Mount Victoria at the time and my flatmates had all gone away for the Christmas holidays. I couldn't have told them; in fact, I never did tell them. When they came back I engaged in all this subterfuge so they wouldn't guess what I was doing. If a call came in for a job, I'd suddenly pretend I had a depressed friend I was going to take out for a drink and I'd get dressed up and rush out the door! Or, since my bedroom was by the front door, I'd say I was going to bed, get changed and sneak quietly out of the house. It was really important that nobody knew what I was doing.

Anyway, the first call I had was for a job at the Plaza International Hotel. I was terrified at the idea of going to this flash hotel in case people might recognise me. What if I knew someone in the bar? I was also really frightened that people I didn't know would realise what I was doing.

There's a driver who takes us to the jobs, and sometimes he'll go up to the room with us and get the agency's fee, which is $50 an hour. Anyway, that night I was so nervous I really needed him to take me up there. The client was a middle-aged man from the country somewhere, who was passing through Wellington. He was a quiet little man. I don't feel like I did a particularly good job, but I don't care either.

I'd still find it a difficult job, even now, having to spend two or three hours with someone who's not very socially skilled and with whom I don't have much in common. We spent very little time in bed. It wasn't really sex he was after — he wanted a companion. He ended up paying basically for me to watch TV with him, because he was lonely.

He was my first client, and I've worked with that agency ever since. It's run by a couple, with the woman mostly doing the interviews and the guy doing the driving. They work from home, using a private telephone and everything. It's only small, about fifteen women maximum, with maybe only two or three working on any one night. I've only met one other woman who works there, apart from Penny, and that's just because she was picked up at the same time as me one night. Sometimes I think that's a disadvantage of escort work, because it's so isolated and there's less support. But it also seemed like an advantage when I started, because I felt so uncertain about the whole thing that I liked the idea of being able to keep myself anonymous.

The clients I've had fall into a number of categories. Some are just lonely and want someone to talk to. Sometimes it seems they're after that rather than a fuck. But they still have a fuck because they've paid for it.

Then there are the clients who are in Wellington on business, staying in hotels, and it's obviously just part of the way they operate — that when they go away on business they will get a girl up. It's just normal practice for them. They've usually got wives and families at home and they're quite together.

And then there are occasional ones who want a particular kind of sexual fantasy which they can't get otherwise, like they want two women together. I did a job like this on my first night. After doing the hotel job, Penny and I did a job together at this army guy's place. It was a two-hour job, kind of a *ménage à trois* situation.

We do a lot of calls to private homes, and about a third to hotels. Most of the men in the private homes are single, or separated or divorced. Occasionally their wives may be away somewhere, but often they'll be very guilty and panicky and don't want to go through with it when you get there. I tell them I'm quite happy to have a cup of coffee and a chat, but they'll have to pay me for it, otherwise I'm leaving immediately. In fact they always end up fucking me. Nobody wants to shell out $100 just to have a cup of coffee with somebody — despite the wonderful scintillating company!

I also had one really odd call where I went to a young guy's place and he really freaked out when he saw me. I think he expected a prostitute who was a real stereotype. But I usually make an effort to be nice and chatty, and I think it quite shook him that I was so normal. He started trying to convince me that I should get out of the industry. Why was I wasting myself like this? I should be doing all kinds of good things with my life, and he couldn't possibly do this to me and he felt so terrible. But when it came down to the $100, he did anyway. After all the drama and tragedy, he still fucked me. It was quite unnerving though, having him go on at me like that.

Sometimes I think it would be easier working in a parlour. I'm interested in trying it to see, because sometimes it drives me bloody crazy having to talk to them. One guy fucks pretty much like another, whereas the conversation can be really hard work. Sometimes I've thought they've got their money's worth just from me having to talk to them.

I always think this work is very similar to the kind of thing you go through if someone picks you up hitch-hiking — starting with the terrible fear about being raped and murdered by the first lift, until you don't feel bothered in the least about it. And the kind of relationship you have is similar in some ways — all the small talk and everything.

Some of them are quite interested in me and want to know all about what I'm doing. Before I started I thought that I would make up a completely different persona and background, but I don't really feel the need to do that. If it was somebody I really disliked or didn't trust for some reason, maybe I would.

A lot of these guys ring up because they don't want to be seen walking into a parlour. And they don't want to be seen by all the women working there or by other clients. Sometimes it's just comfort and laziness — they simply can't be bothered going out.

I've also been in situations with men where they either haven't been able to get it up, or they have but they haven't been able to come, and it's dragged on for ages and ages, sometimes because they've been drinking. But if it gets to the end of the hour, I'll get up and put my clothes on and go. They've already paid at the beginning of the session, so there's nothing they can do about it.

I feel they've got to have some responsibility in terms of getting what they want. I don't make any kind of move on anybody, partly because I'm quite happy to get out of the sex if I can. If they just give me a cup of coffee and talk to me, I'll just sit there and talk back, and if it gets to the end of the time, I'll just go. That's never happened yet. They usually finally get around to saying, 'Let's go into the bedroom.'

It's actually extraordinary how conservative most of them are — that really startled me when I first started doing it. They would just go into the bedroom and turn the light off, pull the sheets and blankets down, quickly take their clothes off and get in under the bedclothes. I think I'd expected that they would want more exotic or interesting kinds of sex, but in fact it's pretty boring, mundane sex, and far more ordinary than I would have in my private life with anybody.

A lot of the services we provide to clients aren't just sexual anyway. We provide a bit of company, a listening ear, whatever. I did this extraordinary job the other night for a young Swiss guy who was having difficulties in his relationship with his girlfriend. He was a very clinical sort of person and had decided that since he wasn't satisfying her sexually he would get a prostitute in to teach him what women needed and wanted in bed. I felt really thrown when he told me that was what he wanted. I just thought, 'Oh God, what do I do here?' We went to bed and I gave him a guided tour of my cunt and showed him which bits were which and what you could do to them. But then it turned out that what he really wanted was to talk about the relationship, and the sexual side of things was probably the least of his worries. It was probably more to do with his being such a cold and clinical person than anything else, so I tried to tell him that as kindly as I could. And he was really pleased. He was a very satisfied client indeed.

I've been doing escort work for about three and a half months now, and none of my clients have given me any trouble. The advice I was given about safety was fairly paltry and useless, though. Basically it consisted of, 'Just give me a ring if anything goes wrong.' But obviously if you got into a really difficult, violent situation, you might not have access to a telephone, and besides, you'd have to wait ten minutes at least for the guy from the agency to come and pick you up. At least this agency has a driver. Most of them send the girls out in a taxi or expect them to provide their own transport.

Something that can be a real pain in this work is bogus calls. The agency does try to check calls, but for all that we can still end up being sent on them. I was taken out on one call, in the middle of the bloody night, right out to the Hutt and when we got there, it was obvious somebody was home but nobody answered the door. We'd driven for bloody miles out there, and then we had to drive for bloody miles back home.

I got a bogus call the other night to a hotel where some of the staff had given the number of a non-existent room. The duty manager approached me and asked which room I was looking for, then told me he suspected the staff had been fooling around. He asked if I was from one of the agencies, and began asking me about the work and everything. Then he said to me, 'Do you do hand relief?' So I ended up giving him a quick blow job in one of the hotel rooms. I just had to think of a price off the top of my head and I'm sure it wasn't enough. We get paid by the time, you see, and I've no idea what parlour prices are like for different acts.

In terms of safe sex, I've always insisted they wear condoms for everything. Essentially I just say that I won't do it unless they put a condom on.

KATE

I provide my own condoms, which I get free on a doctor's prescription. I wear a diaphragm in case the condoms break, so I won't get pregnant. I had an AIDS test when I first started, but apart from that I haven't had any check-ups — I'm not even really sure what I should be getting checked up for.

Some of the clients feel very strongly about safe sex, but I think that's often because they have really negative ideas about prostitutes and think we're all carrying round thousands of diseases. Some of the guys can be quite grotty, though. I've seen some who could have done with a wash, but I let them get away with it. I wouldn't stand for that now — I've become more and more assertive as time's gone by.

I don't enjoy being fucked by men who are unpleasant and sleazy. I don't enjoy it; occasionally I feel a bit disgusted by it. But I handle it mainly by just switching off. I keep myself cool and detached, whereas normally if you're having sex with somebody out of desire or love or whatever, you get involved, presumably in a passionate or sexual way. And I just don't do that. I remain as clinical as if I was a doctor examining somebody. And I'm quite passive — I'm only as active as I need to be to get them off.

Often I think about the time. I look at my watch over their shoulders quite a lot, thinking that in ten minutes I can get out of bed and go and have a shower and the driver will come and pick me up and I can get out of this place. I hate it if they don't come quickly. And I can get quite sore too. I haven't learned any tricks for hurrying them up — that's the kind of thing I feel I'd like to have more contact with other women in the job about.

I won't kiss or anything like that. Sometimes they want me to, but they're usually not too difficult about it if I don't. I have had one or two who haven't had prostitutes before. They were accustomed to having relationships with their wives and actually found it very difficult and disturbing to have sex without being able to kiss. But kissing them is very unpleasant — their slimey mouths and horrible breath. It's a lot worse than actually being fucked and it's a bit too personal. I also have a sense that I have to set a limit somewhere. Even if it's just a little bit of my body that's off limits, it's still quite nice to have that. Maybe it's necessary to have that.

I've never felt as though I needed to take anything to help me handle it all, though. I'm not a very druggy sort of person, whether it's alcohol or anything else. The most I'll have is a drink or two with them. I think I would probably feel less able to handle it if I was out of it on something.

Having us both working has been quite good for Penny and me. If anything, it's made us closer. We've been together about eight months now, and when we started working it was just after we'd broken up for a short time. But then it was like we really needed one another to talk to because we were going through the same things. We both became obsessed with prostitution when we first started doing it. It just seemed like such a big deal that it was all we could think about. We were both quite worried about safety to begin with, and nervous going to jobs, and very protective of each other.

We pretty much work on the same nights because it means we sit around home together while we're waiting for calls. Sometimes the agency might say the guy has asked for a blonde or whatever; other times either of us could go, so whoever is feeling like it takes it.

When we started working, the agency told us they had received one or two calls from women clients in the past, and Penny and I both said that if anything like that came up again, we'd be happy to do it. But I don't actually know if I would be now. I have a certain amount of detachment towards these men which I think I would find it hard to maintain to the same degree with a woman. I also think I'd feel strange, in a jealous kind of way, about Penny going with a woman.

It's hard to say if working has had an effect on our own sex life. I do know that when we first started, if one of us had been with a client and came back late at night and got into bed, we would get very sexual very quickly. It was like reclaiming your body. I used to have a real sense of needing to do that, but I don't as much now because it doesn't seem like such a big deal any more.

When I first started I didn't want anybody knowing what I was doing, or only people I knew I could trust. It was as if I didn't want to become part of this whole world of prostitutes. Now it's important to me that the people I'm around are accepting of sex workers. I really like being around the women I know in the lesbian community who have done it, or whose lovers have done it, because I can be quite open.

I also know when and where to keep my mouth shut. I don't get into situations where I'm liable to be attacked for what I say. I'm aware that most people tend to view prostitutes as a kind of alien breed, a separate group outside society, and you can't escape that stigma. So deciding to be a prostitute obviously carries far more emotional weight than going and getting a job as a waitress.

I'm still incredibly conscious of that stigma. I mean, I'm accustomed to being a lesbian and working in straight situations where I don't feel comfortable about coming out. But it's like this is the ultimate thing you have to keep your mouth shut about. And there's no way I can talk to all the feminists and lesbians and socialists and people that I hang out with at varsity about this sort of thing. There's only a small select group of people I can be open with about this, and that pisses me off.

There is an enormous stigma attached to prostitution that doesn't attach itself to you if you choose to barter your sexuality through marriage or through being a model or a waitress wearing a short skirt or whatever. And that means 'prostitute' and 'non-prostitute' are two distinct categories.

Before I started doing it I was still in the position that a lot of feminists are in, which is where they will accept prostitutes but refute prostitution. Many feminists still think that prostitution in itself is a really bad thing, and prostitutes are just women who were forced into it or are doing it because there's bloody good money in it.

But I'm not so sure now that I think prostitution in itself is wrong. A lot of radical stuff has been written in recent years about how sex has been treated as something apart from everything else in Western society, and how because of Christianity it's been treated as if it should be sacred and holy. So while everything else has been accepted as a commodity under capitalism, sex hasn't been. Yet marriage has very clearly been a barter around sex in the past, even if sometimes different factors operate today.

I don't see it as necessarily bad for someone to hand over cash in exchange for sex. I think a lot of feminists have been affected by that very romantic idea of sex and sexuality, and continue to think that it needs to be linked with love and that kind of thing. So they see it as outside acceptable boundaries for sex to be used in a straight cash transaction. But it's actually a very honest transaction. Some people pay to have therapy or counselling; they pay for all kinds of services — I don't see any reason whatsoever why people shouldn't pay for sexual services.

There was a time when I would have seen prostitution as the selling of women per se. The whole female sexual slavery bit. I don't see it as that now. I see myself as selling a service, in the same way as I might sell myself to carry plates in a restaurant or look after disabled people or work in a law firm.

There are definite aspects of objectification in it, because you're trading on your body and your looks. And that does depend, though only to a certain degree, on conventional notions of beauty and stuff. I'm certainly no perfect Barbie doll, but presumably you can't be too far from the ideal — if I was seventeen stone and covered in acne I wouldn't be able to get a job doing this. But then that's true of a lot of professions for women.

Before I started I used to be disturbed by the idea that through prostitution men could order women around and have a woman totally under their control. I had this idea that if they gave you $100 you were theirs for the next hour. But that's not how it is at all. I feel I have quite lot of control over what goes on. I'm quite definite about what I will and won't do, and what I will charge extra for, and I refuse to give up those limits. In some ways this whole job gives me a sense of being quite sexually powerful — I find it extraordinary that they're willing to shell out such large sums of money for nothing so fantastic really.

I do enjoy the variety in the work. And there's something quite appealing and wicked about being driven around town and going into flash hotels in the middle of the night in my best clothes. I get something out of being able to dress up like a lady and put on a different persona and be a bit glamorous and everything, because I'm not really like that in my personal life. Although, interestingly, I've become more like that since I started working again.

When I was a teenager I used to dress up a lot and wear lots of make-up and high heels, but through feminism and everything I stopped. But now it's like I've rediscovered that part of myself and the part of me that likes wearing lacy underwear and stockings and things and enjoys feeling attractive. And Penny quite appreciates that side of me too, so I've discovered, which is really lucky. So now I will dress up like that sometimes to go out to dinner with her or to go dancing or whatever. Working has given me that back, which was certainly something I didn't realise would happen.

This work is not exactly exciting, but compared with being a waitress or a cleaner it is interesting and varied. And of course there's the money, because that's what keeps me working. And it's quite a good way to be earning money, because it doesn't really require me to be focused or putting a huge amount of effort into anything. Prostitution will always seem like a possibility for me, and it's good to know that I can do it.

Kate went on to work in a couple of Wellington massage parlours, where she found the money was better, but disliked the atmosphere and the long shifts. After several months she gave up work entirely, feeling angry with men, disillusioned and depressed. Kate is currently living in the Wellington hills with her lover, tending to their garden and cats, and working at an assortment of casual jobs. In the last few months she has entered into a 'deep healing process' involving meditation, therapy and making peace with herself and the world. She has recently acknowledged early sexual abuse and now feels that prostitution 'isn't a very loving thing to do to yourself'.

JULIA

Julia was a thirty-four-year-old mother of two when she first began working for an escort agency. Since then she has also worked in several South Island massage parlours.

I grew up in a professional, academic Wellington family and then hitched around Europe for about nine years. Later I lived as a country hippie and came back to live on the land at places like the Hokianga, Coromandel and near Nelson. Eventually, about eleven years ago, I moved to a southern city, primarily to be near a good school for my children's education.

I had often thought about working in what I now call the 'sex industry'. I always knew I would enjoy it, but I didn't quite know how to go about it. When I came to the city I started thinking more about it. Then I met somebody who was doing outcalls, and thought that this was exactly what I'd like in my life.

In those days there were only two outcall services in the city. We had RT in the car and would just get picked up from one person and taken to another. It was quite a busy, lucrative business. I did outcalls for three years and never wanted to work in a parlour — I couldn't imagine being with somebody for only half an hour; it just seemed like too short a time. Outcalls last for at least one or maybe two hours.

I can remember the first call I did. It was to a hotel, and to quite a young person, somebody younger than myself anyway, because I was thirty-four when I started. I remember thinking, 'I really shouldn't let it be known that this is the first time I have ever done this. I've got to be a bit sophisticated here.' I'd borrowed all these clothes, shoes, the whole thing, because I was a hippie. I went into the hotel, and I remember him asking me at one point how long I'd been doing this sort of work. I just said, 'Oh, for a while,' being fairly blasé. After that it was easy, and I didn't find it at all difficult to be with somebody I didn't know.

When I started I thought that being an escort involved going out to dinner and all that sort of thing, and I knew I didn't want to have anything to do with that. There may have been two parallel situations going on with escorts at that time. The agency I worked with offered an outcall massage service, but I think all the clients I had assumed there was going to be more than massage involved.

What they wanted was my charming company. I loved doing erotic massages, and I liked to think that perhaps they would enjoy that and whatever happened afterwards. During those years we had spent living in the bush I had taught myself to massage. When I started working I realised that this wasn't the sort of massage I was supposed to be doing. I was doing it in too therapeutic a way, so I just adapted it and have constantly refined my technique since then. *All* massages are therapeutic if the person receiving them gets some sort of benefit from them. But I used to give much firmer ones, whereas now they're definitely softer, and I'll suck toes and do all sorts of things that I wouldn't consider doing before.

I did outcalls for about three years. At one point I was working for two or three services at once. Sometimes we had no driver and I used to drive myself around to grotty old factories in the middle of the night. I led a totally charmed life — it never occurred to me that anything could go wrong. I look back now and think that things were really different then.

Now I won't do outcalls in any shape or form. I got mugged in America, almost killed, just walking down the street in broad daylight while I was over there on holiday, and it changed my entire life. I suddenly realised that there were crazy people out there in the world, when up until that point I hadn't even known they existed. After that I came home and put a lock on my back door, which I'd never thought I needed before, and gave up outcalls. That was eight years ago, and I've worked in parlours ever since.

When I started working in the parlours, I found it very strange that I was with people for such a short time, and I was expected to give them a massage and whatever else in that space of time. But I just adapted my massages so they were shorter and it was fine. At first I was working in a small inner-city parlour which was quite busy. It didn't take long before I had lots of regulars, including some of the men I'd done outcalls with previously. The clients were a mixture of local men and businessmen. They were from every conceivable background. In fact, if you walked down a busy city street, the first ten men you passed could be typical clients.

It was really lucrative initially, in the days before the drought that brought about the economic decline. Up until then we used to get a lot of farmers in the parlour scene, and they're easy clients to have. What happens in the rural community definitely affects the economics of the city.

I've worked in parlours for eight years now, and I've seen quite a few places. A lot are small and dark. Some show blue movies and you have to wear a certain type of lingerie while a big man sits at the front desk — I just don't like working in that sort of situation. Some parlour bosses are bad news, expecting their workers to give them freebies. I've only seen that happen once or twice, but then I don't tend to work for those sorts of people. I did have one boss once, when I was doing outcalls, whom I liked a lot, and occasionally when he was tired and business was quiet I'd give him a massage. Sometimes we'd end up making love, but that was purely my choice.

I really believe men should have no place running parlours. I think women who have worked themselves are generally more sympathetic towards working girls. I don't like seeing a man on the front desk. I'd also like to see more parlours owned by women. I'm not a feminist — I've never thought of myself as a feminist, even though I probably have a lot of understandings that some would like to put that word to. I just want to be a simple human being, and I don't like divisions.

I don't really mind bosses as long as I can respect them. But if they do things I don't approve of, I'm very judgemental and I might leave. I've worked in four parlours in the South Island. One I left after it had a fire. I went to another, but the finance company that seemed to own it began taking away all the furniture and told us we'd been sacked. Another one I left because of a disagreement over principles.

The parlour I work in now is a very large one. It's very upmarket, very tasteful, nice and clean — it's a pleasure to work there; in fact, it's a privilege to work there. I'm very happily ensconced at the place and I hope to stay till my ripe old age. I've always thought I'd go on working until I was sixty-five and retire then. Who knows? I worry because I'm a lot older than all the girls I work with — I always have been — and now I'm forty-five I think, 'Good God, my body's all changing and my face is getting wrinkly and nobody's going to want me . . .' but it doesn't seem to have had that effect at all yet. People often tell me, and younger men tell me this too, that they like someone who will listen, and you often don't get that until you've lived a bit. But we're still an incredibly vain lot, and because there's a lot of money floating around, it often goes in making us look better. I just saw a girl spend $600 on hair extensions the other day. I didn't even know such things existed! It involves glueing on extra hair to make her hair suddenly long. Now that's big bikkies!

The business is certainly not as lucrative as it was, though. Clients talk about their money problems, saying they'd come more often if they could, and what's more, you know that person used to.

The prices seem to be pretty much the same throughout, although sometimes they can vary slightly from city to city. When I first started working I'd never had so much money in my life. I had a great time! I guess I took a fairly Robin Hood sort of attitude towards the money. If people had money and were obviously rich, I quoted the standard sort of price. But if they didn't seem to have as much, I'd just sort of say, 'Well here's my bag — feel free to put in whatever you want.' It was like donations. I remember somebody gave me a dollar once.

At the time it suited me to do that because that's what felt right to me, but it made for terrible relationships with the other girls. Once a client has paid less, he doesn't want to pay more. So there would be guys I'd done who would go to them and say, 'Last time I only paid $30,' and the other girls would come back fuming. They decided that the reason I had so many requests was because I was under-charging. Maybe that was so, although I like to think those men asked for me because they liked me too. Anyway, I discovered that the girls could be very vicious. It took a while but I learned to keep things on the same level as them, and that's the only way I can do it.

I won't do unprotected oral sex nowadays. When I first started working, though, I wasn't very good at using condoms at all. But I got gonorrhoea one or two times too many and that changed my behaviour. I went for tests at the STD clinic every two weeks, so when they picked it up it was always very new. If I'm absolutely truthful, I'd have to say I didn't stop working when I had it — I carried on, only I used condoms. I took heaps of antibiotics, so that I look back now and wonder what I have done to my system, pumping all that stuff into it.

Men are much happier about using condoms now too. It's only occasionally that they'll try to bribe me to have unsafe sex, but I just say, 'Well, we're talking about my life here — do you think it's only worth $100?'

I think AIDS has had a big impact on the industry. It's another reason why things have quietened down. When we first heard about it, there seemed to be headlines in the paper every week and the clients became much more willing to use condoms.

We all talked about it a lot too. I used to march to work with the morning paper and we would read the articles out and pass them around the staff room to each other. I was worried about AIDS because a lot of working girls used needles, and that seemed to be the way it had moved into the heterosexual community.

I'm not sure how many working girls are using, because often you don't know unless they come to work really out of it. And that could be from pills anyway. But sometimes you'll go to work and find that somebody's been sacked because gear was found in the toilet, and you think, 'God, I didn't even know that person was using.'

They get given the sack because all that sort of thing brings the heat on a place, and besides, they often just aren't very reliable. They might not turn up at all, or else they will but they'll be sitting there having a cigarette and they'll nod off, or you get clients mentioning that they seem a bit weird. Some parlour owners tolerate it more than others; some won't tolerate it at all.

A lot of what's held up to be important is image. That's why I look very different when I'm working than I do at any other time. And I quite enjoy the dressing up. But sometimes clients will tell you how they've been with somebody who looks the epitome of what the real high-class working girl should look like, yet she was very cold or acted unprofessionally, or whatever. But then who's to say what sex appeal is? It's a vast thing. We have the stereotyped image of what we think men look for in a woman, but everybody is so highly individual.

I like to think that clients don't just want sex. Occasionally I'm thrown by having someone who obviously only wants that. I find that especially with the Japanese, although I rarely get them because they like very young girls — they'd like blonde, blue-eyed fourteen-year-olds if they could get them. But what I've always found with them is that not only did they not want or understand the verbal communication, but they didn't want kisses or cuddles or any of the things I like. Sometimes they didn't even want a massage — just one, two, three, bang, 'Thank you very much,' and they'd give you heaps of money and go. I was always left sitting there thinking, 'What's this all about — this is awful.' But that's exactly what a lot of working girls like from a client.

A lot of my clients told me I was different from the other women they'd been with. I've always felt, though, that since they were paying out a lot of money, it was up to me to put my everything into that situation. I see myself as a paid lover, with the emphasis being on the love. My aim is to dance with that person in a physical and loving way.

I have had the odd relationship with a client, but I try not to. I had the most beautiful love affair I've ever had in my whole life with a man who had been my favourite client for six years. He was very well known in political circles, and when he left his wife and came and lived with me, there was a lot of flack for several months. It was the strongest relationship I'd ever had, and it was the first time he'd ever really been in love with anyone. It was quite magical. But then the old pattern that I always develop set in, which was me wanting to be on my own again. He went back to live with his wife, and I just hope all's well in his world. I don't see him any more, but I wish I did. I think he may still be a little bit more involved with me than is comfortable for him, so if it's easier for him not to see me, that's fine.

I kept working while I was with him, and he was just wonderful. He adored me. He thought I was the most wonderful creature that walked this earth. He'd deliver me to work and pick me up, and he totally understood it. I think he may have felt different if we had been together before I was working.

I find the constantly changing variety of clients exciting. I'll often feel that magic about them, butterflies in my tummy, the works. I've always been a very physical person and tend to get sexually bored with one person. But then I know a little secret inside me — I know who I am inside. Maybe there's somebody in front of me I'm not particularly physically attracted to, but I look into his eyes and see that the same energy keeping him alive is what's keeping me alive, and then I understand. And my heart melts, so that what we've got between us turns into something special. And it always, always works.

I feel love for every single one of my clients. I have to, because that's what I'm there for. Sometimes people say to me, 'Do you do sex?' and I just say, 'No, I'm sorry, I don't. I can make love with you, but I can't just do sex.' Because I'm there to have the experience for myself. And I'm constantly falling in love. Maybe it's just for that night and I'll never see them again. But then there are others I've seen for eight or nine years on a fairly regular basis and I love and adore them. I often think about them, when they're not there, and then they'll suddenly show up an hour or two later, and I'll say, 'I knew you were coming — I felt you.'

I tell them I love them. I just say to them, 'Look, right now I am totally in love with you,' because that's exactly what I'm feeling. And I tell them, 'You'll go out that door and maybe we'll never see each other again, and that's okay too.' But I think they come to me for some sort of loving contact. And that to me is what working is all about.

I'll have lots of kisses and cuddles with my clients. I couldn't imagine being with somebody without kissing them. I know most working girls don't do that. Even if they only want hand relief, for me it's still kissing and cuddling and doing it in a way that's as realistic as possible. It's still like making love for me, only using my hand instead of my vagina. When clients tell me how someone else will just sit on the bed at arm's length and wank them off, that sounds awful to me. I can't understand someone not being able to participate and share in what to me is an act of love.

This job, to me, is all to do with caring and communication. That's why I think my older daughter would be brilliant at it, if that's what she chooses to do, because she's a real communicator. People open up to her, and talk to her a lot. She's also very stunning and has a lot of style, and she's an extremely caring person — both my children are.

When I first started working, my daughters were aged about three and seven. I knew that one advantage of my working would be having the money to pay for all the things they wanted to do. It wasn't easy coming to live in the city after living so simply in the country. I'd been used to making soya-bean coffee for health-food shops, trotting around them all for days on end and making only a very small amount of profit. So

JULIA

I doubt whether I'd have started working if there wasn't any money involved.

The hours are long, and I had to pay for somebody to be with the children when I wasn't there. When I started doing outcalls, most work came in after eight at night. I had a dear friend who lived next door, and sometimes the children would sleep over there and she would get them up in the morning and send them off to school with her children. At other times somebody would come and sleep the night at our house. I was in the position of being able to pay people quite well to do these things.

When I went into a parlour situation, I worked two double shifts a week for about five years. I'd go in at half past ten in the morning and work right through to about three the following morning. I did that twice a week, because it suited me to do it that way. That way I didn't get tired. Also, the shifts changed over at six thirty in the evening, but when you've got young children that's a terrible time to be either going to work or getting home from work. So I would pay various friends quite well to be there after school when the children came home, have dinner with them, sleep the night, and get them up and off in the morning. Then I would wake up about ten o'clock and stagger around for an hour or two. I'd be just coming right two days later and then I would go through it all again. But that was the way I worked that one out around the children.

They were both told what I did when they were about nine, by older children. I was sad about that, because I was into the magic and wonder of childhood, and sex and love are totally intertwined in my life. My eldest one coped extremely well when she was told. She came home in tears and said, 'Claudine says that you're a prostitute and you do nasty things with men with no clothes on for money.' She'd gone to see William, who was one of the teachers, and told him. He said to her, 'Nonsense, your mother's a very loving woman and I admire her greatly.' She and I had a wee talk, and later on that night I rang William up and said, 'That was very nice, what you said to Jodi.' He replied, 'That was the truth.'

What I told her was, 'Look, there are a lot of lonely people out there who have got no one to love, and then there are people like me who just love loving people. I do make love with people and they do pay me to make love with them, and that's a very special thing and I have a lovely time.' She looked at me and said, 'You're probably quite good at it,' so I said, 'Well, I think I am.'

I mean, there had been various people through my bed all their lives when they were growing up. It wasn't as though there were no men in my life, and they just took all of that with a grain of salt. What she asked me now was, 'Well, what happens when other parents don't understand and I don't get invited to their homes?' So I said, 'I'm really sorry if that happens. All the people we know feel all right about us, and we know a lot of people. It's just that I'm playing around with people's two biggest hang-ups — sex and money — and I'm combining them, so there's bound to be people who will react, and I'm sorry about that. But it's not something I can do anything about.' And she came to terms with it a bit in that way.

My younger one found it harder. She tends to bottle things up inside her. Other people would tell me she was having a hard time at school, and I'd get it out of her that it was because they were doing things like singing the Maggi soup ad, 'My mum's a Maggi mum.' Instead they would sing, 'Your mum's a prosti mum. Prosti mums have much more fun,' and things like that. It was awful. I considered stopping work at that point, but realised that even if I did, I would still be the mother who *had* done it. I just feel very sad, though, that I've put my children through that.

The girls both have a very good attitude to it now. They're really supportive of me. My younger one still doesn't talk about it very much, not to me anyway. My other daughter's very sophisticated. I can remember two or three years ago she used to say, 'Some of my friends think it's a bit strange that you work in a massage parlour, but I think it's neat.' She admires me for what I do. She asked me to come and talk to her Women's Studies class about working — she wanted me to tell them all about it. So I did. A lot of girls might not have wanted it known that their mother was doing something that that. But then she's very exceptional.

My working is a very important part of my life. I have high standards for my own personal relationships, and I think one of the reason why I've never been with one person for very long is because the magic often lessens and I can't tolerate that — I'd rather be on my own.

Sometimes I think there should be places where men work for women to go to, although it would probably be a trickier sort of place to run. There aren't many men who could be with a lot of women in busy times, although I've met some in my life who could cope, so I know they do exist.

Very occasionally we've had women come to the parlour wanting to go to bed with another woman. I've done the odd outcall in the past to married couples, but each time it was the man's idea and the woman wasn't very comfortable about it. I used to tick him off about what he was putting on her. He wanted the great male fantasy — two women — to feed his ego, and I don't like that.

I did have a whole physical relationship with a woman myself once, a few years ago. It surprised me, but I was pleased that it happened. It makes things more open and brings more barriers down. It was just that this person came into my life whom I felt a lot of love for, and it just happened to be somebody of the same sex. It had never happened before, and it hasn't since, but who knows?

But doing outcalls with couples tended to be always for the man's benefit, and I didn't feel very good about that. I won't do anything that doesn't feel right for me. To me, that's 'prostitution', as society likes to see it, and I won't have any part of it.

Julia is still currently working in a South Island massage parlour. Recently her interest in AIDS led to her becoming actively involved in NZPC and she feels very positive about being able to make some practical input into the AIDS prevention and education arena.

TRACY LEE

Tracy Lee is now in her forties, and it was many years ago that she first began working Wellington's streets. Since then she has also worked in Auckland, as well as in Wanganui, where she was living when I met her.

Over the years I've been involved with all sorts of men and in all sorts of situations. I got married once, to a seaman called Klaus. When we were first together I was going in and out of psychiatric hospitals, and later we lived in Samoa with my kids for a while. I found out he'd been living with someone else over there up until the day I arrived. We had a huge row and I sailed back to New Zealand without him. Later we got back together again, but in the end I realised I couldn't cope with the relationship any more, mainly because he was too good for me — he never hit me or anything like that.

I've lived with a lot of top criminals at times. I actually found out months and months later that one of the men I'd been involved with was that guy who was found in an English quarry with his hands cut off, as part of the Mr Asia drug ring. But he didn't even smoke dope when I was with him — I couldn't believe it!

In the last two years, since I've been back in south Taranaki, I've lived with two different men. One of them I loved very much, and he'll probably be the only man that I will ever feel that much for, but he belted me all the time. I can't live with a man who does that. Years ago I would never have thought that, but I do now.

It might just be me — I've got to be free. I don't think I'll ever have a really lasting, good relationship. I'm too stuffed in the head where men are concerned. Maybe one day, if I go to Hanmer and get some help, I'll be right, but not in the meantime.

I've been raped quite a few times. I'm a prostitute, so I can take it. But to me rape is rape. I've even been raped where the two guys used joeys — I thanked my lucky stars, I can tell you! I haven't been raped by clients — maybe I've got the right outlook with them, because they always seem to want to treat me right. Sometimes I've been raped where it's been my own bloody fault because I was in that situation and knew what I could expect. I can cope with rape now, because rape is no different than having sex really, except that it's against your will. It's better not to fight it, just let it happen. When you think about it, it's just another man having sex with you, isn't it? So let's be blunt about it.

There's been three or four times where I've been forcibly raped, or I've been in situations where I've been made to feel that I should have it or otherwise something could happen to me. Then I've just gotten away from it quietly and said to him, 'Bye bye, dear — that was very nice. Come round to my flat — let's do it again.' And his ego has been that big that he's come round and I've had a couple of men waiting to beat the shit out of him. Why not? I didn't go to the police, because when you're a prostitute it just means a whole lot of shit. No — I'll deal with it myself.

I said to one chap who raped me, 'If I ever hear that you've raped another woman, I'll come after you.' He ended up spending three months in hospital. And I have no regrets about that, because he had no right to do that. Sure, I could take it — I was a hooker. But what about some young woman, or an old lady, who couldn't? So he had to be taught a lesson. You don't live in my scene without learning to deal with your own problems.

When I first started on the streets in Wellington, prostitution was just something I graduated into. There weren't any parlours in those days — you either took them to your own home or you went to a hotel. Most of the time I was stripping, and after I'd done an act I'd go out and stand around on the street. And of course the cars would start pulling up. If a man wants you, there is a look he gives you, so you just say, 'Hi, love, would you like a bit of fun?' and it goes from there. From the streets you usually took men to your place or went in the car with them — a very dangerous practice, actually. I never had any problems, although I know a lot of the girls have.

More recently, I did the streets up in Auckland, although mostly I worked in parlours up there. It had been thirteen years since I'd been on the game in Wellington, and it was hard going back to that life, because I'd never worked parlours before. I was very frightened, because I didn't know if I could do it again or not, and I didn't feel particularly good doing it. It was so different, so much harder from what I remembered.

To be on the street seemed a lot more dangerous. I never went out up there without carrying a slug gun. They're safer than a knife because if you carry a knife the other person is liable to get it off you and use it against you. There are very few men who will keep walking towards a slug gun, though, to see whether it's a real gun or not. I've never had to use it, but there were a couple of times when I got quite frightened.

That's why I stayed with the parlours mostly, but if you don't do as the parlour owner says, then you lose your job. I've never allowed a parlour owner to touch me, because they won't use joes and they fuck every other bird there, and God only knows what they might have. I think I got away with it because I'm older. I wasn't into drugs, and I worked well, so the parlour owners didn't want to lose me.

Sometimes, in Auckland, I had to work twenty hours a day or else I would have got the sack. There are five million other young women out there who are going to walk into your job if you don't do the hours, so too bad. Klaus and I had broken up and I had a $250 a week mortgage and two kids to look after, and the DPB just wasn't enough. Now I don't believe in a lot of benefits or in people who abuse them, but I really don't think the government helps women enough. Not women in a situation like that. So I had to go back on the game — it was as simple as that. I didn't want to, but what else could I do?

You have to work long, hard hours, seven days a week, to earn big bikkies on the game. It's hard work. Unless you're top priority and you work the top hotels, but you don't hear about those ladies. I used to be one in Auckland. I was approached in the parlour by a man who asked if I wanted to do the hotel circuit. You must be perfectly groomed and dress top class all the time, because you're wining and dining with top men from all over the world. You must be prepared to go away for weekends, or go out on the yachts. It's a wonderful life.

I could have married two millionaires in this country in my time. One of them I said no to, and he is now a very good friend, but I was afraid I might bring him down because my face is too well known. Mostly I'd meet these men in the bar, or the hotel person may arrange it and give me a room number to go to. Often you go and dine with them, and you're expected to stay all night. If he likes you enough he'll be a regular client, and he'll be like a sugar daddy. You don't have too many, only one or two or three. They buy you everything and maybe take you overseas.

Some of them may even set you up in your own flat, but if you have a sugar daddy who does that it can be dangerous. He'll want you to have only him. If those men don't want you to have boyfriends, you can't. So it can be quite a lonely life. It's like having a husband who pays for absolutely everything, except you're only the mistress.

The men who do this are normally here on business, often regularly in town once a fortnight or whatever. And you're expected to be their companion and hostess on the days that they're here. Some of these men are wonderful gentlemen and can be fantastic to talk to. I enjoy intelligent conversation, and these men know how to hold a conversation, and they know how to treat you like a lady.

Hotel management was always aware of all this, but they turned a blind eye. They knew it was good for business to have some nice, discreet ladies in the house. The guy who invited me into the hotel circuit presumably invited other women too. I think the hotels did that because a lot of the street girls used the hotels otherwise. They're better off handpicking who they want to be there.

You always get money for sex from these men, but a lot more as well. Bottles of Möet for dinner — although quite frankly, I hate the stuff. You do have nice things bought for you — but that's being a woman, isn't it? It's the same as being a wife, 'Oh darling, my birthday is coming up, and I saw this lovely ring in the jewellery shop down the road — do you want to go and look at it?' And yes, she knows she's going to get it. It's just like being a wife, except you're only there for an hour or so.

Women do have it over men. You know, they say when men raise a hard-on, all the blood rushes there from their head and they've got to get rid of that hard-on as quick as possible because they need that blood for their brain! So we do have it over them, the poor bastards!

I've always used a joey, mainly because I like being clean. I don't like the thought that I might have two or three men in a night and their sperm inside me — it's not nice. There's also a trick that we've used, and I've taught the other girls too, and that's a sponge. You soak it in disinfectant and shove it up and anything that's in there usually comes out when you pull it out. So if you get a broken joe, you're pretty safe.

In all the years I've been on the game I've only ever once had anything. I got gonorrhoea last year, and I was in bed for two weeks on antibiotics, sick as a dog. It was my own fault because I went with this bloody boyfriend when I knew he was playing around, and he gave me a load.

The AIDS thing is really spoiling a lot. It worries me heaps actually, because it will change the whole course of our future generations, all over the world. Before, you only had the problem of promiscuity. You only had the worry of gonorrhoea, or maybe crabs or whatever. But not now.

Also, a lot of IV users are sharing needles still. That's the biggest problem. That's why I think prostitution should be legalised, so that a law must be passed whereby prostitutes must have a check-up every four weeks, and if they suspect that anything might be wrong, like a broken joe, they shouldn't be allowed to work until they're cleared. But we should have a fund and a prostitutes' union available to help any lady through that time. Like sick pay. I think we do need a union where all the pros put a certain amount in every week and it will help them in the future.

It's not just the IV drug users, though. We've got the young kids generally and the way they sleep around, running off to nightclubs and getting pissed and going off together. I really feel we should have more panic created in New Zealand about it — there isn't enough fear put into people's minds.

I'm too careful, but there is always the fear. Unfortunately it's the killer, and what can you do? If I meet a really nice guy and go out with him a few times and then go to bed with him, am I going to insist on using a joe? I do now, at first, but you can't keep on insisting, especially if he moves in with you. He might have AIDS from way back, and you wouldn't know unless he goes and has a test, but how do you ask some guy you really like to go and have a test? And once you're in love with him and you want to live with him, what say he has got AIDS? It's a much bigger issue than people realise. I don't think it will kill prostitution, though — nothing will ever stop people wanting sex.

I might have four or five clients a week, and I'll use a joe with every one of them. But I know young ladies who hang around the nightclubs who will have a different man every night and never use joes. Now, who is more at risk? And I know some males who fuck a different female every bloody night, sometimes two. So who's more at risk?

I think NZPC's magazine *Siren* could help educate people, but it shouldn't only be passed around to prostitutes. It can help with preventing AIDS and understanding prostitutes, and it should be available in all sorts of public places, like police stations and doctors' surgeries. And the clients should get to read it too.

WORKING GIRLS

I could tell you some funny stories about clients — I've sure seen a few! We had KY Katie — he was amazing. He did all the girls, on a weekly basis, and you'd only see him when it was your turn again. He always carried a big black bag, like a doctor's bag, and in it he had dozens of bottles of Dettol and dozens of tubes of KY, and a pair of gumboots. I've never to this day found out why he had the gumboots, though I'd dearly love to know! He used to turn up at the flat and buzz off straight into the bathroom, and you would hear all the taps running. Twenty minutes later he would emerge out of the steam and the smell of Dettol, and he would be covered from head to toe with KY jelly. He would then proceed to cover me with KY jelly too, and then, when we were both as slippery as greased pigs, he'd hop on, slide around, hop off, go back to the bathroom, spend another twenty minutes there, then emerge dressed and reeking of Dettol and leave — just like that!

Then there was another one who used to like you to wear a G-string and nothing else. He always brought a big, long ostrich feather with him and you had to put it down your G-string and hop around the room going, 'Cheep, cheep'. That's honest to God! And while you did that he sat there and wanked himself. So you didn't even touch him. I think the going price then was about $40 for that. He was only there ten minutes.

One man liked being locked in a wardrobe. I always felt sorry for him because he was a very well-known politician in this country. He liked to be locked in, then dragged out and booted around, kicked. He said his mother used to do that when he was a kid. It was very sad, but there were a lot like that.

You'd be surprised at the number of men who wanted to be whipped or beaten. And I don't mean just mildly. I was what they called a 'marker' for a while. There are two different types of men who want to be hit — those who just want it to sting, and those who want to bleed and end up marked. One man used to pay me a dollar a stroke, and he would have anything up to a hundred strokes at a time and go out covered in marks.

I had to stop doing it after a while because I used to feel sick afterwards. I knew I was turning into a nasty bitch. It's all very well being able to turn off in prostitution, but imagine getting to the point where you can turn off and hurt someone that badly! No, I didn't want to be like that, so I had to stop.

The men who wanted that came from all walks of life — often normal, married businessmen, or maybe professional men — doctors, lawyers, politicians.

I've got one man at the moment who likes being dressed up in nappies with a dummy in his mouth — he wants to be treated like a baby. It's hilarious! I was blue in the face from laughing in the bathroom the first time I did him!

What's caused a lot of problems sex-wise is that people have been told certain things are dirty and not nice. It's not fair to condition a person to think like that, because for the rest of their life they're going to be stuffed when it comes to enjoying sex. And I don't care what anyone says — sex is one of the biggest and most important things in a relationship, because you can't feel real love until you have feelings physically as well. Friendship, being able to trust — they all come later.

I don't beat around the bush. If I see a man I really like, I tell him, 'I want to go to bed with you now.' I'm not going to wait around for three or four weeks and then find out he's a wonderful man in every way but he's got a dick two inches long! If one partner doesn't feel good about sex with the other, it won't work as a relationship. You look at all the marriages of the middle-aged men who come to prostitutes — they've got everything else but good sex, so it proves my point.

I would say the majority of my clientele are married men, or men in a relationship. Quite a few are being sensible, because if they're not getting what they want from their lady, it's better to go to a pro and have that release once a week than find another lady and have a shit of a marriage break-up and everything, especially when there's kids involved.

But by the same token, I get angry at the men who say, 'Oh, my wife doesn't understand me.' Bullshit! He should teach her a few tricks to make her like it more, or at least try. I think there should be sex clinics. Marriage guidance is all very well, but it's not going to help the sexual side of it. We should have clinics where either partner can go and learn all the ins and outs and not feel guilty.

A lot of men tell me that the reason they come back to me is because they find me easy to get on with, and the first thing I do is go down on them. Now I've got my own reasons for doing that. If a man's got a load or anything wrong with him, like crabs or anything, you can tell. By going down I'm getting a look.

But for them, going down on them first gives them that psychological lift straight away. If a man has trouble getting a hard-on, it's the best way to get him to have one, because he can feel and see at the same time. It's exciting to see what's happening. A lot of people would call it perverted, but I don't believe there's any perversion in sexual relationships — it's only what you feel in your mind that makes it perverted or dirty or whatever.

So that's what I do first, and then I pretend that I'm horny, 'God, you've got to come inside, get it in me now, I've got to have it because I'm going to come . . .' and I guarantee that they come every time. I fake it.

I had to learn to switch off in order to be able to do this work. I would say a good ninety per cent at least of the women who are on the game have been abused either sexually or mentally by a man in their early life. I wasn't abused sexually, but I was abused mentally. Very badly. Most of the young women I've worked with all say they've had some sort of abuse by men in their life. Normally a father or an uncle — usually a relative.

In my case I never believed I was good enough for any man. I already believed that I was, as my stepfather said, 'a fucking dirty little tin goddess', which was his favourite saying for me. And if you tell a kid that often enough, they're going to believe it. Every man I got into relationships with after that was like him. They all treated me badly.

The first two or three clients I had who were older men, I spewed afterwards. I vomited and felt sick as a dog because I associated them with being my stepfather or my father, and it was really hard. But then I learned to switch off. It's survival. But I really do feel there should be a clinic for ladies on the game so they can talk out their particular, specialised problem, in order to have a normal relationship in life.

I've gone too far now. I'm too old. In order for me to get out of all the traumas and the problems that have made me unstable in relationships, I would have to go way, way back, and even my psychiatrist once said he was afraid to do that. How far can you push a person? It's memories. I've managed to come through reasonably well because my mother was a very sensible lady and she gave me a reasonable start. I always think I'm lucky really, because I did have a reasonable start, until the later years, and I've had four beautiful children of my own.

A lot of ladies are into drugs too. I see them sitting there, zonked out, selling everything they've got or shoplifting so they can sell the goods for more money, living every day of their lives desperate for another hit up. All I can think is, 'There but for the grace of God go I.' I could have had anything I wanted, without paying, in Wellington or Auckland or Aussie. I think the only thing that stopped me was seeing them in the toilet with a belt held between their teeth and around their arm, trying to find a vein. Or lying with their heads on the table in the bar, mouth dribbling, nose all snotty, just wasted. What sad lives, now gone. I've seen a lot of potentially very productive young people who are now utterly stuffed. In five years I lost fifteen friends — they all died.

Up in Auckland I've seen some of the parlour owners keeping the girls junked up just to keep them working for them. It happened when I came back to this town two and a half years ago too. One of the girl's boyfriends muscled his way in to the parlour as manager. He got into the drug side and started selling the girls stuff, and some of them ended up with $300-a-day habits, which he cultivated to keep them with him. I complained about him, and next thing I was tripped up and had my head smashed against the wall. I didn't go back to the parlour, but went on the game privately through another lady, and he began threatening me. Then he narked on me, and the police came around, so I decided to stop.

In this kind of work you tend to build up more and more traumas because of the life you live. So after two or three years you're a person with a whole heap of problems which just keep snowballing. That's how it was for me. I had a real bad alcohol problem, and a hatred of men — but not so much that I stopped having personal relationships with them. I've had terrible battles and been locked up in cells. I've actually felt I've been quite dangerous, and it's worried me. Everything builds up and snowballs, until it comes out in drugs or violence or in having a nervous breakdown.

The only thing I would wish is that I'd had help when I needed it — when I was beaten, when I was raped, through all the dramas I've been through. It's a wonder I'm not a lesbian! I've had psychiatrist after psychiatrist saying to me, 'Do you like ladies, Michelle?' And I've said, 'Yeah, I love ladies,' and they've said, 'No, not like that, Michelle — lover-wise?' But I've never been at the point where I've preferred female companionship more than male. Maybe I should have — maybe it would have been better for me. But maybe I've been a bit afraid too — that I might like it better than men. I think that stops a lot of women, actually.

I found the long hours of parlour work hard, and when I got back to this little town, having to work such long hours meant I lost both my youngest kids. These were the two youngest ones who were still living with me. They ran wild. Roxanne first of all — she got put in a family home, and that broke me up. And then my son, Jeremy, was taken off me because he was getting in a lot of trouble, so I sent him up to his father in Auckland. But that didn't work out. He ended up coming back here and doing an armed robbery. He was only thirteen too. He and my daughter's ex-boyfriend robbed an elderly couple at knife-point in their own home. So he ended up in a boys' home, but we managed to get him into a boarding school and he's doing good.

There's no way I would encourage any of my kids to go on

the game. Firstly, I would hope that I'd given my kids a good enough start so they wouldn't need to do that anyway to make themselves feel better; and secondly, it's not good for your mind. You have to live with the stigma. Very few young women can cope with society looking down on them.

One of my daughters, Madeleine, did go on the game. The little bitch blackmailed me. She went down to the parlour one day when I was off and applied for a job. I arrived back to find her there and I said, 'Either she goes or I go. I'm not having my daughter on the game.' She just looked at me and said, 'It's all right, Mum, I'll go. But I'm going to Auckland to work.' So I thought, 'Oh no — what do I do now? She's going to go up there and meet some of the worst people she could ever meet up with — it will totally ruin her.' So I just looked at her and said, 'Okay, Madeleine — you want to work on the game, fine. But you only go with who I say, that way I can look after you.' And that's what we did.

She only lasted two months and then it got her. I knew it would. Madeleine has to have love around her, and liking and respect. And she wasn't getting it on the game. Even now she is finding it hard to cope with the way people here look at her and talk about her because of what she did for two months. But it was a lesson well learned.

It is different working in a small town, heaps different. In Wellington and Auckland you're a non-face. You can walk down K Road and everyone on the street knows you, but they're the same as you. So they don't mind, they don't care. You don't have to feel worried about what everyone else says.

In a town like this, especially if you've got family, you have to be a little diplomatic. I'm lucky in that respect because I got through all that, and quite frankly I don't give a fuck now what anyone thinks. They don't pay my wages or my bills or buy my food, so if a person doesn't like me, I don't have to be around them and they don't have to be around me. It's stupid to even consider working in a small town like this and trying to hide what you are, because it won't work.

There's two escort agencies operating here at the moment

—the parlour just closed down after the guy was busted for drugs. I know about ten or eleven girls who are working here. All sorts of clients ask for us. In the last few weeks I've done a few local men I had as clients last year too. Very nice but lonely men. They live on their own and when I go to their home I usually stay longer if I can, but I'm not worried about getting any more money for it. A lot of parlours and agencies would insist that they pay for every little bit of time, but I don't think that's right. If they're only having sex once, they pay me for that, and they've paid an hour's escort fee already. So if I haven't got another job to go to, what skin is it off my nose or anyone else's if I care to stay with them longer?

I've had men from all walks of life as clients. I recently had a judge who was a very wonderful man, and I've had police, lawyers, you name it. You can't say that any particular type of man or any particular profession is more involved in getting a prostitute out. I've got one man now who every two months will save up his lunch money in order to see me. I only charge him $80, because he's a nice person and I believe I'm helping him out. He is stuck in a bad relationship and can't afford to get out of it, so every two months I provide him with just a couple of hours of fun and that gets him through.

One of the things I've learned about being a prostitute is how to enjoy the company of clients. Too many prostitutes are too concerned with getting them into bed, out, and gone again. Then they wonder why the men don't ask them back. Sure, if you're busy, you may have to finish within the hour, but there's no reason why you can't make the man feel good in that time.

You also learn discretion. I don't ever name names, because it would be wrong to do that to a man when all he wanted was a bit of fun now and then, or to get over an hour of loneliness. Even in the big cities I won't do that, and if I see a client when I'm walking round I won't acknowledge him unless he says hello to me first. I'm not out to wreck a marriage or make a man feel guilty for an hour spent — that's not fair. I've been in a bar here when there's been four or five of my clients drinking with their wives or friends, and I won't say hello to them unless they acknowledge me first.

One thing about working here is that you don't have the danger element. In cities like Wellington and Auckland you've got all the nutters and perverts. Most men who've got a real bent and who could be dangerous end up gravitating to the big cities anyway, because they can't get their kicks in a small town.

I've found it's better for me to work in a place like this. I only do one or two a night now, because I'm trying to get a little shop going and I run that in the daytime. I'll keep doing escorts while I need the money, because I want any debt that's been incurred with the shop cleared up. But once everything is debt-free, I'll give that up because getting the shop going feels like the first time I've ever been able to really know myself. All I want to do now is get it going, settle back, and maybe find a relationship I can feel comfortable in.

I just want to be me. I just want to go on with what I'm doing and not feel guilty for being me. I'm starting to really like me, and that's important.

Whether I'll actually give up the game or not, I don't know. The trouble is, I enjoy their company, and I'm not restricted. I know I can walk out of that room at the end of an hour and if I want to see them again, I can; if I don't, I don't have to.

I see things in black and white. You either live with it, or you change yourself to the extent where life is better for you. A lot of people bellow on that life's a bowl of shit. It isn't. It's not life — it's us. We're the ones who complicate it. I don't think anyone need live in misery, because we've all got the choice to change it. Sometimes we need a bit of help, that's all.

A big thing, too, is having a sense of humour. You've got to be able to laugh at yourself. It's no good sitting down and bitching and moaning, because it just wastes your time. Why waste all that wonderful life? It's already too short. Christ, when I think about the near misses I've had with death. Even now I've got a couple of lumps which I'll have to get cut out. But the way I see it, either I go and get the bloody things cut out, or I die.

There's no in-between. And it's no use sitting around crying and bitching about it.

I believe in Krishna, and karma is another law — that what you give, you get back. So if somebody does something wrong, you either fix it up then and there or you let it go and they'll get it back in due course. The old Hindu religion — it's not bad.

We make such a big issue about how people should be together for a lifetime once they marry. What a load of crap! We're all predators, we're all animals — men even more so. They were the hunters and the fighters. Sure, over the hundreds of years we've changed so that we've become what society says we should be. But look at how unhappy people are because they don't live by their instincts any more but by what other people say they should be.

If I had my life over again, there are certain things I might wish — like that I hadn't had my stepfather, or that I'd done more academically with my life. But I can't really say that I wouldn't like to be a prostitute again, because being a prostitute made me a very nice person. When I look back at all the people I've helped and the situations I've put myself in to help others, I don't regret it. I think we're all put on this earth for a reason, and even if that reason is just that you exist and then die and feed the worms and the worms feed the birds and life goes on, that's fine.

After this interview was done, Tracy Lee ended up going to Wellington for a celebration one weekend, stayed for several months and went back on the streets. She now lives in Auckland and works on K Road.

CAROLINE

Caroline is a lesbian feminist who began working in the sex industry when she was in her early twenties. She has worked and lived in a variety of situations, and has recently been running an Auckland parlour with another woman.

When I was young I had a really excellent childhood. I came from a really good, secure family background with a very liberated father who taught me that women can do anything as good as men. He was way ahead of his time, and I grew up believing completely in equality until I went out in the real world and tried it and it just didn't work.

I came up against sexism, up against chauvinism. People refused to listen to my opinion. I grew up in a family where a woman could do whatever she wanted and feel comfortable about it, but the man I married was not of that opinion at all.

I was very young when I married, only seventeen. I was working as a dentist's receptionist at the time, and my husband was a labourer, then became a wharfie later on. We hadn't discussed values before we got married, and I had just assumed that it would be an equal relationship. It wasn't at all. It was very unjust, very unfair.

We were married five and a half years and had two children. We were at loggerheads continually, physically fighting, him hitting, kicking, punching me up. I refused to have sex towards the end of the marriage. That was my only weapon, really, because I didn't have any money. He kept the money — I wasn't allowed any. So I thought, right, the only weapon I have is to stop the sex, but that didn't work in the end. I just got raped, heaps, all the time, continually. And that was another rude awakening, because at that time the law allowed a husband to rape his wife. I went home to my parents, but they just sent me back, saying, 'Oh well, that's part of being married — a man has his rights.' So I thought, 'Wow, this is living hell. I'm trapped in my own home, a prisoner with a jailer who can beat me, thump me, give me no money and rape me if he wants.' And to me that's what marriage was.

Eventually I got out and ended up in a refuge. I went out and got a job in a boutique and put my children in childcare, and that took over half my wages, because they were very young. I had a little baby of four months and another girl of two, and the nursery hours weren't long enough to cover the hours I worked in the boutique so I also had to pay somebody to pick them up and mind them until I got home on the bus. I enjoyed working, but financially it was just about impossible.

I went from there to living communally for a while. It was a lesbian-type community at Muriwai, and I lived there for two years on the DPB, which was about $58 a week then. I had sort of started to identify as a lesbian when I was married. Right throughout my marriage I was very drawn to women and always thought they had the nicer qualities. I think I'd known and felt that for a long time, but they didn't discuss it in schools and I hadn't read any literature and had no way of knowing it could be an alternative.

All I had was a lurking feeling all the time. We used to go out to parties and I'd spend all my time talking to the women. My husband used to say, 'You're a real woman's woman, aren't you?' If only he knew how much of one! I was just not interested in flirting with the men at all.

I probably fell in love with women a couple of times when I was married. There was a woman who lived next door who was a single parent. She'd get very lonely during the day, and I would too. I used to spend a lot of time at her place and I got closer and closer to her. One time I got really drunk and kissed her, and that's when she distanced me. She said, 'Well, I think you had better look at your sexuality. I think you might be gay, and I'm not.'

Caroline

When she said that it felt wonderful. I actually went back and told my husband, and that I really liked how women felt and everything. So I knew when I was quite young, about twenty or twenty-one, but there was just nowhere for me to go. I didn't know how to make that sort of contact.

Finally, when I was working, I found out there was a gay bar. I started going there and talked to some women there. I was really struggling financially and knew nobody to share a house with, because my husband had been really possessive and I had no friends. I was going under, and these women said I could go and stay with them on their land. It was Maori land, and there was only one other Pakeha woman there besides myself.

During those two years I actually made friends with a woman who used to come up and visit quite regularly, and I just fell in love with her. My self-esteem was really low at the time, and she asked me to come back to the city and live with her. I kept ringing her up and saying, 'You don't *really* want me to live with you, do you? Do you *really* want me? And my children?' I'd found out that once you told people you had children they didn't want to know, and there weren't other lesbians around with children then either. I hadn't met any at that stage.

But this particular woman loved children, and she was a very caring and lovely person. So I moved from Muriwai back down to the city and lived with her. She was a Polynesian woman and I lived very much a Polynesian lifestyle with her. I lived with her for four years and went out with her for another two after that.

I had started working as a prostitute while I was living with her, and the relationship fell apart. I couldn't handle it. I'd done that, though, because she was a Polynesian woman working in a factory for a really low wage, and I was still only getting my $58 a week or whatever it was, and we were really struggling.

Men put the idea of prostitution into my head. I was working in a Chinese restaurant at the time, and one day the guy who owned it put $70 extra in my wages and said, 'Well, if you pop out with me once a week I'll keep your wages at this level.'

I didn't even take offence. I find men's excitement over something like that amusing rather than offensive. But the seed was planted, and the next time an offer came I would say, 'Well, I hope you've got at least two to three hundred dollars.' Subconsciously I was digging to find out just how much is this worth. And I was really amazed when the answer came back, 'Yes, yes — fuck, yes.' And in 1979 that was a lot of money.

Men were always offering me money. Even when I was managing a boutique the same thing happened — the owner said, 'Well, how about coming away and staying in a motel with me for the weekend and I'll pay you?' Men continually made me into a prostitute.

The first time I accepted was with the boss of that Chinese restaurant, and we just went to a motel. It felt really easy. I'd had lots of practice at putting up with things being done to my body and not allowing that to affect my mind and my emotions. That's how I survived the last two years of my marriage.

I went with that Chinese man regularly, but his wife found out eventually and made a terrible scene — forced him to sell the restaurant and go away. He told me, 'Don't worry, I'll find somebody else to look after you,' and he actually found another quite wealthy Chinese man to help me out. So I got into prostitution completely outside of the parlour scene or any known prostitution circles.

I got a high out of the power of getting the money. I had never had access to good money, so who cared whether the sex was dull? The excitement was that I was going to have all that money in my hand at the end. Eventually he had to go away too, because he was actually part of some Chinese triad. And I was stuck then, because I'd been used to this additional income. That's when I first went out and looked for a job in a parlour — a very exclusive place called Fanshawes.

Nothing was actually legal in this place. It had a bar but no liquor licence, and there was gambling. Very wealthy Arabs used to fly in and put thousands and thousands of dollars on the gambling tables at a time. It was very up-market, and had floorshows and everything.

Caroline

People don't realise New Zealand even had a club like that back then — this was about 1980. It was the sort of club people would like to have in New Zealand now. It was run by New Zealanders, but most of the men who came were overseas visitors. There was a little password to get in. There were men rolling thousands of dollars out of their pockets continually.

I found out about it through a friend working there. It was really good. All the girls just went in whenever they wanted. You'd go in and chat up clients, and then they paid a fee to go through into a room with you and you made your money. And the prices were good because it was such an up-market place.

But it only lasted ten months before it was closed down, mostly because of the gambling. There were actually armed gamblers at the table, and a couple of big shoot-ups over debts that weren't paid. It was all over the papers when it got busted, all over the front of *Truth* and the *Herald*. I was very lucky I wasn't busted too, because my friend was. She was a schoolteacher at the time, and it was quite devastating for her. She had her name splashed over the papers and lost her teaching job. She's never been the same since.

I'm more instinctive than her, though. Three days before the place got busted I could smell undercover detectives. I told her, 'They're sneaking round, they're checking it out. I'm not coming in.' She told me not to be ridiculous, but I just knew that the guy I'd been talking to was an undercover, and sure enough he was. I've always had very sharp instincts which have stood me in good stead for surviving.

During that time I'd moved out from my lover's and gone to flat with a gay guy. He was wonderful and he's still my best friend. He helped out by looking after the children while I worked. He taught me all about bondage, because he was very interested in being a slave to a mistress.

I was quite bossy with him. I would come home and go, 'Your room's a bloody pigsty — why don't you get in there and bloody well clean it up?' and he would go, 'Yes, yes, all right.' One day he came up with a great big leather strap and said,

'Well, if you give me a really good hiding I might remember to keep it tidy.' So I did. It just got more and more formal from then on. He would say, 'If you give me a hiding regularly I might keep the house really good for you,' and then he suggested that if I bought him a nice little serving pinny and a pretty little dress, he might do the dishes and keep everything nice and clean, and gradually I learned all about it.

The psychology of bondage and discipline is really amazing. You have to understand all the fetishes. For some men it's the feel of silky material against their skin; for others it's the sight of a fish-net stocking and a fine stiletto shoe; for other men you dress up in a really androgynous manner and you look quite threatening.

After Fanshawes got busted I got a job doing straight parlour work. I found the job good. I found the money amazing, that's all I can keep saying. The money was really amazing. There's no other way that a woman can make that kind of money. It gave me access to a completely different lifestyle. I liked the women I met too — most of the women in the parlours were really strong and really alternative and took no shit from the propaganda that society sets out for women. I liked their mental strength and felt that I fitted there.

While I worked there, though, I also advertised and let it be known that I specialised in bondage and discipline work. I used to go out to private clients. I had a huge suitcase that I took a great amount of pleasure in painting my own designs on, all in black and silver, and I got a designer to make a whole lot of costumes for me. I had chains and locks and straps and cat-of-nine-tails and collars and all different kinds of whips.

You can just chain them up in any old position. You don't even need to have things to chain them to. You can just lay them flat on the floor on their face, and chain their hands up to their ankles behind their back and they're absolutely helpless. Then you tell them what disgusting, ugly, horrible, little, inferior creatures they are. And all the time you make them lick your boots, literally lick them. Sometimes that really turns them on; at other times it may cause a lot of anguish and despair. Usually they've been humiliated like that before and they like what's happening, even though it's scary. For them this is a release, almost like therapy.

Often with this sort of client there'd be no sex involved at all. That's why a lot of lesbians I knew approved of this particular form of prostitution. A lot of the clients were married, a lot were businessmen. A surprising number of very young men requested it. It was a whole cross-section of people really, but especially those like magistrates and lawyers who are in quite powerful jobs.

I've had some of the same bondage clients coming to me for six or seven years. It makes it easier for them, because I know their whole history and why they like this, what they like, and how they like it. I quite enjoy the role because it makes me feel powerful. It comes naturally to me because I really do believe that women are superior and I really do think that men deserve to be whipped by women from time to time. I don't see why we shouldn't have certain male sacrifices where they're punished by a high-powered woman who teaches them a lesson.

It's the B and D work which other lesbians seem to approve of more, though, not just because it often doesn't involve sex, but because it's a complete role reversal. It's a female being utterly chauvinistic to a man — lick my shoes, fetch this, fetch that. The woman is the dominant one and he's being belittled to her. He's her slave.

I found it exciting. I've never felt uncomfortable about having to have sex with a man or felt as though men have dominated me terribly, but that's because I'm strong. I've always carried a knife and I've used it when I've had to. I won't take shit from anyone.

I maintain that all prostitutes should carry weapons. Once I went out as an escort to a motel where there was a guy who had served in the Vietnam War. He was absolutely crazy, off his head, and tried to drown me in a bath.

I've got a scar up through my eyebrow and under my eye where another client attacked me. He broke two ribs as well as splitting my eye open. We were fighting over a condom. He wanted not to use a condom, and it got really violent, just fighting over a condom. I've always insisted on condoms being used, before AIDS or anything.

For all the rough times I had with clients, I never once reported them to the police. I should have, but I didn't. I was intimidated a lot by the law, and I guess I didn't really want to expose myself as a prostitute. I was also frightened that I wouldn't get a job in any other parlour if it was known that I stirred.

It really annoys me, though, that women are not allowed to carry a knife with them. I carry one all the time, and I don't give a fuck if the police want to prosecute me. I just think it's ridiculous that we're expected to walk around absolutely unarmed and trying to fight against men who are physically bigger than us. No matter how many self-defence courses we go to, if a man's sixteen or seventeen stone and you can't get away from him, then that's all there is to it. Being able to use a knife makes all the difference.

It's important to me to be able to be a warrior and a prostitute. Like being a lesbian, a mother, a feminist and a prostitute. I think it's really neat if you can be all those things. Why slide yourself into one little category when you can actually have a whole range of skills?

It wasn't always that easy. My lover couldn't cope when I started working, and she got nastier and nastier as time went on. She'd tell all her friends that I was working in a parlour, and they'd just have nothing to do with me. I'd go down to the pub or the women's club and everybody would get up and leave the table. I felt really angry, and ended up with quite a few drunk and disorderly charges during that time.

Some of it was because it was a strongly Polynesian community I was mixing in, and they had these strong Christian values, ironically, even though they were Polynesian. They're absolutely anti-lesbian a lot of the time, let alone anti-prostitution. And at that stage I didn't really know any other gay women, so it was a very hard and lonely time for me.

It's changed now only in the sense that I'm more aware and won't tolerate that sort of bullshit from women any more. Those same women are still around. They're still just as rude and arrogant, but it doesn't bother me now. I needed acceptance then. I needed support, and I never got it. Now they can say whatever they like and I just smile nicely in their faces. But I still sometimes feel alienated.

It's still true, though, that any lesbian woman who wanted to earn her money through prostitution would have to be prepared to lose a lot of support from the lesbian community. She'd have to think very, very carefully about whether the partner she's with at the moment could cope with it all, and what the long-term effects could be on her relationship with her lover.

I don't mean in relation to sex, because I think that side of it is easier for lesbians to handle. It's still relatively hard for me to find lovers who are accepting, though. I tried having relationships with other prostitutes, but that got very messy, and difficult once in that she had clients and I had clients, and she was away and I was away . . . Ideally you'd think that might be the answer, but I didn't find that it was. I still tend to like a partner who's very self-assured in her own lesbian identity. When I was involved with other prostitutes it tended to be more bisexual women, and I found their bisexuality really difficult to deal with.

A lot of people say to me, 'Well, you're bisexual anyway, or else you couldn't do your job,' but I'm really strong in my identity as a lesbian. Outside of my work I'm not interested at all in having affairs with men. I haven't actually met another lesbian like that in the business. I have met a lot of bisexual prostitutes who will go with women, but I find in the end it's out of amusement, curiosity. Or they've had a really bad patch with a man and they might do it for a year or so, and then they go back to a man. And I got hurt in relationships like that.

So I've never really met another lesbian prostitute, one who's really adamant about what her sexuality is. I did have a partner, a lesbian lover, who tried prostitution with me, but after a couple of months she just couldn't handle it. She saw it as belittling having to serve these men, and she decided it wasn't worth the money just to have to compromise her beliefs and ideals.

I guess it *is* compromising. But I look at it from the point of view that as lesbians we compromise in all aspects of life. If, as lesbians, we want to make a living, if we want a comfortable standard of living, then I believe we have to make compromises. It depends on the level of work you're in as to how you make those compromises.

It's not only lesbians working as prostitutes who compromise. A lesbian working in advertising, for example, may use her sexuality and her flirtatious appeal to win herself a contract, and if she needs to do that, she will. I know women who do that regularly. That sort of thing happens all the time.

The way I see it, being a lesbian prostitute is quite a revolutionary thing to be. If *every* woman charged *every* man, including her husband, for *every* fuck, then the whole ownership of the world's resources would start shifting to female control. Let's face it, men have most of the power in this world because they have access to more finance.

Men are quite silly when it comes to sex. A woman can win out every time. Women have always had that power. Feminism tries to play it down, though — it's much better to be unadorned, it's much better to be pure. Why not let's look at the areas we *have* got power in and encourage our sisters to manipulate away? I think that's absolutely fine. After all, what's wrong with a shrew? If we would only learn to feel comfortable with that power and to feel comfortable about being a shrew, then we could enjoy a much more comfortable lifestyle. So I really think the feminist movement needs to look at that particular area.

Besides, it's true that a lot of the lesbian community's support systems and nightclubs have actually had money donated to them by lesbians who worked in that way, or who have been mistresses to rich men, or who have married rich men and divorced them. If lesbians can swindle money out of men and put it back into the lesbian community, it has to be acknowledged that they're doing an important job for the lesbian community. We all have different jobs and we all have different roles in life, but I think the 'lesbian shrew' is a really important one.

I can think of one nightclub that was owned by a lesbian who had made all her money by being a mistress to an old man and then she opened up a club for lesbian women. I know some lesbians would be outraged at knowing where the money for their club had come from. But I think those particular women are really short-sighted. They're on idealistic, little bullshit trips that aren't real. It's not what life's about. Most property is still exclusively owned by men. Most of the big buildings around town are owned by men. If you're going to open a club for women, the chances are ninety-eight per cent that it is going to be a man you lease the building from. I mean, what can you do that is completely free from men?

So that's why I see women who charge men for sex as being quite strong and quite revolutionary. If I hadn't been a prostitute, I might not still have been able to be a lesbian. I was a lesbian with two young children and no skills. It would have been very hard for me to live out the rest of my life as a lesbian. I would never have been able to get enough money to own a home, and the chances of my meeting a lesbian who was actually willing to give me some money or put a house in both of our names were not very good — especially since I had children of my own, who might get half of that house. I might easily have decided, 'Oh, what the hell — I'll just bloody well get married.' I think the likelihood of that happening would have been very high.

But the fact that I've been able to earn an independent income has allowed me to live a lesbian lifestyle. That issue is the crux of why I am a prostitute. To stay a lesbian I have to have some good income coming in. I've seen hundreds of working-class lesbians go and live with men, or marry men, and it's not because they change their sexuality.

I don't think any woman goes out there and knowingly

decides she's going to be a prostitute forever. It's a means to an end. And I think you'll find it's the same for most women. Why else would somebody want to keep doing that over and over again if there were alternatives?

Some aspects of it could be seen as attractive. The glamour of it appeals to some. Prostitutes are nicely dressed and they usually know people who drive around in Mercedes and Jaguars, go out to fine restaurants and have lots of opportunities in life. There are a lot of prostitutes who travel abroad with wealthy gentlemen, and that can be a really nice perk, but it's also well earned. You're spending up to a week or two weeks away with someone that you're not particularly attracted to, and that can be quite hard work — you deserve your money.

I've just come back from having escorted a gentleman over to Sydney for a few days. He had to pay for my time as well as for all my expenses, so men have to be quite wealthy in order to be able to do that.

Some men probably feel that gives them a right to be very demanding of you sexually. But if you're a wise prostitute, you wouldn't go away with that sort of man. Most of the women I know who travel overseas on a regular basis tend to go with older men who can't do a great deal. I think if you did go away with somebody who was really sexual, you would have to at least quite like them. There are situations where prostitutes are mistresses to men they are quite close to and actually have loving feelings towards, and they get on quite well. Normally those relationships are quite exclusive, though, with a woman having one man who basically keeps her. He's usually a married man, typically a high-powered businessman with a really good expense account.

When I lived like that it wasn't with New Zealand businessmen. For me it tended to be with Japanese men. Mostly such arrangements are made with businessmen who have foreign investments overseas and like you to travel with them when they go away on business. Most New Zealand men just aren't wealthy enough to be able to afford a mistress-type relationship.

CAROLINE

I was New Zealand mistress to a Japanese businessman who probably had mistresses all over the world. I met him while I was working at Fanshawes. He sat down and worked out what it would cost me every week to run my home and bring up my children, and then he would write me a cheque once a month. So I actually had a wage from him. He also gave me a $10,000 lump sum. If you are a mistress and you're a really good shrew, you can usually organise lump-sum extractions out of them, which is something you can't do in a casual one-hour session with umpteen dozen clients one after the after. I've always found exclusive mistress relationships to be really lucrative. That's how I got my first home, through him. He actually gave me the deposit.

I was his mistress for three and half years, exclusively his, as far as men went, although I had women. He came around and caught me in bed with one once, because he had a key to the house. He was actually quite all right about that, though. It didn't worry him.

I spent quite a lot of those years with him, and the wages still came in whether he was here or not. They were enough for me and the children to live on, and were probably more than I could have earned in paid employment at that time.

I liked him and became really fond of him. And he was very much a gentleman, a very suave person, with quite a brilliant intellect. He had a number of university degrees, and apart from other things, I used to pick his brains. I learned a lot about international business and economics through him.

I spent a lot of time just being his companion and talking and listening. A lot of time is just spent listening, because these men get really stressed out doing big business deals all the time, and they often chat to you about it. It had to be all very secret, though, because he was very well known in New Zealand and so we had to go to out-of-the-way restaurants.

That sort of thing didn't worry me, though, because regardless of how I felt, I always concentrated on the money. I didn't care if he felt too embarrassed to be seen out in public with me, as long as I got paid. I did travel with him sometimes, although that was quite complicated. I also got pregnant to him, which was very messy, but I chose to have an abortion, which he knew about.

I did use condoms with him, so it was really bad luck that I got pregnant. I used to have to hassle with him about it because he felt he was above all that. He felt that using condoms was fair enough if you're turning tricks in a parlour, but a mistress should be above all that sort of paraphernalia.

I found it difficult to keep my own private life going while I was with him, and we did have some terrible fights about that side of things. He would come round when I'd be having a party with some friends, and I just didn't want him there. Once he came around with a big bouquet of flowers, and I just picked them up and threw them all over the floor and stomped on them. I yelled at him, 'I told you to ring before you come around . . . you ring before you come home . . . now get out,' and I slammed the door in his face. We had quite a few scenes like that. Just because he was paying me money, he needn't think he owned every hour of my day.

My children liked him immensely, because he was a very good man. Maybe in terms of morals he wasn't, because he was married and probably had other mistresses, but he was very good to my family and myself, and the children sensed his goodness. He was very sensitive and loving towards them.

Perhaps he was not so good for New Zealand's economy, though. In the end he set up a lot of deals here for Japan to buy into our companies and things. I used to give him a hard time about it. I was quite radical and he was a high-powered business operator and taught me lots about business, and I taught him lots about what happens to other people as a consequence of business deals. So we educated each other.

I found it very difficult at times reconciling what I believed with my relationship with him. I probably never did reconcile it completely. I just decided that I needed to survive, and that's what I was doing. But I knew a lot of my friends didn't approve — my personal friends have always tended to be pretty radical people.

CAROLINE

The relationship only ended because he had to go back to Japan and then move on to America. I still have contact with him occasionally, though. He was a very good influence in my life. I think, as long as you are not in a permanent relationship with somebody, then the mistress relationship can be a very good one, provided that you are compatible with the person.

After he left I went back to parlour work again. That was how I managed things, actually. I'd work intensely in parlours, then I would find a nice man and be a mistress for a while, have a rest, then go back into a parlour again. That's a pattern I've used to survive over the years. If you work flat-tack in a parlour, continually, you just get absolutely exhausted and become a mental wreck. Eventually I got sick of that pattern and decided that I would like an income without having to work all the time, so that's when I looked at setting up a place.

I first started thinking about running my own place a few years ago. I'd be busy working in a parlour and I'd say, 'God, there's not much to this.' Most of the parlours I worked at were owned by men, and their attitude was pretty terrible. Some of them insisted on sleeping with you first, just to see if you were any good at the job. They tried out every girl before they employed her, and some still felt that they had free access to the girls whenever they wanted. If you refused, you lost your job.

If it was known that I was a lesbian, then often there'd be special interest in me and the owner would expect me to put on a show with another girl for his titillation, whenever he wanted, for free. I did do that once — I picked up with some other woman and we did that. But I started getting really pissed off, and then I became more low-key about my sexuality being known.

What I really wanted was to set up a parlour along feminist lines. I hoped that it would be an environment where there was a bit of dignity for the women. If a place is decked out nicely, you feel a lot better about yourself. And if you're not intimidated every minute by somebody pinching your bum and making rude remarks to you, which is what most of the male owners do, your working conditions would be a lot better.

I also felt that women in the industry needed support — they needed to be able to talk openly and get support, which never existed in the parlours. They also needed knowledge. A lot of them were quite ignorant about sexually transmitted diseases, and about who the liberal doctors were around town they could talk to openly. Some were messed up about their sexuality. There were just a hundred thousand areas, really.

Working out the structure was difficult, because I knew from experience that to run it collectively could be really hard. And I was also looking to my own future, since I do need income for the rest of my days. So I didn't see it being run totally on a socialist philosophy with all the girls having a share in it and us all working together. I'm not that self-sacrificing. I looked at it as a business proposition. We'd hold a monthly meeting and chat about what's happening in the business, and they could air their opinions about how we could improve things. Consulting them about changes, not just implementing them without finding out how they felt.

And that's what I've tried to stick to in the two years or so since the place has been opened. It's a rap parlour and escort agency, and it will have to stay that way because I've had a prostitution bust, so I certainly couldn't get a massage parlour licence.

I usually have about twelve or thirteen women working for me. They're almost all part-time, because I think to do this sort of work full-time is too much. You get really grumpy and overworked and short-tempered, and can't possibly give your best if you're working day in, day out.

Some of them live with a partner who brings in the bulk of the income, so they're just earning money for extra things. Some have a day job and just do a shift or two in the evenings. Heaps of them are on the DPB, subsidising it with part-time work.

Almost all of the women who work for me have children, and we've organised things so that most of the mothers look after each other's children. When one's off she'll look after another's children, and vice versa. And we've also got a really wonderful cleaning lady who has made herself available to look after children when necessary. We also have quite a few women on call who will look after children. It's sort of a support group. It works out really well.

At our monthly meetings we end up with babies there and all sorts. The little children come along, with bottles, nappies, the lot. It's quite informal, and usually held on a Sunday afternoon. It generally lasts about an hour, and we cover a whole wide range of issues. There's always new people starting who don't realise we've got a health clinic in Manukau that is free for the girls to go and have their test done, so we chat about that. If there's somebody who hasn't been before, we organise one of the other girls to take her over there and make sure she has her checks okay. We talk about prices, and discuss any clients who have been real bastards.

I think it is very difficult to be a prostitute, and especially to be a prostitute and a mother at the same time. A lot of the women that I know have chosen to live a continual lie to their children. They tell them they work in a cake shop or a florist shop or whatever. But you can only sustain that until the children get to about ten or eleven and they start finding things out for themselves.

I lied a little in the beginning, but then my children got to about ten and began hearing me chat to people about work or the 'parlour'. They did some of their own inquiries as to what a parlour was, and one day one of them said to me, 'You work in a parlour don't you, and that means you do things to men for money, doesn't it?' So I was confronted directly by a ten-year-old, and you have to be really strong to be able to answer those questions. And then you go through all the pain of whether it's right or wrong to teach your children about such issues at such an early age.

That whole area is really difficult for a prostitute. Most women I know say they're going to get out of it before their children are that old, and some do that. For a heterosexual woman it's maybe easier to go off and marry some man and only need a small income. But there are a few women who work in the industry almost all their lives, and they have had to deal with that.

My own children's attitudes towards it all have changed over time. When my oldest daughter first asked me if I 'did things to men for money', I asked what she thought it was I did. She giggled and said, 'Oh well, wank them off and things like that,' and I said, 'Yes, that's quite true, that's what happens,' and it was left at that. She went off and didn't say anything about it again for quite a long time.

A bit later I said to her, 'Well, now you know what I do. That's fine, between you and me, but don't go around telling a whole lot of people, because you'll find most people can't handle that or won't allow their children to come and play any more.' They'd already had to deal with my being a lesbian and a lot of children not being allowed to come to play.

My children's lives have been very hard because of the choices I've made. They've had to grow up really fast and they've had to learn heaps. And I've always felt a bit sad about that. Like, why should they have to suffer because of what I chose? But the good part is that now, at ages fourteen and sixteen, they're really amazing. They've worked through all their initial anger and shame and they're teaching other people really incredible things. They're really non-judgemental.

If they did choose to do this sort of work, there would be nothing I could do, except to teach them the best way of doing it. I would live with a lot of flack — everybody would say, 'Well, what do you expect? Their mother's a whore; her kids are whores.' And that's always worried me, that they'll be tarred with the same brush and not get the right to be judged for themselves.

One of the reasons I put them in a boarding school was to give them that space away from me and to give them a sense of developing their own identity. And in that sense I think it's been the correct decision. Children are cruel. And if you've been in the industry a long time and you're quite well known in the area, there will be children who will give your kids flack about what their mother is.

They've never had any trouble coping with my choice to be lesbian or with my choice to be a prostitute. But they did have trouble coping with society's bigotry, because they were put on the spot by their own contemporaries and ended up fighting my battle on my behalf. And when you're thirteen or fourteen, it's really heavy to be defending your mother's choices when intellectually you're not really prepared for it or you haven't got the insight to really understand a lot of the reasoning behind it.

One child tells nothing. She's very conservative and wants everything to be absolutely hush-hush. The other daughter is a bit more outrageous and brave, and she will tell select people what I do. She's learned a lot from that process.

I think my one sadness is that my children have had to live through my battles; they've had no choice. Either that, or they left me. They actually tried that at one stage and went to live with their father, but they only lasted a year then they came back home. When they left I felt really weepy and distraught and very angry — I cursed feminism a lot. I felt as though I had supported all the right groups and I expected more women to support me than actually did through that period. I was very alone. I kept having dreams all the time about holding a baby and then dropping it on the floor and watching it break. Like my children had been pulled away and they were breaking the bonds. I would wake up in the middle of the night crying a lot. I felt hopeless. I felt a failure. I felt like I couldn't do anything right in life. I had fucked everything up. I couldn't be straight. I couldn't be a good mother. And I felt really ashamed.

That was a very, very hard year for me. I didn't communicate with people, didn't want anything to do with lovers. I was full of hatred. I learned that although I had often been angry at how difficult it was to be a lesbian mother, nevertheless my children brought a lot of richness into my life. And I learned to understand the position of the lesbian who never has any children and just works. If anything, it taught me the value of having had children. I felt really lost without them because I had been used to a very strong connection with my girls.

Anyway, it didn't work, living with their father. I had done all the groundwork with them; I had raised them single-handedly. I'd imparted my own value system on them really, and it was totally at odds with their father and his new wife. I'd taught them to think and have their own opinions, but in their father's home they had to go back to being children, acknowledging authority, not having the right to debate issues, and they found it absolutely impossible. Besides that, *he* found it impossible. They were too strong for him, mentally.

We still have difficulties because of my work, though. There are certain people they'll bring home and say, 'I don't tell them what you do, Mum.' My eldest daughter in particular struggles. She says, 'I love you, Mum, I really love you, but I can't handle the business you've chosen to be in. I just can't.' She gets these conflicts in her mind that she loves me but I'm a bad woman, because the world tells her I'm a bad woman. It's really difficult for her to cope with.

Both my daughters have to be radical thinkers if they're going to survive. The life I've chosen has shaped the future of their lives, really. They say they want a good education, and they tell me, 'I don't want to be a prostitute. I don't want your life. I've watched what it's cost you, and I don't want to live like that.' They've really learned from my life, and I might have these really straight, together, absolutely amazing daughters.

They've got a lot of tolerance for people, though. They're deeply compassionate, and they defend lesbians a lot. Sometimes they make me laugh. One of them told me, 'One of the teachers at school is gay, Mum, and the kids were talking about it and saying all lesbians have hairy legs and never wear bras.' She said, 'I just sat there giggling, because I know different. I know there's all kinds of lesbians.' And she asks them, 'Well, how many lesbians do you know?'

In that respect they've become teachers at a really young age. Even though they argue with me privately, publicly they actually defend lesbians, they defend prostitutes, and they teach people. And in that respect my children are really doing a wonderful thing for society.

I do think they've been born into a really difficult situation, and I'll never, ever, quite get over that guilt. I just hope it doesn't affect their lives forever. What if they want to get married to some nice man and they bring him home to meet me and Mum's a lesbian that runs a brothel? Could be the end of the relationship. If so, then maybe he wasn't worth knowing anyway.

Sometimes I think prostitution must run in our family. My grandmother has been a prostitute almost all her life. My mother was fifteen when she had me, and my grandmother raised me for the first four years. She always had a beautiful home, full of really lovely things, and she spoiled me endlessly — she always seemed to have heaps of money coming out of her purse. I never understood where any of it came from, but apparently my grandfather and her had worked as a team. They'd been married for years, but they were really naughty. She used to go and sleep with some rich man, and he would walk into the bedroom and pretend to catch them. And then they would blackmail him for so much money per week not to tell his wife. They conned heaps of money out of people that way!

They were operating in Wellington, and a lot of my mother's sisters worked down there as ship girls. Some of my cousins are striptease artists and prostitutes. There's actually heaps of them in the family, on both sides. My parents have known for years what I do, and they've always said, 'As long as you're happy, that's all we care about.' But I think it hurt my father sometimes — it must be really difficult for any father, or mother, to handle the fact that their daughter's slept with thousands and thousands of men.

There are certain conservative friends my parents have who just wouldn't be able to handle it, so I've learned to respect my parents' friendships, just like I've had to learn to respect my children's friendships. When they ask me not to let people know that I'm a lesbian or that I own a parlour, I have to respect that. I used to say I ran a little health and beauty centre up in Auckland, which was fine, except that one of the girls' mothers from their boarding school sold all sorts of facial products and she wanted to call and see me in case I could sell some of her products for her!

So my children have learned to be quick-witted, as I have. Initially I was really angry and thought that I didn't have to hide what I do. But I've learned that it's respectful to value somebody else's space, and that you don't really have the right to just storm in and say, 'I'm a lesbian and a prostitute — so there!' It doesn't get you anywhere.

At different times in my life I've had a real battle with using drugs and alcohol and stuff. If you're really wound up and you've worked really hard, it's sometimes nice to get a bit drunk and escape from it all. And there are lots of stresses in this business.

I found it particularly stressful getting my own business going, because there were a lot of unexpected problems. A lot of them arose from my not discussing values with my business partner first. She was Maori, heterosexual and not a feminist, and the two of us had very different approaches to it. I wanted to run the place more in the interests of the women working there. I wanted to make enough to live on, but I never wanted to be a millionaire. But my partner went absolutely overboard. There was never enough money coming in for her. A lot of it went up her nose, on cocaine and acid trips. So she'd take it out on the girls by devising systems where she could extract more and more out of them, like, 'Well, I think you should pay $10 a week towards the tea and milk now,' and 'I think you should pay another $10 a week towards getting the laundry washed,' and finally, 'Well, perhaps you should pay us $20 a time to use the rooms.' She just got really mercenary and would take out her own lack of being able to manage her personal life and her money on the staff.

When she came in, she would yell and scream and boss everyone around in the parlour. If you haven't been through a management course before, it's a whole different ball-game to be suddenly owning and running a business after having been just a worker. It took me over a year to adapt to that, and to find my strength, and to learn to have a certain amount of command and not to let people exploit my compassion and exploit my feminism. There were a few women who would tell me all the lies under the sun, and not want to turn up for work, and just try to completely exploit my caring for women. That was quite a rude awakening for me, to realise that not all women respect the fact that you care for women, and that some just think you're an idiot.

Some women sat down and told me that to my face. That was good for me to see, though, because it taught me to have a good long look at what women were really like out there. Over the years I'd selected friends who had similar feminist values, and to a degree I'd been sheltered from all that. So I'm a bit more cagey now about who I wish to associate with. Now I want to give my energy to those who appreciate it, not just those who think I'm a soft touch.

I've learned the hard way that there are really very few business owners who care to look at what's happening to their workers. Most parlour owners see their employees as money-making commodities who are disposable and replaceable. If one gets troublesome, get rid of her. Get the more passive ones, whom you can exploit. I had that problem with my business partner.

Our relationship had to come to an end because we fought continually. Things got so bad that we had a punch-up, and obviously two people can't go on like that. We sat down and talked about it and she said, 'Well, I don't feel the same way you do about the business. I want to make a lot of money and I want to make it fast. I had a hard time when I was working, and these girls can just learn to put up with it the same way I did.'

So we split up and now she's going to start another business around the corner, and it's going to be much bigger than mine . . . It doesn't worry me. So okay, she might take a lot of my customers away for a while and I'll have less money, but I think in the long run I'll be happier knowing that at least the women who work for me are really happy with their job. And I think that if you've got happy people working for you, that will reflect on your customers too.

Another issue for me concerns the extent to which I can run a women-only business. It would be nice if it could be absolutely women-only run and organised, but I don't think it's possible now for women to run this sort of business alone. You do have to have connections with strong male power. There are thugs moving into New Zealand from Australia now, and there have been bits in the paper about them bashing strip club owners and taking their money. I've got connections so I can get help if I need it.

We had one woman — a client bashed her around the head with a baseball bat, knocked out her two front teeth, stole her money, and forced sex on her. It was an absolutely terrible situation. And the women in the parlour looked at us and said, 'Well, what are you going to do about it? We want him fixed up.' But by law, if you own a business, you're not allowed to use standover tactics. The police will come down real hard on you if they hear you've been using them. Morally those sorts of things are heavy to cope with and work out.

After that issue, we now have drivers for the women going to escorts, and they actually have to stay there and wait. I've instructed them now to go into the house and check it out properly. If it looks seedy and there is more than one person in the house, they are to sit right there in the lounge in case the girl calls.

We've employed men part-time to do this, and they get paid per call. It's unfortunate but true that men seem to be more afraid of other men than women. That's just a fact. Not a fact I like, but you've got to be real. It's idealistic to think you can run this sort of business without those connections. Otherwise people go under, or end up like that girl who worked for us. And incidentally, we did get him back. He got a baseball bat, and his own teeth were knocked out.

Any woman who wants to get her own business going in

future would have to be very, very strong mentally. There's a phenomenal difference between being a working prostitute and running a business. You'd have to be prepared to lose a lot of your social time; be prepared to be very tired; be prepared to listen to a lot of people's problems and do a lot of counselling; be prepared to get a lot of rude shocks about the reality of life. You might have thought you knew it all when you were a prostitute, but when you actually get to owning a business, you learn heaps more.

If you're a woman who has come from a working-class background and has really struggled to get there, then you also have to be prepared to deal with jealousy and anger from people you thought were your friends. All the women who used to be my friends are no longer my friends, mostly because of jealousy. They came from the same background and didn't survive; their lives fell apart on drugs and alcohol. They're actually filled with viciousness towards me now. And these were women I gave years and years of my life to, helping, listening, being supportive. Any woman who gets into a power position of any sort is destined to feel a lot of envy and jealousy from other women because it's so hard for women to get in to power positions in a male-dominated society.

What keeps me going is just a deep gut feeling that what I'm doing is right. A lot of us were ground-breakers in the feminist movement, and we all learned a lot in those early years. Then we went off in different directions. This has been my direction and the territory that I'm meant to work in. I'm meant to learn the things that I'm learning. And also I do meet some really amazing women in the business who come back two or three years later and say, 'What you told me back then actually happened,' or, 'I thought about that and it was really neat what you said to me.' And those things make it worthwhile.

Sometimes when things get difficult I look at other avenues and think I'd like to give up and go away and buy a little bit of land on an island. Leave it all behind. But I feel like I'd let a lot of people down. People in the industry who knew me when I was really poor believe in me, and they're still watching me. I was angry and powerless, and that's what drove me to do it. I would look around and see the most amazing women managing parlours, but never owning them. And I'd ask them, 'Why don't you want to own it?' and they'd say, 'Oh no, it's too much responsibility.' There was always a man at the top keeping them, and it was always a man who had the ultimate power. I used to just about cry watching these women and thinking, 'You're brilliant, you could run this yourself — why aren't you? Why have you got this stupid belief that only a man is strong enough to do it?'

It was a bit idealistic, though, because I've learned now that you have to work with men to a degree. I still have the ultimate power. Nobody comes into my business I don't like — I throw them out. If they don't like my rules or my value systems —down the stairs, matey. I wanted to be free of male power. And I am. But what a battle. Other women now, single lesbians, tell me they're free of male power. 'No man tells me what to do,' they say, and I think to myself how lucky they are. They didn't have children to be blackmailed with, but if you've got dependents, most men try to manipulate that situation through your children.

I am lucky now in that I get on very well with the Vice Squad, and they actually help me. If I have problems I can ring the police and they'll come down and remove people from the business for me. I had a theft one time, from a parlour, and the police actually got the money back and gave it to me. As long as you're straight up and you genuinely care about running a good place, then the Vice Squad are excellent.

In New Zealand it hasn't been a life-threatening business up until two years ago, but I believe that's changing. There are too many heavies moving into the industry now. And in order to survive it's going to become a much more vicious game, and you've got to decide how far you're prepared to go to survive. If I find I've got to start getting people beaten up on a regular basis in order to keep my income, I may decide I don't really think it's worth it.

CAROLINE

But probably I'd choose to arm myself and fight. For years I've tried to free myself from male power, and I'm not going to lie back and watch male thugs take it away from me again. It's not women coming over here, using standover tactics and extortion and demanding money from my business — it's men. And why should I give it to them?

I know a lot of people out there disagree. They think we should all be pacifists. But where does that get us? Okay, I know there's a place for being a nice little environmentalist and writing letters of protest and that sort of thing, but what we're talking about here is real street-level stuff. The guys who are moving in on the industry fight rough and dirty, and if that's what it takes to keep what I've worked for, I'll do it. It's just a bit ironic that I've spent all these years trying to live as a lesbian and feminist and raise two daughters — but I'm sure as hell not going to let anyone just walk in and take it all away.

The lovers I choose have to be like that too. I've learned I have two kinds of women as friends — the fragile ones who are nice to visit and talk with, and those who are tough enough to live at street level and cope with the way I live.

I know a lot of women feel that if women fight to keep what they've got, they're using male weapons — but if it's a choice of doing that or losing all you've got, I'd rather fight. I've worked for years to free myself from male power, to get my own business and to run it in the interests of women — I'm not going to give that up lightly . . .

I know I'm not suited to a life of servitude. Still, I don't think I would want to come back a prostitute in my next life — I'd like to come back as something a bit easier next time around!

Caroline has now sold her share of the rap parlour and escort agency she was running. She has recently opened her own business, specialising completely in heavy bondage and discipline. She communtes to work several days a week from the rural women's community where she now lives and is happily involved in a new relationship with a lesbian lover who is very accepting of her life as a sex worker.

Conclusion

The women whose accounts appear here challenge conventional stereotypes of prostitutes. What strikes me most about these women is their diversity — they come from different ethnic groups, have different sexual preferences, and have worked in different geographical locations. Some are from urban working-class backgrounds, some from a farming heritage, and some from professional or academic families.

They became involved in sex work at different times in their lives, in different ways, and for different reasons. Harley and Bridget began their involvement in the industry when they were very young, while Julia and Victoria, on the other hand, were in their mid-thirties before they started 'working'.

Most have worked in massage parlours, but the transitory nature of this industry means that many have also done escort work or worked the streets. Some women only ever work in one arena — Julia, for example, works in parlours and prefers to see clients only in that context. Sarah and Caroline would do outcalls as well, when a client phoned a parlour to request that someone be sent round. What many of these women's experiences suggest, however, is that they come into the industry at one point, but move in and out of a variety of different arenas over the years, often changing cities or even countries as they go. Gloria, for example, came into the scene via the strip clubs, spent time on the ships, worked in various parlours and brothels in Australia, and had a succession of sugar daddies on both sides of the Tasman. Harley also had sugar daddies, did escorts, worked the streets, and had jobs in parlours. Liz and Caroline moved from working to running parlours, and Sarah went back and forth between working and doing reception duties. Thus the different contexts in which individual women

CONCLUSION

work can be highly diverse and demonstrate their acquisition of a wide range of business skills and expertise.

Their experiences prior to work in the sex industry are also very different. Sarah had been employed as a secretary, Caroline had been living in a rural lesbian community, and Jasmine was still attending a Catholic high school at the time she began working. Victoria already had children when she started; Genevieve had her children during the years she worked.

The women's family backgrounds were diverse also. Hinemoa was raised in a large Catholic orphanage; Hilary described her family as being 'split', and Gloria called hers 'broken'. Caroline, on the other hand, described herself as coming from a 'secure family background'. Desna had been adopted as a baby, and both she and Victoria had been raised in strictly religious households, while Bridget grew up in the midst of a more unorthodox, drug-based lifestyle.

The link between drugs and prostitution is strong for some women but not for others. Jasmine did begin working for that reason, and Liz, Harley and Bridget all speak about having a heavy drug problem. But it is not always clear whether they started working to get money for drugs, or used drugs in order to be able to cope with working. While Harley says she could not do what she does without being 'out of it', Kate and Alexandra do not use drugs and say they would 'feel less able to handle it' if they did.

One experience common to many of the women is a history of sexual abuse. Bridget, Desna, Jasmine, and Harley are among those who describe having been sexually abused as young children, while Sarah, Genevieve and Lee recount rape experiences from their teenage years. It is also quite likely, since they were not directly asked, that some of the women chose not to disclose that they had been abused, or may not yet have even accessed those memories — Kate, for example, relates in the postscript to her account that it is only very recently that she has been able to acknowledge childhood sexual abuse.

Such diversity of experience in the women's lives suggests

that is impossible to identify any single factor underlying entry into prostitution. Indeed, a range of contributory factors exist, none of which alone is sufficient to explain involvement in sex work. Early childhood experiences of abuse and rape are, for example, common to many women in our society — even if one rejects the 1987 Telethon campaign figures suggesting that one girl in four is abused before the age of eighteen as being too high, the most conservative estimates still suggest a figure of at least ten per cent. The majority of these women, however, never become involved in sex work. Conversely, some sex workers have no known history of childhood sexual abuse.

Attempts to explain prostitution have often sought to identify pathological features in the backgrounds of sex workers, but since such features are frequently common to many non-sex workers also, such explanations have limited value. *All* individual women make choices about their lives in response to their current social circumstances, and any woman's career decision reflects a complex interaction of factors, both past and present. Such factors *influence* rather than *determine* her choices — hence the diversity in these women's lives and backgrounds.

Some background experiences, while by no means inevitably leading to involvement in sex work, may nevertheless provide women with early learning that can later be translated into the sex-work context. The ability to engage a switch-off mechanism, for example, is learned by many little girls as they struggle to cope with the abuses perpetrated on them by older boys and adult men. Most of the women describe this mechanism as enabling them to make their body available to the client while distancing themselves from the situation. It is as if they disconnect their mind from their bodies, so that they are not fully present. This enables them to maintain a sense that *they* are the ones in control still, that they give the clients access to their bodies only. Sarah expressed it this way: 'They didn't buy me because "me" is my head. That's what is inside me and nobody can ever buy that.'

The need to retain something of themselves is also associated with the women adhering to a no-kissing rule. Kate describes kissing clients as 'a lot worse than actually being fucked', and maintains that, 'even if it's just a little bit of my body that's off-limits, it's still quite nice to have that'. Likewise, Sarah is emphatic that, 'you can switch off to the rest of your body but you can't switch off to your face'.

Keeping themselves separate from the proceedings involves many of the women in acting. As Bridget describes it, 'You fake a moan here and a groan there and pretend you're really loving it.' If needs be, the women will even fake an orgasm, but as Sarah said, 'You only fake an orgasm as an absolute last resort, because it's very embarrassing.'

However, while by far the majority of the women describe their job as acting, and rely on the switch-off mechanism to cope with it, the occasional exception exists. Julia, for instance, says she cannot imagine *not* kissing her clients and describes what she does with them as an act of love in which she fully shares and participates. Victoria also, although she acknowledges the need to act and stay detached, nevertheless describes needing to be able to find something in each client that she can love. Like Julia, she gives them lots of cuddles and affection. Both these women had no prior involvement in sex work until after they had experienced a variety of relationships, had borne children, and were in their mid-thirties. Maybe these factors contribute to the different attitude they show towards clients, an attitude that may itself be another useful coping mechanism. Neither of these women referred to themselves as 'prostitutes' — Victoria called herself a 'mistress', and Julia 'a paid lover' — and it is possible that their emphasising the love and affection aspects helps to make their exchanges with clients more acceptable to themselves.

Their descriptions of the interaction they have with their clients certainly differ quite markedly from those of most of the other women, who usually want to keep the level of contact they have to the bare minimum. Far from enjoying cuddles with clients, most are emphatic that the only enjoyable aspect of what they are doing is the money. If they acknowledge any emotional feeling towards the men at all, it is typically one of disgust and revulsion. For, as Sarah says, 'Who wants to be there? Who wants to be nice to this creep?' Often there is simply no feeling at all — as Alexandra expressed it, 'I used to feel nothing.' Jasmine maintained that for parlour women anyway, the real communication is between the women — and what goes on with the men, apart from its financial merits, is purely 'peripheral'. The appearance of a client may even be perceived as annoying if it interrupts the good conversation flowing between working girls at that particular point in time — 'The men coming in were what was disrupting us.'

Maybe women who are lesbians are able to enforce the switch-off mechanism even more effectively than heterosexual women. Certainly, from the accounts given by Caroline, Bridget, Hilary, and Kate (who identifies as bisexual but is living in a lesbian relationship) it seems easier for them to keep their working life and their private life separate. Not having sex with men in their personal lives reinforces even more strongly the notion that this is *work*. It is a job, and the nature of the encounters they have with clients are so different from those they choose to have with their lovers that the latter are seldom contaminated by the work experience.

For some heterosexual women, however, there are obvious difficulties involved in trying to move from being switched off to the men at work to being switched on to the man at home. Sometimes the problems associated with this are so great that heterosexual prostitutes decide it is simply not feasible for them to sustain a personal relationship while they are working. Hence Sarah says she tends 'not to have personal relationships with men while I'm working', opting to stay 'celibate' instead.

The clients are just as diverse as the women. They can come from any background, any walk of life. Lawyers, businessmen and politicians are just as likely to request their services as soldiers or seamen, yet popular images of prostitutes' clients often fail to acknowledge such diversity.

The men who visit sex workers also vary markedly in their motivations and purposes. While some simply want straight

Conclusion

sex, others see it as an opportunity to have a secret fantasy fulfilled. Bondage and discipline sessions are popular, but so also is a hand job. As Kate said, often the ordinariness of the men's sexual desires was amazing. Encounters with clients are frequently towards what many would describe as the mundane, boring end of the continuum of sexual experience.

Some men may, on occasion, request a straight massage only from a parlour, or even book in with a woman when their desire is simply to talk. As Victoria acknowledges, many of the clients who want to talk are of an older generation who would find it difficult to accept a need for counselling. Their self-image and role-modelling more comfortably allows them to seek the services of a prostitute than a therapist, but in some encounters the boundaries between these roles obviously become blurred.

The women's own perceptions of their involvement in the sex industry vary immensely. Hinemoa and others who were part of the ship scene may have never directly sold sex for money. Yet they still engaged in an exchange relationship with the men, by making themselves available as female companions to seamen who in return would buy them drinks, food or presents. The boundary lines here become very unclear as to whether such exchanges constitute 'prostitution' or simply reflect the give-and-take involved in any relationship. That then raises the question of the extent to which all male/female relationships contain an element of sexual exchange in them. Is it only women who work in the sex industry who use their sexuality for personal gain? What about the young woman who goes nightclubbing and lets a man pay her way all night, knowing that the tacit assumption for both of them is that she will later 'deliver'? Or the traditional dinner date, with its similar exchange arrangement — he will pay for her if she sleeps with him? Or the flirtation and seduction games that can accompany acting auditions, scholarship applications and other job and career moves?

No female prerogative is attached to such tactics. Men also often engage in flattery and gamesmanship in order to win contracts and sign deals. However, women's structural powerlessness in our society places them in the position of often having to negotiate with male employers and gatekeepers. These men frequently persist in viewing women as sex objects, thereby making it extremely difficult for women to avoid using their sexuality in order to gain a position of advantage. Men may have the financial power, but Caroline, Sarah, Victoria and Tracy Lee maintain that men's biggest weakness is sex. That is why Caroline suggests: 'If *every* woman charged *every* man, including her husband, for *every* fuck, then the whole ownership of the world's resources would start shifting to female control.'

Women in our society are still often regarded as men's sexual property. Their social value can be 'cheapened' by use and enhanced by chastity. The wife in a traditional marriage arrangement is making a bargain around her sexuality in ways that parallel the exchanges negotiated by a sex worker. It is for precisely this reason that Sarah comments: 'I see very little difference between housewives and prostitutes. A lot of housewives are doing the same sort of job that we are . . . They're saying to their husbands, "I'll give you sexual favours and give you children if you support me and feed me and bring me home money!" They're doing it for their livelihood as much as we are.'

Other women may make exchanges around their sexuality that are less blatant. Even lesbian women, as Caroline acknowledges, may use their sexuality, if only flirtatiously, to gain a position of favour. In so doing they are responding to men's definitions of women and to the structural power advantages associated with being male in our society. While for most of their lives lesbians will choose to live outside of such definitions, at times collusion may appear to be a necessary survival strategy.

The illusion cannot therefore be maintained that it is only sex workers who use their sexuality for personal gain. They clearly make such exchanges more overtly, but what many of them have done is make a conscious decision to reject a climate of innuendo and harassment for one in which they can capitalise directly on their sexual assets.

Conclusion

While it is men's definitions of women's sexuality to which the women respond, issues of power and control are central to how they negotiate *within* that context. In the sexual encounters between sex workers and their clients it is the woman who establishes the rules governing such interaction. It is she who sets the price, determines what she is prepared to do, and establishes the limits of acceptable behaviour. The risk she takes, of course, is that the potential exists for the client to violate that code of acceptability. She may then end up raped, abused, infected, beaten or even dead.

The code of trust governing such exchanges is similar to that which operates in any situation of intimacy. For the sex worker it may be only an illusion of intimacy that is being offered — nevertheless it carries with it a certain degree of vulnerability and a set of expectations concerning how such exchanges should be conducted. The rules themselves, such as 'no kissing', may be different, but essentially what is being negotiated are the conditions that will enable each party to obtain what they want from the encounter without feeling exploited, violated or compromised.

The set of contractual understandings governing these encounters in many ways parallel those characteristic of other workplace agreements. Where problems may arise, however, is when discrepancies occur in the perceptions held by clients and sex workers as to the nature of the transaction being negotiated. Caroline, for instance, found her Japanese businessman objecting to the use of condoms once he felt he had moved from being a client to taking her as his 'mistress'. Often the women find the most problematic clients are those who approach the encounter as if it was one of mutuality — Hilary complains about the men who 'want to please *you* in bed too, so the idea is to train them very early on'.

For the client, what is being sought may be sexual relief or a fantasy fulfilled, but for the sex worker the goal is always financial reward — regardless of whether or not she obtains any personal satisfaction, emotional or physical, from the encounter. While the client puts the emphasis in 'sex work' on the 'sex', to her the emphasis is on the 'work'. We have been given insights here into an *occupational* world. What frequently confuses the issue, however, is that the label 'prostitute' has for so long been used as an overall identity tag — it has been used to denote moral worth rather than occupational reality. The word's Latin derivation demonstrates that it did originally mean 'to set up for sale', but common dictionary definitions now describe it as 'devotion to base purposes' and the prostitute as one who is 'given over to evil'. Economic and occupational considerations are thereby minimised, or even excluded, by such a focus.

The fact that so many of the women found prostitution attractive because of the money highlights the extent to which women are still relatively economically deprived in our society. Caroline, for example, took in her first clients because of the inadequacy of the DPB, and Lee began her involvement in sex work when she decided 'it was only money that was stopping me [from getting] a decent lawyer to fight for my child'. As Bridget said, 'Where else can a young woman get that much money in a job?' and not surprisingly had her income reduced by two-thirds when she gave up sex work. For those reasons Harley was emphatic that she saw no other work prospects for herself — 'Why should I get a straight job and work eight hours a day, five days a week, when I can earn more than that in just one night on the streets?'

Moving out of sex work into another occupational arena is often very difficult for the women. Sarah and Bridget describe the money and the lifestyle it affords as 'addictive' — 'It's the most seductive thing I've ever come across' (Bridget). Victoria recounts stories of months spent trying to obtain alternative employment before turning back to sex work again. Trying to get out can be difficult not only because few other jobs for women pay as well, but also because of the problems associated with trying to present a plausible work history to prospective employers. The stigma attached to prostitution in our society is still so great that, as Kate acknowledges, 'It's the ultimate thing you have to keep your mouth shut about.' Such a stigma may

Conclusion

serve to keep some women out of sex work, but it may also undermine the self-esteem of those who are in it to the point where any alternative seems impossible.

Current debates about pay equity indicate that men are still not prepared to pay adequate wages for such traditionally women-dominated jobs as childcare workers and nurses. Yet many men will regularly set aside part of their income to buy sexual services, although class position may determine the extent to which they can participate in such practices.

Visiting a prostitute is an attractive option for men for a variety of reasons. It, by definition, implies a virtual guarantee of sex, so to many men it appears a 'cheaper' option than the risks associated with choosing a dinner date who may not 'deliver'. Desna had one client who, despite the fact that he was highly attractive, 'couldn't be bothered with all the bullshit of going out, trying to find a suitable female, making friends, trying to chat her up and maybe, just maybe, a date or two away, he might get into her knickers'.

For some men it provides a means whereby they can have sex with other women, or even attach themselves as a regular to one woman, without it threatening their marriage. As Victoria said, 'They know I'm in business. It's a job to me, so I'm not going to tie them up emotionally.' Men with unconventional desires undoubtedly consider paying a sex worker to have their fantasies fulfilled, and physically unattractive men find it a non-threatening way of forming a sexual liaison.

The professional code of discretion exhibited by sex workers is clearly reassuring to their clientele. Tracy Lee, for example, commented, 'I don't ever name names, because it would be wrong to do that to a man when all he wanted was a bit of fun now and then, or to get over an hour of loneliness . . . I'm not out to wreck a marriage or make a man feel guilty for an hour spent — that's not fair.'

The women's professionalism is also evident in their commitment to safe sex practices on the job. Sexually transmitted diseases are an occupational hazard for women in this industry such that, even before the threat of AIDS, most were careful in the precautions they took. Less so are many of the men who visit them. The women often referred to clients trying to bribe or coerce them into having sex without a condom — Caroline, for instance, had two ribs broken and her eye split open while fighting with a client over the use of a condom.

Client aggression was reported by many other women as well. Harley and Liz referred to several instances on the streets where they had been beaten up, robbed or raped by men. Victoria went through a traumatic ordeal while doing an escort when the client attempted to rape her at knifepoint, and Caroline had another situation with an escort where he tried to drown her. Parlour women, while often having more protection at hand, are not always immune from such violence either. Sarah had a man try to strangle her, one of Bridget's clients raped her, and Jasmine was thrown into a mirror which shattered during an attempted rape in a parlour.

The women seldom call the police in such situations. Bridget remarked that, 'It's an unspoken rule in the drugs and prostitution scene that you don't go to the police . . . You go to someone else and get them to fix it up.' Similar comments were made by Tracy Lee and also Harley, who even when she stumbled across a policewoman she knew from school after a particularly savage attack, nevertheless refused to talk to her.

Trusting the police to help them does not come easy to the women. Past experience has taught them to be extremely wary. To take a rape complaint to the police and courts can be a traumatic experience for any woman — Sarah, Jasmine and Bridget all testify to that. Furthermore, in Lee's and Jasmine's cases it was the police themselves who were doing the raping.

The lives of the women in this book provide us with a microcosm in which we can see very dramatically many of the realities faced by all women in our society. They reveal a world in which to be born female carries with it the risk of abuse and rape, in which men's violence is a constant possibility, and in which economic survival can be a daily struggle. That these women's lives also contain massive contradictions should be no

CONCLUSION

surprise, since so too do our own.

Hinemoa was involved with the ship scene for years, yet found it impossible to accept her husband going with a prostitute. Kate, in identifying as a feminist, rejects conventional stereotypes of feminine beauty, yet agonised that the escort agency would refuse to employ her for being too fat. As a lesbain, Caroline acknowledges the compromises she makes through her involvement in sex work, but sees them as necessary for her survival in a male-dominated world. Sarah also recognises the contradictions which face her as a feminist who chooses to work in prostitution: 'As a feminist I don't like pornography; I don't like men whistling; I hate the whole way that women are treated as sex objects — which prostitution is.'

With the clients also we can see a range of contradictory attitudes. Just as society has for so long been ambivalent towards prostitution, regarding it simultaneously as evil but necessary, so too the clients demonstrate a similar ambivalence. The prostitute is both forbidden and desired, she who attracts because she is other than a wife, but whom many men nonetheless may try to fashion into a wife substitute. Victoria describes one regular client of hers in particular to whom she feels like a 'surrogate wife', and mentions a range of domestic 'extras' she provides which include sewing on his buttons and washing his curtains. The ambivalence men feel towards prostitutes is often apparent when, even if they are dating a sex worker and telling her how wonderful she is, the bottom line for them whenever there is a disagreement is to turn around and say, 'You're nothing but a whore.' Sarah's husband was sufficiently impressed by her income as a sex worker to marry her for her money, yet verbally abused her almost daily for being 'a whore and a slut'. Similarly, Alexandra's boyfriend maintained she had no right to question anything he did since she was 'just a whore'.

Dividing women into two camps, madonnas and whores, has been an effective regulatory device for centuries. The fear of being ostracised as a whore has persuaded many women to refrain from any behaviour that could earn them that tag, whether it be as fleeting as indulging in a one-night stand or even simply dressing in a manner deemed provocative.

Traditional explanations of women who ended up in the whore category have often presented them as unwilling victims, forced into prostitution by unscrupulous men or because of excessive drug habits. Undoubtedly there *are* elements of coercion and exploitation in the sex-work industry. It is the typically male parlour owners, for instance, who reap the greatest profits from the women's work. Bridget and Harley also describe an expectation on the part of these men that they are entitled to free sexual access to their workers. As Harley says, 'If the guy owns the place and you want the job then it seems like there's not much choice but to give it.'

The evidence from these accounts, however, suggests that perceptions of prostitutes as exploited victims acknowledges only part of the reality of their experience. Harley herself says, in relation to male bosses demanding free sex, 'I've always refused — I figure they can get stuffed.' The women were divided at times as to the extent to which they believed women entered prostitution by choice. Bridget considers that even 'if you go into prostitution because you're desperate for money, I don't really think that's much of a choice'. Jasmine, however, maintains, 'it's something every woman has as an option', and Sarah says that for her, 'working was about freedom and money'. Hilary also is emphatic that, 'The image of poor women being coerced into becoming workers really annoys me because most prostitutes do it by choice . . . It's a conscious decision they make.' Their options may seem limited at the time they make their decision, but all of us, sex workers and non-sex workers alike, are faced with limited options. How many women clean other people's offices or cook other people's meals by choice?

Many of the women are also adamant that they exercise considerable control within the sex-work context. Kate remarks that, 'Before I started I used to be disturbed by the idea that through prostitution men could, even if they had to pay for it, order women around and have a woman totally under their control. But that's not how it is at all.' It is the women who set

CONCLUSION

the rules and fix the price, and, in Bridget's experience, the longer they work, the more assertive about such issues they become. As Sarah says, 'It's a matter of experience . . . the longer you're in the game, the tougher you get, and the more you learn that you can in fact just slap their hand away.'

The issue of exploitation is a difficult one. Bridget acknowledges, 'I know some women think they're the ones exploiting men. I don't, because I still think that no matter how much they're going to pay me, it's not enough.' Harley, on the other hand, maintains, 'I don't think we get ripped off . . . if anything we're ripping *them* off.' Sarah also says, 'You see yourself as exploiting *them* more than they're exploiting you. You have to see it that way, or you couldn't do it otherwise.'

At times the women suggest that sex work provides them with a means of trying to reverse the usual male/female power imbalance in their lives. Jasmine talks from the stripping context about experiencing 'a feeling of power . . . as I moved down to my G-string', and Kate similarly comments, 'In some ways this whole job gives me a sense of being quite sexually powerful — I find it extraordinary that they're willing to shell out such large sums of money for nothing so fantastic really.'

Sometimes it appears that charging men for sex provides the women with a means of trying to recover some of what they consider men have stolen from them. Lee, in discussing her decision to become involved in sex work, acknowledges, 'Although I didn't particularly like men at that time, I saw a way to compensate and secretly revenge myself for all the pain and insults I had received from the men who were responsible for my situation.' This desire to get something back from men is probably strongest in those who have been sexually abused. As Genevieve says, once she realised that her father had raped her, 'After that you could say that in some respects I wanted everything out of men. I wanted to take, take, take everything a man had. If it was *their* money, I didn't care how long it took me to get it, as long as I got every cent they owed me.'

It is impossible to generalise about the effects of sex work. While it may confirm some women in their victim status, undoubtedly for others it provides a context in which they can, maybe for the first time in their lives, exercise some control over whom they have sex with and under what conditions. Although by no means all of these women declare themselves feminist, they share commitment towards appropriating personal power in the sex-work context.

Sex workers collectively are also taking more and more steps to empower themselves within the wider social context. The New Zealand Prostitutes' Collective (NZPC) is one of many such groups internationally that are seeking to support women in the industry and represent their interests socially, legally and politically. It is appropriate that the last section of this book has been written by members of NZPC, for its emergence not only reflects the commitment to safe sex shown by these women, but also their determination to build a place for themselves in a world that is still overwhelmingly ambivalent about their existence.

APPENDIX

Off Our Backs and on to Our Political Feet!

A statement by members of the New Zealand Prostitutes' Collective:

The end of 1987 saw the beginning of what was to become the NZPC (New Zealand Prostitutes' Collective). A core group of sex workers, although we had not yet learned to call ourselves that, began to meet in pubs, private homes, massage parlours, on the street and, typically New Zealand, on beaches, to discuss in a semi-serious way the forming of an organisation specific to the needs of sex-industry workers.

> I'd always thought a union was needed. After eight years in the sex industry, forming the collective, although not a union, seemed like a positive step forward towards empowerment for sex workers.
>
> — Sarah, founding member

At this time a few sex workers were invited to meet with the AIDS Task Force of the Department of Health. AIDS, of course, was something we had all heard about. Our wallets were beginning to register its effects, and certainly it was becoming another reason for the wider community to stigmatise us further.

We started to gather material on sex work organisations from around the world. In particular, descriptions of the work carried out by PCV (Prostitutes' Collective of Victoria, Australia) provided us with cultural clues on how to proceed.

The Department of Health started to woo us in earnest. They were quite clearly committed to enlisting sex workers as educators for the prevention of HIV/AIDS. We felt if AIDS was to be kept out of the sex industry, then the sex industry would have to be brought out of hiding.

We agreed with the department on objectives, signed contracts and eventually funding started to trickle through. We set about establishing community bases, first in Wellington in October 1988 and then Auckland in March 1989.

> It was hard in the beginning. The funding from the Department of Health endorsed our right to exist, however, we still had to deal with practical problems like persuading landlords, office suppliers and the telephone company that we were a legitimate organisation. It was a time of coming out.
>
> — Catherine, founding member

One of our first tasks was to alert other people in the sex industry to our existence. We solicited throughout New Zealand for their support and distributed a circular inviting contributions to what was to become our magazine, *Siren* (Sex Industry Rights and Education Network).

> When I first saw the circular for the collective my initial response was, what a great idea. My next thought was one of 'pity it will never get off the ground', knowing how much people in this industry hate exposing themselves. Then I thought it is attitudes like this that ensure that they don't, so do something.
>
> — Letter to first issue of *Siren*

Siren has since grown in readership, providing not only information on HIV/AIDS prevention but also a forum for other sex-industry-related issues. Today in any one issue there will be contributions from masseuses, escorts, managers of parlours, transsexuals, transvestites and even clients of sex workers.

Support for the NZPC came from other areas too — in particular the New Zealand AIDS Foundation and Auckland Drug Information and Outreach.

APPENDIX

Support also came from a more unlikely group. It was perhaps appropriate that our first discussion with the police on the role of NZPC took place in a massage parlour. Until then we were not encouraged to talk openly even amongst ourselves about sex work.

We were all operating under the Massage Parlours Act 1978 — playing the game — pretending our business was to massage, nothing to do with sex work. It was a significant step forward. Even more significant was their encouragement. However, the sex industry will still continue to be policed, both appropriately and inappropriately.

— Catherine, founding member

Advocacy remains an important part of the work of NZPC. In 1989 we presented a submission on the Crimes Bill to the Parliamentary Committee on Justice and Law Reform. NZPC accepts that society will require that there be some legislative controls on our industry, but at present some of the controls tend to push parts of it underground while other controls are simply ineffective. In all, they create considerable difficulties for AIDS education in the industry.

We would oppose any attempt to have a legalised but more tightly state-controlled sex industry, which would actually have the effect of driving further underground those workers and clients who were outside the state-controlled sector. NZPC feels that changes to the law should be careful not to unintentionally encourage the development in this country of a class of pimps who exploit sex workers. We also want to see the existing laws decriminalised so that, for example, it is no longer an offence for a woman to solicit custom.

At present it is the client who approaches me and asks me for extras, yet I'll be the one who gets busted.

— Sue, sex worker

It is important that as prostitutes we have control over what we agree to do, with whom, and in what circumstances. One of our most important aims is to support women in the industry, both those who want to keep working and those who want to get out. That means fighting for the day when there will be no more stigma attached to writing 'sex worker' on our CVs than there would be had we spent three years as a teacher or an accountant.

NZPC is about empowerment, about enabling women who have been scapegoated and victimised in the past to come together and work for our own protection and our own benefit. Our aim is to see all women in the industry working safely, and walking tall.

Any sex workers in New Zealand are welcome to call NZPC:

Auckland   Phone (09) 366-6106
Wellington   Phone (04) 828-791
Christchurch Phone (03) 652-595
Dunedin   Phone (03) 477-6988

or write to:
NZ Prostitutes' Collective
National Office
PO Box 11-412
Manners Street
Wellington

FURTHER READING

Bell, Laurie (ed), *Good Girls/Bad Girls: Feminists and Sex Trade Workers Face to Face*. Seal Press, Seattle, 1987.

Delacoste, Frédérique and Alexander, Priscilla (eds), *Sex Work: Writings by Women in the Sex Industry*, Cleis Press, Pennsylvania, 1987.

Jaget, Claude (ed), *Prostitutes: Our Life*. Falling Wall Press, Bristol, 1980.

McLeod, Eileen, *Women Working: Prostitution Now*. Croom Helm, London, 1982.

Perkins, Roberta and Bennett, Gary, *Being a Prostitute*. Allen and Unwin, Sydney, 1985.

Pheterson, Gail, *A Vindication of the Rights of Whores*. Seal Press, Seattle, 1989.